BE YOUR OWN
DECORATOR

BE YOUR OWN DECORATOR

Carleton Varney

A PLAYBOY PRESS BOOK

Library of Congress Cataloging in Publication Data

Varney, Carleton.
    Be your own decorator.

       1. Interior decoration—Handbooks, manuals, etc.
I. Title.
NK2115.V316   747′.8′83   78–10242
ISBN 0–87223–514–9

For my wife, Suzanne, and for my sons,
Nicholas, Seamus, and Sebastian

Contents

BE YOUR OWN
DECORATOR

Introduction

During the past twenty years I've traveled each year around the USA on lecture tours to talk about the subject I know best—decorating. The title of my lecture—to be specific—is "Decorating Around Your Personality." And you know, I believe everyone has a unique personality and that your personality should show in the way your home is decorated. Molly and Norman Rockwell's house in Stockbridge, Massachusetts, is filled with furnishings that make it look like a combination of old and new *Saturday Evening Post* covers. Ethel Merman's apartment reflects her personality too: a big brass bed, and bright colors—lavenders, pinks, reds, and greens. When Van Johnson decorates, he brings his love of Rhode Island schooners and nautical memorabilia into his home.

The style and decoration of one's home should not be left solely in the hands of a professional decorator who arrives at the front door and after five minutes of looking about your rooms declares, with hands on hips, that "the sofas are too big, the drapery treatments all wrong, the bedroom furniture of an 'unchic' era, and, in general, everything, but everything, must go." If you should have such an experience, remember one thing: It is not the furnishings that should go; it is the decorator.

When decorating, you should consider all existing furnishings for possible use, for possible reuse—perhaps in another room—or for discard. Yes, not every piece should stay. I never advocate using pieces that have "had it," nor do I believe in filling up every inch of space in a home for the mere sake of "saving the old." I believe in using what is of value—whether it be from a monetary, spatial, or sentimental point of view. I have certain pieces of furniture that I would not part with for just these reasons.

There are lots of professional decorators in America who always consider the likes and dislikes of a client before planning a room. They are the decorators to choose when you are decorating your home and call in professional assistance.

Professional decorators work in many ways. Most calculate fees on a percentage of the decorating and furnishing costs, others on a time basis. Top professional hourly fees can run anywhere between seventy-five to a hundred dollars per hour. But, when on lecture tour, I have been asked thousands of questions about the hows, whys, and how-much of decorating. Obviously, the availability of good decorators in many areas of the country is limited. Many homemakers must look to themselves if any design job is to be done at all.

This book is a compilation of twenty years of my decorating ideas. Many of the ideas have appeared in my syndicated newspaper column, "Your Family Decorator"; others have been part of my lecture series. The ideas in all sections of the book have all been used by me, in one home or another. So I guess you could say they have been put through the test kitchen. And they've come out winners. What good is a recipe unless the ingredients really work!

Be Your Own Decorator is not a textbook. There are no graphs and cutouts to show furniture sizes. While I do write about scale and how to lay out a room, I do not believe nor have I ever believed that the exacting and regimented way of space-planning a room via the textbook method is the answer. Floor plans for furniture placement are very helpful aids when determining how many chairs, sofas, and end tables to purchase. And floor plans are essential when you are making decisions about the scale of furniture pieces. But can you tell where and how to hang a picture from a drafted floor plan? Should you really place a potted palm tree where the floor plan says? The spot designed "for tree" may be badly lighted.

Many is the time that the floor plan is useful as a guide only. The sofa, on the plan, can look best in front of the window. In reality, it might look best on the long living room wall. An actual room is quite different from a floor plan room.

I suggest throughout the pages of this book

that you consider the floor plan useful, but not infallible. The decorating rules may be many, but I have found that all of them can be broken.

It is my sincere hope that *Be Your Own Decorator* will give you lots and lots of ideas to experiment with in the everyday planning of your own home. It is also my sincere hope that the book will give you confidence to do things you haven't done before—possibly because you were afraid to do them. Maybe, after you've gotten confidence, you will paint the drab bedroom ceiling mauve and those dull bedroom walls pink—with bright white trim of course. Your imagination will be liberated!

In closing, I want to say that you will not be turned into a professional interior designer just by reading this book. If it should start you on the road to becoming a professional decorator, that's to your credit. I am all for getting everyone in on the job of making the home environment as pretty as possible. My major intent, however, has been to make more people aware of the potential for beauty in the home environment, since home is the most important place there is.

CARLETON VARNEY
Hillandale Farm
June 1978

1

Entryways—A Hearty and Happy Welcome

First impressions count. And the first impression a visitor gets of your home is the entryway—it must be beautiful. In addition, in these days of cramped living quarters, the entryway must often be useful as well as beautiful.

I know people who have turned their entry foyers into work areas, complete with desk and storage shelves. Others use their entryways to display hobby collections. Some people build floor-to-ceiling closets in their entryways to store out-of-season clothing, as well as bicycles, skis, and such. These closets look super when the doors are mirrored to expand the hall's narrow space.

One friend of mine turned his square entry hall into a "mini-museum." The walls are hung with many favorite objects collected on his travels over the years. The display is dramatically mounted on walls covered with fudge-brown vinyl suede. Each group of objects is illuminated by track-mounted ceiling lights. Underfoot, there's a beige sisal carpet.

If your hallway is too small or narrow to be useful, make it beautiful with color, paper, carpeting, and lighting.

A designer wallcovering that would cost too much to use in a large space might be affordable in a small hallway, and rich, dramatic color that would overpower you in your living room might be just the thing to liven up an entryway. In a tiny hallway I once saw, the walls were lacquered black, the ceiling covered with shiny gold leaf, and moldings and doors were painted white with brass hardware. The look was rich, dramatic, and just right for a space that was too small to be useful.

Before decorating your foyer, remember the elements of design you have to work with. What will the floor treatment be—colorful tile, printed nylon carpeting, a fine oriental rug? Will you paper walls from ceiling to floor, or will you choose a grass-cloth wallcovering above a painted or stained dado? Perhaps you will line foyer walls with bookcases, or maybe you will think felt is the best wallcovering.

Think about ceiling treatment, too. Perhaps you will paint the ceiling to match walls or a contrasting color. Or maybe you will want a tented ceiling to give the entry hall a dramatic look.

Lighting also plays a big part in entryways. The overhead chandelier is popular in foyer decorating; a wrought-iron fixture would be perfect in a foyer with a practical Spanish-tile floor, or, perhaps, if your home is full of rich woods and leather, the fixture you want is an English lantern.

The best place to start, however, is with the largest elements—walls and floors.

Wall and Floor Treatments

It's fun to start with lots of good color in the foyer. Colorful walls are making a big comeback, so you needn't be afraid of using an intense Chinese red, a deep eggplant, a true daffodil yellow, or a fresh emerald green.

One of the handsomest entryways I ever saw had lots of black accents. There were shiny black doors leading to the rooms beyond; and the polished floor, accented with jewel-tone oriental rugs, was stained black. Walls were painted rich coral, and the ceiling was pure white. The ornate moldings were painted shiny black.

And would you believe that a room with black walls could be cozy and cheerful?

Personally, I like dark walls to be glossy, so if your wall surface is free of cracks and lumpy plaster, paint on color using a glossy paint, or use varnish over a matte-finish paint.

If you prefer a lighter mood, what about an entrance hall with a white painted dado and upper walls covered with an eye-catching wallcovering of a vivid green and white stripe? Against the facing wall I would like a jonquil-yellow lacquered console table with a handsome mirror or picture grouping above it.

One of my friends chose fire-engine red for her foyer walls with a white ceiling, and it was smashing. Flooring was terra cotta vinyl laid in a herringbone pattern. The foyer furnishings included a colonial chest (which in addition to being handsome offered valuable drawer space) on one wall, and above it hung small walnut wall brackets on which a collection of Revolutionary War soldiers was placed. The red-walled foyer led into a living room with colonial furniture, walnut-paneled walls, and a plaid carpet of red, white, and dark green.

Many fans of prints, and particularly of things Early American, do not realize that fabrics and wallcoverings called "documentaries" exist. Documentaries, quite simply, are designs directly copied from, or inspired by, old fabrics and wallcoverings. Documentary fabrics and wallcoverings may be inspired by museum collections, private collections, or by historic landmark preservations, such as Williamsburg or Historic Charleston. A documentary may copy an English floral chintz or an Early American coverlet.

True fans of the old days like to furnish their homes with antiques or with exact replicas of furniture from their favorite periods, and to enhance the authenticity, they use documentaries for walls, draperies, and upholstery. The entryway shown is an example of Early American carried through to the last detail. The documentary wallcovering was inspired by a handwoven wool coverlet circa 1855. The trim and door color was picked up from the paper's subtle blue motif, and a deacon's bench was painted to match.

If you prefer an eclectic look to an authentic period look, you can still use documentaries. I think that cotton jacquard documentaries have the kind of geometric look that is super with contemporary counterpoint.

Let's take prints a dramatic step further for foyer treatments. Thanks to wallpapers that create the architectural look, many unusual effects can be achieved in your entryway. You can have a stone balustrade around your foyer walls, or you can have Gothic, Ionic, or Corinthian columns at each side of your front door. A New Orleans fireplace-screen wall, a pair of gates, or a wall of louvered shutters—all can be created by wallpaper to give your foyer a theatrical flair.

There are wallpapers that feature Roman buildings, New Orleans houses, and Beacon Hill brownstones. The wallpapers are large in scale and add great architectural interest, particularly to dark, drab foyers. Wallpaper architectural details, needless to say, are far less costly than the real thing.

Recently, in decorating a round foyer, I used the architectural look for interest. A thirty-inch-high wallpaper dado, simulating wrought iron, was installed around the wall. I used the same wrought-iron wallpaper detail under the crown molding. Large wallpaper columns, giving the effect of plaster or concrete pillars, were applied at each side of the double entry doors and also flanking the doors leading to the dining room. Wallpapers featured three shades of green—Kelly, forest, mint—against a white background. On the floor I used brilliant green vinyl with a white star center and strip border.

Documentary-print wallcovering inspired by a nineteenth-century handwoven indigo-and-white-wool coverlet gives this Early American entryway a welcoming look.

Greeff's "Jerusha Bartlett" documentary print wallcovering

Paneled walls are wonderful in a more spacious foyer, or a paneled dado with a wallcovering above. I recently saw an Oriental-style foyer which featured walls covered with prefinished hardwood plywood paneling. The mellow wood paneling was an effective background for traditional Oriental furnishings—a handsome console table with a floral arrangement and brass candlesticks, a bamboo-frame mirror, and red-lacquered chairs with powder-blue cushions. A burgundy-red, beige, and powder-blue Oriental area rug was placed on a floor of diagonally laid black and white tiles. More on the Oriental look for your foyer later—and more also on the dramatic possibilities of checkerboard floors!

I am also a patent enthusiast—patent vinyl, that is. It's a great way to camouflage cracked, pitted walls with flair. But your walls needn't be eyesores to get the slick patent treatment—any wall will do.

Granted, patent vinyl is not the cheapest way to decorate a wall, but it's one of the most attractive and practical of all wallcoverings, and there are colors galore to choose from. My favorites are the dark, rich colors—chocolate brown, ebony, burgundy, navy, emerald green, and the tortoise-shell looks. Did I say a moment ago that I like dark walls to be glossy? Come to think of it, I guess I also like glossy walls to be dark. Somehow, the lighter patents don't do as much

This distinctive foyer is paneled in 4' x 8' boards of hardwood plywood paneling whose mellow color serves as background for traditional Oriental furnishings. Burgundy-red, beige, and powder-blue Oriental area rug is placed over floor of diagonally laid black-and-white-square tiles.

for me. The corridor walls of my office are covered in shiny chocolate-brown patent vinyl. The trim and carpeting are punchy tomato-red!

Try one of those dramatic dark patents on your entryway walls—perhaps my chocolate-and-red combination. Or how about reversing the scheme —fire-engine-red patent vinyl on the walls, with chocolate carpeting, chocolate trim, and a beige painted ceiling?

Small entry halls can easily be given a lift with wallpaper remnants that cost a fraction of the by-the-roll prices. For a small foyer I frequently choose open-design wallcoverings such as trellis and fretwork patterns that give the illusion of greater space. Sheet mirror is even better for visually expanding a small foyer, especially if you mirror the doors as well as the walls. If your budget won't allow this, however, even a small painted foyer with many doors and little wall space will look larger if you paint the doors and doorframes the same color as the walls.

Underfoot, bargain-decorate a wood floor with

paint-on stencils. You can buy the stencils in kit form in a variety of patterns and use them on bare wood or painted wood. Just make sure your design is well protected with a few layers of polyurethane.

If carpeting is more to your liking, shop for a large remnant and use it over wall-to-wall sisal matting, or directly on the wood floor.

And how about tiles for foyer floors? Anyone for checkers? One of my favorite floor-tile patterns is the checkerboard. The black and white squares—be they of marble, vinyl, or carpet—are both traditional and modern. Many traditional homes have black-and-white checkerboard floors in the foyer, and many a contemporary entry hall has a black-and-white checkerboard area rug under a brilliantly colored Parsons coffee table.

If you play checkers, you may have noticed that today checkerboards have gone multicolored. There are blue-and-green boards with colorful yellow and white checkers. There are pink-and-purple boards with turquoise and pale-green checkers. Look at the number of decorating schemes that today's checkerboards can bring to a foyer. When thinking of something new for flooring, think multicolored checkerboard.

Decorate the Foyer Doors

You don't see many interesting doors in today's homes, since most builders favor the hollow-core ("flush") door with its flat, no-personality facade. But there is one thing those uninteresting doors are good for: dressing up. And nothing could be easier than decorating such a door in a hallway.

If you have a flush door in the entryway that simply leads to another door, why not decorate the door and the walls on either side with a wavelike supergraphic design? Think of the door and surrounding wall as one surface and paint waves of color right across the entire elevation. The wavelike design can be sprayed on via the masking-tape-and-paper method, and your waves might be bright yellow, emerald green, and azure blue for the sunshine look.

If your entry is wallpapered, you can paper the door, too, and install an interesting doorknob while you're at it. For added appeal, nail narrow moldings a few inches from the door's edges.

Wallpaper inside moldings and paint the doorframe, molding, and room trim a contrasting shade.

This was done in the entrance foyer of a home I visited recently. The wallcovering was a chocolate-brown patent vinyl printed with a white bamboo design. The front door and closet doors were papered, too, with moldings and trim painted shiny chocolate. Carpet was a soil-hiding off-white nylon shag.

A final word on doors: Don't overlook door hardware when foyer-decorating; I like big and important hardware in the entrance hall, no matter what the style.

The Large Foyer

All too often the large foyer becomes the final resting place for all the odds and ends, the furniture and accessories that don't fit elsewhere in the house. You know what I mean. When you enter, you're greeted by a sad-sack dresser that should have gone to the junk shop ten years ago. and sitting on that dresser is a frilly boudoir lamp that was moved to the foyer when the master bedroom went Danish modern. The "decor" is completed by the worn living-room carpet, cut down to fit. Then there's a bicycle, a set of skis, and assorted galoshes strewn about, too. The effect is grim, drab, depressing. But it needn't stay that way.

After you've transformed those drab walls and floor, you might use the foyer to experiment with a new decor or furniture style. If you're a traditionalist who also admires the clean, contemporary look, why not go contemporary in your foyer? You won't have to invest in a great deal of furniture—two chairs and a glass-and-chrome console table will do it—and you'll have the best of two decorating worlds: the traditional you love in your living room, bedrooms, and family room, and the contemporary you've been dying to try.

Or perhaps you've been thinking of going Oriental in your decor, but hesitate to invest in expensive living-room furnishings in the Oriental style. Why not try out that Eastern look in the foyer? Start with an Oriental rug in rich reds and golds. Cover walls in an Oriental gold-and-red-patterned wallcovering. For furnishings, how about a white lacquered campaign chest and

wicker chair? And for pizzazz, why not paint the door leading to the room beyond a hot Chinese red? Accessorize your Oriental foyer with ebony-black Oriental vases, lamps, and plant stand—and banish the forlorn foyer forever.

While we're thinking Oriental, let's expand. These days I'm in the Persian decorating mood. Who hasn't admired the delicate beauty of those exotic Persian carpets with their colorful all-over patterns of birds, leaves, and flowers? Now, picture that rich, exotic look translated into the brilliance of a formerly drab foyer. In a hall I'm doing now for a client, I've done the walls in ceramic tiles of rich mustard, royal blue, black, and white. The high ceiling is painted royal blue and the trim is white. The foyer floor is tiled in Spanish-look vinyl tiles of rich royal blue and white. It's a delicious effect, and one I've carried right into my client's living room.

Alternatively, you might paint walls a rich mustard and door surfaces and trim shiny red. How handsome the look of mustard walls and red doors would be with a parquet floor decorated with a gold and beige Oriental rug and a Chinese-red coromandel console table.

Place a Chinese-base lamp on the console table and above it hang a mirror with a carved gold-leaf frame.

For another new look for the larger foyer, consider this scheme. Paint walls rich deep blue and all door surfaces and baseboards white. For a rugged floor covering with style, choose printed nylon carpeting with latex foam backing. With deep blue walls, I would like a flooring pattern in deep blue and bronze-gold tones. A tortoise-finish Parsons-style console table would pick up the muted bronze tones in the carpet print. Best bets for accessories would be a white Chinese-framed mirror above the console, a white Chinese-style lamp on it, and lots of potted plants. And why not add an interesting antique clothes tree of bentwood design painted white?

Storage

A COZY LIBRARY IN YOUR ENTRY HALL

Books and bookshelves are very much a part of decorating these days, and in my opinion a wall of books, or even a table display of books, can be just as interesting a part of any room as the colors, fabrics, and furniture. With book jackets more colorful than ever and bookshelves available in every shape, size, and style imaginable, there's no reason not to have decorative as well as practical book storage. And there's no reason not to use it to brighten that forlorn foyer.

It's easy to create practical, attractive book storage-plus in your entry hall. Build wall-mounted bookshelves to hold your books and some well-chosen accessories, and under those shelves mount a wider shelf for storage. Picture white laminate shelves against tangerine walls, or sunny yellow shelves against sky-blue walls, or natural wood-finish shelves, protected with polyurethane, against fresh white walls.

If you don't want shelves that hang on the walls, think stackables—they're favorites of mine in colors or wood finishes.

However you shelve your books, you can turn that neglected foyer into a cozy library. I saw it done in a rather large hallway that had handsome wood-framed windows. Except for some hanging plants, the windows were left bare to let in the sunshine. Stackable cases held books on one side of a window. More books were arranged decoratively on a set of antique library steps. For lounging, there was a curule chair with seat pad of zippy leopard-skin fabric. And contributing to the mood of cozy relaxation was a multitoned blue carpet.

A word on seating in your foyer: Cane chairs, too uncomfortable for hard, everyday use, are wonderful stop-off seating in an entry hall; and bergères, those graceful and comfortable "occasional" Louis XV pieces, work beautifully in

A formerly forlorn foyer in the Eastern style features an Oriental rug of rich reds and golds and an Oriental wallcovering in the same vibrant hues.

Stacking bookcases, a conversation-piece chair, and a blue multitone carpet turn a once neglected hallway into a cozy library.

Bigelow's "Orleans" carpet

foyers too, especially when they flank a contemporary glass-and-steel console table.

FOR LOUVER LOVERS

Are you a louver lover? I am. I love louvered window shutters with fixed or movable slats. And I love louvered doors on closets.

If storage is your problem, louvered-door closets in the foyer might be the solution. Here is how a friend of mine solved her storage problems beautifully. In a long, narrow entryway of her city apartment, she had shallow louvered-door closets built in. Since the doors went from floor to ceiling and from one end of the hall to the other, this airy slatted look was a must; otherwise the hallway would have been much too closed-in and dreary. My friend had the louvered doors and the walls painted fresh white. Then, to give an illusion of width, she stenciled her floor with bright crosswise stripes of sky-blue and grass-green from wall to wall. (The paint job was protected with several coats of clear polyurethane.) For more airy brightness, the ceiling was mirrored to reflect those happy stripes.

What a fresh, welcoming entryway it was! And

Let your foyer say welcome! Walls of this inviting foyer are painted a rich deep blue to match dominant color of nylon carpeting. Tortoise-finish Parsons-style table picks up the muted bronze-gold tones of carpet print. Antique clothes tree, Chinese mirror, and other accessories in white, along with white doors and baseboard, give fresh accents.

what a practical solution to a city dweller's storage woes.

Special Furniture in Your Foyer

Chairs and an occasional small table are not the only furniture that can make your foyer distinctive. I love, for example, to see a grandfather clock in the foyer of an apartment or single-family house. Grandfather clocks seem to fill that special decorating bill. If you have a spot in your foyer that has to be filled, consider a grandfather clock. The "old guy" will not only tell you the time, he'll bring a lot of charm and color to the entry of your home.

Try a walnut-finish clock against a wall with a white dado above which a green and white damask wallcovering is hung. If you are very modern, consider a Plexiglas grandfather clock for your entry foyer. Grandfather in any suit of clothes will always be welcome there. He's special, unique, and everlasting.

Breakfronts and secretaries are also big in today's decorating. The breakfront and the secretary—that tall piece of furniture used as a desk and storage place—are more or less the same. A secretary has a writing surface, a breakfront does not; the breakfront is used for storage only, but often has the same look and proportions as a secretary.

I like to see a secretary, complete with a bench or pull-up chair, in an entry foyer. The top of the secretary, sometimes with clear glass or wire-mesh doors, is filled with colorful accessories and books. I like breakfronts and secretaries with grille doors, and I also like to see the top doors decorated with sheer fabric.

Antique mahogany and walnut breakfronts are very often deep, thick pieces of furniture and therefore look well only in large foyers. There are on the market today, however, a host of breakfronts and secretaries with streamlined profiles that can bring a lot of character to any entry hall.

If you have an old mahogany secretary and you need storage space, why not utilize it in the foyer? Paint it a bright color—perhaps the color of your walls, or consider painting it light blue with clean white trim. Paint the interior of the upper portion a sparkling color to complement your decor—maybe zinnia red, canary yellow, or brilliant emerald green. Get some bright white or brass hardware for the drawers and doors, and your secretary will look like a custom-made built-in unit.

For a different look in hallway seating, why not choose a bench? There are many bench styles on the market—colonial deacons' benches with stenciled backs and English refectory benches in oak come to mind. But I think it's even more fun to take an old bench and find a new use for it.

Old church pews can be found in antique shops and junk shops, and so can old park benches with slat seats and iron scrollwork legs and arms. Even old rectangular piano benches can take on many new looks.

Recently I saw a great rectangular, two-seat oak bench with the back pierced with charming heart and flower designs. I would have covered the seat with a colorful Early American calico or patchwork fabric. What a perfect look for the entry hall in a warm, cozy home!

For another hallway look, I enjoy seeing a long narrow bench. Church pews are perfect for this purpose. Friends of mine who used an old church pew in their entryway kept the pew's original black and white paint, and it looked stunning against their goldenrod-yellow walls. On the seat of the pew (you know how hard they can be) my friends placed a thin foam cushion covered in a small-figured tapestry fabric of black, gold, pale yellow, and orange. The floor was painted a gleaming charcoal, accented with shiny brass planters holding lots of green plants.

If you choose an old park bench, paint it white and use a large-check gingham for the cushion. You can soften the look even more with ruffled toss pillows in a smaller gingham check, and to carry the park look further, why not a grass-green shag carpet underfoot?

You can cover the top of that old rectangular piano bench with homemade needlepoint and paint the bench a bright color, using sturdy polyurethane paint. You'll find it's mighty handy in the entry hall, since the storage space beneath the hinged top, originally meant to hold music books, can just as easily be used to hold mittens and scarves, or whatever you will.

Accessorizing Your Foyer

I am sure that many of you have heard the old decorating commandment "Never use two prints in the same room." This rule has given way to more modern thinking; several prints are now very often used in the same setting. As for that other old decorating edict—"Don't, whatever you do, hang pictures or paintings on a print wallpaper"—that's another rule that has definitely seen its day.

A New York townhouse dweller transformed the entryway of her apartment into an inviting gallery by hanging all types of paintings and accessories on a printed damask wallcovering. There were modern paintings and prints along with cameos and traditional portraits, mirrors, and a coat of arms in a gold-leaf frame. The wallpaper print in bronze tones complemented sunny gold shag nylon carpeting.

Continuing the gallery look was a collection of crystal objects displayed on a colonial hope chest, used on one wall instead of a console table. How handsome the crystal bottles, antique candlesticks, and sparkling cubes and prisms looked on the colonial hope chest, particularly exciting at night when the candles were lit. You see, the days are gone when the foyer required a vitrine (glass showcase) in which to display such accessories.

Now that you've seen the hidden potential of your entryway, whatever its size, I hope you'll be inspired to capitalize on it. Whatever you choose in terms of color, style, wallcoverings, flooring, furnishings, lighting, and accessories, remember that the most important thing is that the entrance to your home should express character —yours—and it must say welcome!

Lees shag carpeting of Allied Chemical nylon

The gallery look is achieved in this entry foyer by hanging all types of paintings and accessories on printed damask wallcovering and adroitly assembling a collection of crystal atop a colonial hope chest. Bronze tones of the wallpaper print complement opulent nylon shag carpeting in a rich golden color.

2

The Living Room

Starting Out

Many newlyweds will be using this book as they decorate their very first house or apartment. My advice: Use something old, something new, something borrowed, and something blue.

Decorating with something old and something new is the eclectic way of decorating that I have been advocating for years. That means no matching furniture suites, please.

The something old you choose could be an antique armoire. Armoires, in my opinion, offer unmatched versatility. If your newlywed nest is a one-room affair, the armoire, with all its storage space—for wardrobe, bar, TV, stereo—could become your apartment's focal point. Flank that armoire focal point with "something new"—a pair of matching love seats, or a pair of armless chairs facing a love seat. Upholstered pieces, in my opinion, should always be bought new; antiques have a look, but their often-frail frames don't stand up to everyday use. When purchasing your first upholstered chairs or sofas, please buy classics and buy quality. A tuxedo or Lawson-style sofa and club chairs are always good choices. Depending on the upholstery fabric you choose, those upholstered classics can take on a variety of looks, from contemporary to Early American to elegant French.

The something borrowed in your new home might be track lighting, an idea borrowed from the theater for use in the home. A ceiling-mounted track on either side of a room, with spotlights aimed at paintings, at bookshelves, and at your room's focal point—whatever it may be—can turn a drab room into a dramatic one.

And for that something blue—the choice is yours. Is there a color in nature that doesn't harmonize with that beautiful blue sky? If you love blue, go blue all the way on walls, floor, and upholstery. If a beigy natural look is your decorating choice, use blue as an accent. Paint walls soft aqua or sky blue. Then coordinate: Accent a beige sofa with pillows of blue batik and solid blues, ranging from blueberry to aqua; go blueberry blue for lamps and ashtrays; skirt a table in the blue batik.

If you're starting out with some leftover or hand-me-down furniture, first try rearranging. Rearranging your living-room furniture can save you lots of dollars and at the same time give you a new look in your home.

I have always been a great advocate of decorating rooms with the things one loves. I also like to hold onto the things I enjoy and have collected over the years. There are times when I do think about getting rid of an old but good piece of furniture that I've loved and had around for years, but every time I get into this mood I stop and ask myself, "Do I really want to exchange the old friend for the new?" Generally, my answer is no. So instead of buying new, I start rearranging the old.

For example, instead of buying a new sofa, I move the old one from the wall position and place it in front of the draped window wall. I give the sofa a new look—maybe with slipcovers —and freshen the drapery, maybe with colorful new braid. I'll take the throw pillows from the library and zipper slipcover them, too, with a new print for sofa accent. The round drum table from the library may also go into my new in-front-of-the-window sofa grouping, used as an end table instead of the former rectangular table, which then moves to the library. I might even skirt the drum table for a new look. The club chairs, instead of being used at right and left of the sofa, will be rearranged and placed beside each other with a small cigarette table between. Finally, I'll rearrange the picture groupings. Maybe the mirror that hung in the dining room over the server will become a focal point in the living room—over the fireplace.

There is hardly a room I've seen that I cannot rearrange interestingly for a new look, even if the pieces I have to work with seem to clash with one another. The secret is coordination.

One of the best ways to pull a room together, whether you're rearranging or starting out fresh, is with matching wallcovering and fabric. I like rooms that are decorated with coordinated fabrics and wallcovering, and I have coordinated rooms all over the home. Coordinates make a room less cluttered-looking, especially important in small rooms. If you have a small living room—and many of us apartment dwellers do—pick a soft wallpaper and fabric combination. Bold, multicolored, patterned coordinates are dramatic, but I'd avoid them unless you want a pop-flash effect and are planning to use lots of modernistic Space Age accessories. Coordinates with a soft look are long-lived, easy to live with.

If you want to coordinate a small, cozy living room, choose a soft floral design of russet, melon, and umber (yellowish or reddish brown) on a creamy beige background for the wallpaper and fabric, using the fabric on your sofas or love seats, on club chairs, and for window draperies too. Choose a beige or cream-color carpet for this setting, and use mellow, warm hardwood furn-

ishings. Accessorize the room with umber-tone pieces, such as a copper tea kettle filled with flowers for your coffee table; copper lamps for end tables, or lamps of aubergine-color porcelain, or (one of the handsomest lamps I've seen recently) a tortoise-finish lamp with a licorice-black shade—actually a copy of a 150-year-old K'ang Hsi dynasty candlestick. Oriental is certainly in.

Small, coordinated living rooms can be visually enlarged by other means, too. One exciting way to create an illusion of more space is by arranging furniture on the diagonal. Because a room's longest measurement is a straight line from one corner to the diagonally opposite corner, furniture arranged on the bias forces the eye to follow that long, long line.

To achieve this effect easily in a rectangular room, lay a perfectly square area rug on the diagonal, leaving the room's four corners uncovered by the rug (you can, of course, lay your square rug over wall-to-wall carpeting). Arrange your conversation grouping—sofas, chairs, occasional tables—so that they parallel the diagonal area defined by the rug. The corners of the room which remain can be used as work areas, for plants, storage units—you name it.

High ceilings also give the illusion of space. But if your ceilings are the more common eight-foot variety, don't despair; simply select low, floor-hugging furniture to make your low ceilings appear higher. Mirroring that ceiling will also raise it visually, just as mirroring a wall will seem to push out that wall. And today's precut mirror tile is so inexpensive that mirrored walls and ceilings are no longer the luxury they once were.

You can color your room spacious, too. The all-white room is a good example. I like an all-white treatment for the one-room apartment occupied by the single man or woman. Floor can be white vinyl tiles. Cushy sofa and chairs can be slipcovered in sturdy, washable white cotton with sofa wall mirrored. For occasional tables, clear Lucite is a good spacemaking choice. Hang white matchstick blinds at windows. Add warmth to the white room with chairs in warm, dark wood with seat pads of the white slipcover fabric, and with small accessories of wood—boxes, dark-stained baskets for plants, picture frames.

And don't be afraid to eliminate, to enlarge and simplify your living room. Most people talk of buying furniture when they redo a room, but few think of discarding furniture that is too large,

Stiffel's K'ang Hsi candlestick la

The great coordinates—wallpaper and matching fabrics—give this cozy, small living room a look of oneness and spaciousness. The umber, russet, and beige tones in the coordinates are charmingly lighted by a candlestick lamp in a tortoise finish.

too shabby, too fragile to be childproof—or just not quite right. Believe it or not, discarding furniture and accessories can sometimes be just as effective as buying something brand-new—and a lot less costly. Not only do you save by not buying, but thrift shops will give you a tax credit in return for donated furniture. With a garage sale, you can even turn a profit. And the profit to your decorating can be tremendous.

Here's a young couple's story. After living for several years with a house full of sofas, tables, chests, and such, which they had purchased as newlyweds or had received as hand-me-downs,

these young parents decided they wanted a more liveable, easier-to-care-for decorating style.

Out went two sofas! Out went a hand-me-down recliner! Out went a too-small coffee table! Out went all but a few dust-catching—and not very childproof—knickknacks. Out went the heavy draperies! And out went one plaster wall! That's right. This enterprising couple loved the rustic, natural look so much, they stripped an outer plaster wall down to the brick.

To redecorate, the couple—who have one child and a large dog—decided on light natural-finish woods, natural charcoal-gray upholstery fabrics for sofas, and pure white painted walls. To combat the problem of dust and stray toys under the sofa, the built-in cupboard-back sofas reach right to the floor. For color, a built-in bench extends the full length of the window wall and is covered in warm wine red. Simple wall-hung cupboards display the knickknacks between tall windows—left bare except for bushy hanging plants. Underfoot, a chocolate, marble-patterned rug provides a warm—and easy-care—surface for child's play and grown-up comfort.

Stripping down can mean replacing two tiny, useless coffee tables with one generous-size table. Or it can mean putting up one big painting or wall hanging in place of a grouping of tiny pictures that look lost on that big wall anyway. Stripping down might also mean replacing an elaborate window treatment wih simple roller blinds or shutters.

I know it's time to strip down in my own home when I realize that I no longer enjoy an item in a room, or when it's not useful. While in a client's apartment, I noticed that her two tiny coffee tables were barely large enough to hold a drinking glass and ashtray. When I asked her about it, she admitted that at parties, drinks and ashtrays often ended up on the floor, or on the arms of the sofa. I told her to strip down and replace those two coffee tables with one big table. The look was neater, and now my client has a coffee table she can use.

When a friend of mine complained that her swag drapery treatment was difficult to keep clean, I told her to strip down and replace those draperies with simple Roman shades. I love elegant draperies, but not if they don't suit one's life-style.

Stripping down can also be accomplished by rotating possessions as the Japanese do. Instead of displaying all your treasures at once, store

Evans & Black Antron nylon carpet

A pared-down living room for an active family was created with ease of care in mind. Built-in cupboard-back sofas can't collect dust or stray toys underneath because they go right to the floor. And floor care is simplified by a carpet of soil-hiding nylon.

some away and display others. When you tire of one display of accessories, pack them away and bring out a new group to show!

Use Your Imagination

Not all of us are born with a family fortune *à la* Vanderbilt or Rockefeller, but most of us are born with riches of another kind. I'm speaking of imagination, which is the birthright of everyone. And when applied to home decoration, that's a commodity that can put any home on a par with the stateliest mansion in terms of warmth, charm, and just plain fun.

I've seen many instances where imagination and ingenuity in living-room decoration proved an extremely good substitute for cash. For example, fifteen years ago some newlywed friends of mine couldn't afford a sofa or even an armchair, so they bought colorful fabric remnants and used them to cover giant pillows to create fun floor seating. Today, as you know, that idea has caught on big, and manufacturers now commercially produce "pillow furniture."

Another ingenious idea that's caught on commercially is the stacking crate. I remember the days when many people painted and stacked orange crates for use as storage. Today, commercially made plastic crates in super colors are all over the market.

If wall decoration on a shoestring is your problem, take a cue from a young friend of mine. He recently complained to me that the walls in his high-ceilinged living room looked bare. "I can't afford to buy a painting that size," he explained, "and framing a large poster or a bunch of prints would cost an arm and a leg."

The next time I visited my friend, he had found a solution. On a one-week vacation in North Africa he had purchased a colorful striped blanket in shades of wine, pumpkin, emerald green, and purple that filled the wall space to a tee—no costly framing required. I'd say he got a lot of decorating power for the $10 he paid for that blanket, wouldn't you?

A wonderful place to let your imagination run free is in a junk store. I love browsing in them on rainy weekends. My first find was a pair of rattan armchairs of 1930 vintage. With new cushions of white washable canvas, those chairs look right up to date flanking a client's white canvas-covered tuxedo sofa.

Another junk-store find for the same client—a young lady of musical talent—was an upright piano, which we lacquered shiny white. I find a coat of white lacquer or paint can hide a multitude of sins and make even a homely cast-off look like a glamour girl. I often use paint to lighten the look of heavy junk-store pieces (like the piano) or to cover a badly marred finish.

Thrown over that piano is a touch of brilliant color—a white Spanish shawl covered with bursts of purple, red, orange, and sunny yellow embroidered flowers and birds. I found the shawl on one of my junk-shop junkets, too.

I completed my client's apartment with inexpensive acrylic-cube end tables and a coffee table of plate glass on a white-lacquered pedestal cut down from an old dining-table base.

Walls were pure sparkling white with moldings and doors of softest peach. Underfoot was an area rug of straw-colored sisal squares. Windows were hung with white bamboo blinds and peach draperies made from cotton sheeting. Green plants in white wicker baskets completed the look. And the cost? The greatest expenditure was that priceless gift we all have—imagination.

Ideas for the Large Living Room

Americans love wide-open spaces and often build or remodel their homes to include large living rooms. But, alas, those wide-open spaces can be oh-so-cold and uninviting unless they are planned properly.

If you feel as though your living room resembles a big, drafty barn, and you would prefer cozier, more intimate surroundings, here are some dos and don'ts that may help you tame those wide-open spaces.

• DO paint walls a soft, warm color—ripe cantaloupe, vibrant sky blue, fresh grass green.
• DO have several furniture groupings for entertaining and leisure activities. I like a central grouping plus a corner for reading, a corner for your game table and chairs, and a conversation corner with a couple of comfortable chairs and a lamp table. (More on conversation groupings later.)
• DON'T fill your room with "leggy" furniture. Better to have a few massive pieces than lots of dinky, spindly pieces that create clutter. Try large

cube tables, skirted chairs, and plump sofas to give your room a solid feeling.

• DO arrange your main furniture grouping around a focal point such as a fireplace or super painting.

• DON'T feel you must arrange furniture against walls. If your room is large enough, furniture can go in the center of the room.

• DO fill that empty corner with a large plant, a dramatic free-standing sculpture, or a handsome armoire, desk, or bookcase.

A room I saw recently illsutrated how some of these do's and don'ts work in an actual setting.

The room's major furniture grouping focused on a brick fireplace topped by a bold abstract painting. Chairs were upholstered in a large-scale print of chocolate brown and white. The sofa was covered in tobacco corduroy. A jungle of tall green plants filled one corner of the room. And pulling the whole room together was an earth-toned patterned carpet, treated with a carpet protector for easy cleanups—a plus when you have a large area to keep clean.

Let's talk for a moment about intimate conversation groupings for your living room. According to the experts, cozy corners promote conversation. I couldn't agree more. At large parties or on family evenings at home, it's nice to be able to sneak away to private corners, apart from the main conversation group, for a tête-à-tête.

In my house we have many cozy conversation corners in the living room, family room—even in the bedroom. Take a look at your own living-room corners—at least one of them should have a place for private conversation. Perhaps you could select the corner nearest your telephone and have that corner serve double duty—as the telephone spot and conversation spot. Furnish your corner with everything two people might need to be comfortable—let the accompanying picture be your guide:

Against a backdrop of eighteenth-century damask-look wallcovering of golden beige and sky blue are two Parsons-style armchairs and a pretty skirted table. The chairs are upholstered in a mini-check of beige and white to complement the beige tweed sofa and golden-beige table cover. The table is a handy place for sociable conversationalists to perch drinks and coffee cups. It also holds a pretty, glass-based lamp

that casts a warm, inviting glow. And notice something else about this corner: Although it's private, it's close enough to the sofa so that when the private conversation is over, the two conversationalists can join the larger party centered around the main conversation grouping.

Conversation Groupings and Other Furniture Arrangements

In the small living room, you can use the corner of your room for a main, right-angle conversation grouping. I use the right-angle arrangement quite often in my decorating projects, preferring it in a small room to the customary look of a long sofa, two matching end tables, and two matching club chairs. The customary arrangement is acceptable, but isn't it more interesting to use one club chair and one love seat (maybe one that opens into a bed for the occasional overnight guest), along with the long sofa?

When cornering a right-angle conversation grouping, I suggest a 30-inch-square end table for the space between the love seat and sofa. In selecting your table, pick one that is as high as the sofa and love-seat arms.

For upholstery in your right-angle group, select an airy print, maybe one of a floral-and-bird design. The lighter and airier, the better. Heavy tweeds and/or dark upholstery will make your conversation grouping look too massive in a small room.

And think movability in a small space. Don't, whatever you do, furnish with big, heavy coffee tables. Choose easy-to-transport tables such as white Parsons-type tables. Separated, the tables can be used individually for cocktails, for a buffet, for coffee. Placed together, they can make one long table for use in front of the sofa.

To unify the small room, use wall-to-wall carpeting, in a rich color if you like.

Now to the main grouping for the larger living room. Well-arranged main conversation groupings always need an end table or two at hand on which to place lamps, ashtrays, and accessories, and certainly the main conversation grouping in your living room must have a large coffee table.

In my day I've seen many poorly planned main conversation groupings. In these groupings the

James Seeman's "Deauville" wallcovering

sofa generally sits on one side of the room all alone with, perhaps, matching end tables at hand. The chairs in the room unfortunately do not nestle up to the sofa; they are far away, on the opposite side of the room.

Main conversation groupings are easy to plan once you realize that the reason for them is to arrange furniture so that people can sit comfortably and speak softly to one another. The sofa on one side of the room with the chairs on the other means that people have to call back and forth. Many times I've told a client to examine the living-room seating arrangement the day after a party. If chairs and tables are moved all around the room, the conversation arrangement is wrong,

wrong, wrong, and something should be done about it.

Many people like to arrange a main conversation grouping in the round, with a long rectangular sofa, skirted end tables, and three club chairs gathered around a coffee table.

Others prefer the square shape. Why not arrange a group of sectional sofas in the center of the living room—a comfortable, cushy U-shaped sofa arrangement is most effective. The sofa grouping, covered in a striped tweedy fabric, can be lighted from above, or you might try backing up the sofas with some chrome-and-glass tables on which you can place a lamp or two. Complete the grouping with a pair of upholstered armchairs.

A cheerful bird-and-flower-print fabric, lightweight Parsons tables, and a bright blue nylon carpet keep this right-angle conversation grouping from looking massive and dark.

Here's a panelled entrance foyer with plenty of style. Trellis rugs were designed for the setting and were woven by Edward Fields.

An entry foyer with a black-and-white floor always says welcome. Floor tiles should be laid on the diagonal.

The spiral staircase is popular all over America. In the living room of our St. Croix condominium we have rattan furnishings along with lots of big island-flowered chintz.

A lattice ceiling in a family room is a popular look. This porchlike setting utilizes other popular decorating items: a ceiling-hung fly fan, cocoa mat and rugs, and a green-and-white fern print on sofas and chairs.

Carleton Varney

Botanical prints make handsome statements in English country-style houses. Walls in the living room are covered with green strié paper. Carpeting is soft pink.

Pattern on pattern was the rage in the late Sixties. The look is still with us—and will survive several decades to come.

A living room of grandeur is decorated with lemon-yellow damask on curved-back tufted sofas. Furnishings are a mixture of French periods.

Small library is enlarged by use of mirrored wall behind sofa. Tangiers—a modern fabric—works well with Moroccan accessories and with flame-stitch rug.

Intimacy and spaciousness—you get both with a squared-off conversation grouping built around cushy, tweedy sofas. The turned orange wooden legs and arms of the chairs add a whimsical note.

Now that you've thought about conversation groupings for your living room, let's talk about a problem you might encounter as you plan.

Is there a traffic jam in your living room? I'm speaking of a furniture arrangement that impedes traffic—that is, the movement from place to place —in your home. Because home and room layouts differ, I can't give you any hard-and-fast rules for arranging your furniture to best advantage other than the do's and don'ts I've already mentioned. I can remind you, however, to start with a floor plan. Look at it; study it. Where are the doors? Where do people enter the room? Where is the heaviest traffic? Now decide where to place your furniture to accommodate the traffic patterns. Just as you wouldn't build a garage in the middle of your driveway, you shouldn't put a sofa or chair where it will block traffic.

In the room pictured, the fireplace conversation grouping and the dining area are both arranged so that there's easy access to the nearby patio door. A traffic corridor leading to the door was left between the two areas. A sturdy carpet in a tight frieze texture handles the heavy traffic to and from the patio without showing footprints or wear.

Choosing the Living-Room Sofa

Many people find themselves in a quandary when choosing sofas for the living room. "Our living room is twenty-one feet long and eighteen feet wide. Should we buy two sofas?" one person recently asked. Another stated her problem this way: "My husband and I have been arguing about the length of the sofa we should buy. I want a four-seater, but he says a four-seater is a waste because only two or three at the most use it anyway. I frankly want a four-seater for looks. What's your opinion?"

To answer the first question: I would hesitate to purchase two sofas for a 21' x 18' room. One three-seater sofa would be ample, perhaps placed at a right angle to a companion love seat with a square end table at the connecting point. The room would have a simultaneous openness and coziness that might not be achieved with two sofas of the same size, either placed at a right angle to one another or facing one another.

If you have an extra-large living room, say 30' x 20', two facing sofas might be most effective. For small spaces where the face-to-face sofa grouping is desired, I would recommend love seats with two cushions.

Now for my opinion of using four-seater sofas

A large room is broken up into cozy conversation groupings, leaving traffic corridors free for easy access to patio beyond. Heavy traffic won't dim the beauty of a tighly woven carpet in a soil-hiding tweed.

Tightly woven Burlington carpet

—I do find four- and five-seater sofas somewhat long and not the best for conversation. In my own home where three-seater sofas are used, I generally find that they are occupied by only two, rarely by three.

Don't overcrowd a room, either small or large, with too many sofas. One of the nicest sofa groupings I have seen recently followed the flexible approach. The sofa sections were actually club chairs fitted together. One chair had a right arm and one chair had a left arm. Used with one armless section between the two chairs, a three-seater sofa was created. Used with two armless sections between the two chairs, a four-seater sofa was arranged.

Another sofa grouping I liked was a three-seater sofa and one love seat placed at right angles in a cozy country-style living room. The handsome sofas were covered in a cheerful melon-and-blue bandanna print—very striking on the bright copper-tone shag carpet (with its own backing of latex foam rubber). Rich brown walls

This country-style living room has both openness and coziness with an arrangement of one three-seater sofa and one love seat placed at right angles. The handsome sofas, covered in a melon-and-blue bandanna print, are striking on the bright copper-tone shag carpet of nylon with its own backing of latex foam rubber. Walls are rich brown, and built-in bookshelves are filled with objets d'art and collections of books.

Enka's "Super Bulk" n

Rooms require intimate conversation groupings; and like people, pairs are better. In this grouping a pair of tufted chairs in tomato red face a white sofa accented with tomato-red and orange pillows. The carpet of spun nylon is in reds, oranges, fuchsia, and gold. Even eavesdroppers are paired— two white china greyhounds, perched on a glass-and-chrome console table, won't miss a word said in this conversation grouping.

Granada chairs by Selig

added a bit of drama to the room, and there were many different *objets d'art* as well as collections of books setting off built-in bookshelves.

Let's get back to modular seating for a minute. Modular seating is a great space saver in small living rooms where a big, bulky sofa won't fit comfortably. In a small room, I like to arrange modules in the right-angle corner grouping, leaving the rest of the room free for other furniture. When and if you move to a home with a larger living room, the same modules can be placed in an intimate "pit" arrangement in the center of the room.

Add-ons can be broken up and put back together again in any configuration you desire. As for styling, I've seen modulars in styles to blend with every decor. There are elegant velvet-covered modulars as well as plump molded foam modulars covered in washable, childproof sailcloth. And there are wood-framed modulars, too, topped with colorful seat cushions.

Modular seating can solve the party perplexity of seating all those people. Keep a few extra modules in the bedroom or family room. They won't look like uninvited guests at your get-together like folding bridge chairs do.

Foam modules are perfect for a casual living room. They're informal-looking, and lightweight enough to be moved around easily, even by the children. If you like the idea, picture this scheme: The living room features an L-shaped arrangement of molded foam modules covered in sand-beige washable sailcloth. Walls are papered in a washable wallcovering of sand-beige, off-white, burgundy, and chocolate-brown variegated stripes. End table and a wall unit for books, television, and stereo are dark wood. For carpeting I would choose thick burgundy shag and would paint woodwork the same rich hue (for eye appeal and to hide pint-size fingerprints). That same shade of burgundy can be featured in louvered shutters at windows.

Plumpness, incidentally, can be had in non-modular sofas, too. Americans may be dieting and slimming down, but the American sofa is not! The sofa is getting plumper all around. Upholstery is no longer restricted to backs, sides, and arms—now even sofa legs and feet are getting a soft fabric covering. And for even more softness, the American sofa is getting the grand pillow treatment.

As you know, people have been tossing small

pillows on sofas for years—handmade needle-point pillows, solid-color accent pillows, coordinated print pillows. These days, manufacturers are carrying that trend one step further and are designing sofas with toss-pillow backs. And for those who really love to sink into cushy pillows, there are sofas with long wraparound pillows that start at the sofa's center back and cuddle around inside the sofa's arms.

For the ultimate in sinkability, I like a sofa with wraparound button-tufted cushions. The button tufting adds an extra dimension of softness. And if a pretty, traditional look is to your liking, you might cover that sofa in a quilted chintz of coral blossoms on a warm walnut ground.

Two of those plump sofas were the focal point of a restful cork-lined living room I saw recently. The sofas flanked a Chinese-inspired bamboo étagère for books and knickknacks. (A personal collection in an étagère, hutch, or wall unit is one of my favorite focal-point ideas.) And for sparkling contrast to the matte-finish cork walls and soft bronze carpet, there were lots of shiny brass in accessories and glass-topped tables with legs of brushed brass tubing.

You can now also buy modular pillow furniture that snaps together, as well as plump pillow furniture raised off the floor on wood frames.

Consider buying a plump Lawson or tuxedo-style sofa with cushions filled with down or a soft synthetic material. It may cost more than you had planned to spend, but the extra expense is well worth it because a classic sofa with heavenly soft cushions goes with any decor. Moreover, today's down-filled sofa and chair cushions are made with foam cores so that the cushions pop up automatically when no one's sitting down.

Cover your couch in a tiny paisley print if your look is country French; with a nubby beige wool or cotton if you like the natural look; with velvet for a rich elegant setting.

Now imagine trying to do that with a modern-design wood-framed sofa with a squared-off foam slab seat. It can't be done!

LOVE SEATS AND DAY BEDS

I like love seats and use them very often in my decorating projects. Not only are they practical, but in today's smaller-scaled rooms they often look best.

In a large room I sometimes use two love seats. In my own apartment living room I use a love seat–club chair arrangement in front of the fireplace. The love seat sits against a wall, hugged by two large mirrored cube end tables, and there's a large-scale club chair on each side of the fireplace. The love seat and chairs are upholstered in the same geometric print.

Recently I saw a charming apartment living room in which a love seat, covered in an Oriental print of blues and yellows on a beige background, was used for seating, along with two lounge chairs covered in blue velvet. The Oriental feeling was emphasized by a shojilike screen built in front of existing windows, a raised platform for plants in front of the screen, and a bit of indirect lighting. Ancestral Chinese pictures were hung on the wall above the love seat. An Oriental-design rug and an Oriental garden seat and lamp, copies of old ones, also enhanced the setting. The total decorative effect for this underscaled living room was quiet, comfortable, and distinctive.

One career woman/homemaker I know "floated" the love seat in the middle of her living room. A drop-leaf dining table was placed behind the small sofa, and a round coffee table in front of the love seat was hugged by three barrel-back swivel chairs. The love seat–swivel chair arrangement was right in tune with today's comfortable approach to conversation groupings. A popular alternative—a pair of facing love seats at a fireplace grouping—is great for conversation and room arrangement as well.

By using a love seat, more wall space is opened up for end-table pieces. Some people may select 36-inch-wide cabinets for end tables. Others might prefer a desk as an end table at one side of a love seat. A desk I saw used this way in a small apartment living room had been covered with

The love seat is loved by—well, almost everyone! Here is a love seat upholstered in an Oriental design. Shoji-like screen at the windows adds a further dramatic Oriental note. Ancestral Chinese pictures hung on the wall above the love seat, along with the Oriental lamp and Oriental garden seat, complete the setting.

the same colorful cotton fabric that was used on the sofa—a fruit-bowl pattern in yellows, browns, greens, and oranges. The fabric, applied with the aid of wallpaper paste, transformed an otherwise discardable desk into a charming accent piece.

I like day beds in the living room, too, either as sofa substitutes or as supplemental seating. They're hardly a modern invention—they've been on the scene since the seventeenth century—but versatile day beds, or studio couches, as they're sometimes called, are certainly useful in modern settings.

The versatility of day beds is due in part to the fact that they can be used for sitting, reclining, or sleeping. Another factor in their versatility is the multitude of day-bed designs on the market today: In addition to the familiar two-bolster model, there are day beds with fancy frames of all kinds. To name a few, I've seen frames of metal; frames of molded fiber glass; frames of country-style carved wood.

In a handsome, modern living room, I picture a sofa and chair grouping upholstered in a rich paisley of burgundy, poppy red, and forest green, supplemented with two chrome-legged day beds covered in tufted forest-green suede, all against walls lacquered poppy red!

And you thought day beds were things to be relegated to guest rooms or family rooms!

The Sofaless Living Room

In some of today's small living rooms, sofas, love seats, modules, and day beds aren't always practical. No matter; you can have a sofaless living room, and you can make it work beautifully. One I saw recently was in a bachelor apartment. The room was furnished with a Lawson-style club chair in one corner and a wing chair in another. A pair of armless chairs with matching ottomans completed the conversation grouping, all of which was upholstered in a windowpane check of poppy red on sand beige. When this young man entertains, he pulls the ottomans away from their chairs and uses them for extra seating. In that way he can seat six people without a sofa in sight. For larger parties, colorful folding chairs

come out of the closet to supplement the chair-ottoman seating plan.

Another sofa substitute favored by informal folk is the chaise longue. I love the look of a fireplace flanked by a pair of chaise longues, covered in box-quilted cotton.

I've even seen rooms furnished with nothing but chairs. In one, a large circular coffee table sat in the center of the room, with contemporary club chairs upholstered in rich navy blue. The carpet was Chinese in blue and ivory and the walls were white with navy-blue trim.

The chair-table arrangement is friendly to be sure, but it must be done carefully to avoid the "conference-room look."

Now that we've dispensed with sofas, let's move on to some other important elements you'll want to consider as you decorate your living room.

Effective Focal Points

WINDOWS

High on my list of pet peeves is the plain old metal venetian blind. Take down that ugly no-color venetian blind whenever possible.

Today's blinds, you'll be happy to know, are so beautiful they are even being used as elements in great supergraphics. And I've seen venetian blinds used as room dividers and as camouflage for unattractive storage areas in kitchens, work rooms, offices—you name it.

It's all happening because of the color-and-design revolution in blinds—and particularly all those great narrow-slat, tapeless blinds that come in colors galore. I've seen blinds in plum, hot pink, lemon yellow, and scores of other exciting shades, as well as gold, brass, and aluminum finishes. The new gingham-check blinds are favorites of mine for the country kitchen, the nursery, the breakfast room, or anywhere you want a fresh, pretty look.

If you're an antiques fan who also likes venetian blinds, don't spoil your pretty period rooms with ugly, ordinary venetian blinds—look for those handsome old-fashioned wood blinds instead; they'll be right at home in your room. One of my favorite living rooms was decorated in the English manner with natural wood blinds at all the windows. Over those blinds were hung rich tie-back draperies of heavy cranberry silk, and carpet was cranberry, too, topped with Oriental scatter rugs in shades of cranberry, blue, and gold. The two chesterfield sofas were upholstered in brown leather, and there were wing chairs, too—one covered in a damask of cerulean blue and another in cranberry tapestry. Walls were wood-paneled.

If you wish to avoid venetian blinds, there are many attractive and inexpensive substitutes—bamboo roll-ups, matchsticks, laminated cloth shades, balloon shades, and draperies.

And while we're looking at windows, look at your mullions. If you live in a colonial house, or any old-fashioned house, your windows should have mullions (the wooden strips that divide pane from pane). How many times have I seen beautiful old mullioned windows removed to be replaced with single-pane "picture" windows?

If your home is old, please keep your mullioned windows, or replace them if they're gone. If you can't afford to install new windows, look for plastic or wood "snap-in" mullions. They're not my favorites, but they look better on an old house than picture windows.

Picture-*framed* windows, however, can add a new note to your living room. I have always been a believer in the "bring the outside in" decorating theory; I have never believed in overdraping windows that have beautiful views. Why cover the beautiful? I realize, of course, the necessity for privacy; therefore, there must oftentimes be a compromise.

A New York City couple who have a beautiful view of Central Park from their apartment chose the picture-frame window treatment for their living-room windows. They have no draperies—only 12-inch-wide borders of gold Naugahyde framing each of the windows facing Central Park. The young couple did the job themselves. Since there are three living-room windows, each 5 feet high and 4 feet wide, they cut six plywood boards 7 feet in height and six plywood boards 6 feet long for the frames. Corners on all twelve boards were mitered. The boards were covered with the gold Naugahyde, edged with brass nailheads, and then screwed to the wall surfaces around the

three windows. The effect of the gold frames around the windows is exciting and decorative, and for privacy there are venetian blinds that can be lowered when needed. The venetian blinds are a chocolate color with bright orange tapes. The orange, chocolate, and gold color scheme prevails throughout the contemporary-furnished living room.

If you are a do-it-yourselfer, why not consider the picture-frame approach to decorating your windows? You could paint the frames a bright color or cover them with a patterned vinyl adhesive covering. You could also cover the edges of the frames with an exciting braid or with ball fringe. You can hang sheer curtains that draw inside your picture window if you like, or you can install Roman shades or roller matchstick blinds. For the more formal at heart, Austrian shades of a happy print or a solid color would also be effective.

Is your window too wide? Then break it up!

Yes, the wide window is a standard feature of many new apartments and homes. And it's also a decorating problem that is most often handled with a wall-to-wall drapery treatment. I'm not at all opposed to that standard treatment, but I do ask, Why limit yourself when there are so many other imaginative ways to handle those windows?

My favorite way of treating the wide window is to break up the expanse when possible. Breaking up the wide window not only makes the window more attractive, it can also add height, variety, and eye appeal to today's boxy rooms.

One way to break up your wide window is with three or four narrow drapery panels hung at intervals over white sheers. Those narrow panels can be left hanging straight down, or can be tied back. And note, please, that this treatment, unlike wall-to-wall draperies, will add height to your room.

If privacy is not a must for you, make those wide windows narrow by installing small shelves on either side of the window. The shelves should be no wider than one foot. Use the shelves to display colored glass or green plants in attractive pots.

Another way to add height and visually narrow windows is by framing out the window with a fabric- or mirror-covered plywood frame that

A wide, wide window is visually slimmed down through the use of floor-to-ceiling screens and three shades.

extends to the floor. And one of my all-time favorite ways to narrow a wide window is by placing floor-to-ceiling screens on either side of the window. In a handsome, tailored living room I saw recently the floor-to-ceiling screens were covered in a chocolate-brown, camel and cream glen-plaid fabric to match sofa upholstery. The window area was further slimmed down through the use of three window shades. Carpeting was rich cream to match walls. And for color drama, there were four chocolate-brown chairs accented with vivid toss cushions of poppy red, royal blue, mulberry, and lemon yellow.

THE ONE "GREAT PIECE"

Windows aren't the only potential focal points in your living room. Have you ever walked into a room and been bowled over by one super-special piece of furniture—one that outshines the other furnishings in the room? If so, you walked into the home of a smart decorator who knows that a room with one outstanding piece is more interesting than a room crammed with run-of-the-mill pieces.

One of the most effective focal points in a living room, in my opinion, is that one good piece of furniture that lends richness, interest, and personality. It might be a long, elegant sofa outfitted with lots of cushy down pillows on seat and back. Or it might be a wall of built-in bookcases of rich wood. Or it might be an outsize Chinese cabinet lacquered a rich ebony black and inlaid with mother-of-pearl. Expensive? Yes. But with that one great piece in your room, you don't need much more to bring your room to life.

In the living room that features the fabulous Chinese cabinet, for instance, you could use inexpensive wicker furniture throughout. (Even old wicker pieces salvaged from an old hotel or from granny's porch.) Color walls a soft cherry-blossom pink. Paint all trim white. Paint your wicker sofa and chairs pale pink to match walls and upholster them in an Oriental cotton print of soft pink, burnt-orange, red, lemon-yellow, and Mediterranean-blue flowers on a black background. Hang floor-length tieback draperies of the same print over silky white sheers. For end tables, how about clear acrylic cubes topped with pink Chinese jar lamps shaded in white? Believe me, that room packs a lot of punch. And despite the one costly piece of furniture, the total cost of the room isn't excessive.

A friend had her furniture arranged around the perimeter of her living room. There was no focal point. Her furnishings included an heirloom Oriental rug, laid over a wall-to-wall carpet. I advised her to move that rug from the floor to her long blank wall and light it with spotlights for emphasis. Her furniture could then be arranged to focus on the handsome rug: the sofa at right angles to the wall, the club and wing chairs facing the sofa, and the coffee table in between. The opposite wall would then become a perfect spot for a buffet server, topped with a pair of candlesticks. And I would place a mirror above that buffet to reflect the beautiful rug!

SCREENS

Screens are great pick-me-ups for the architectural "blahs." In boxy modern rooms, a screen or two can add personality and softness. Place a couple of brightly lacquered screens, or screens papered to match the walls, in two corners of a boring room, and see it come to life!

I'm using two floor-to-ceiling mirrored screens near the living-room window of a client's apart-

ment. The mirrors will reflect the park view outside and the room's exciting colors inside. In rooms without views, I often use screens directly in front of windows. Better a pretty screen than an ugly view, I say!

If your living room looks more like a tunnel than a room, why not break it up with a screen? It's a pleasant change from the bookcase divider. Place a three-panel screen partway across the room. Arrange your sofa-and-chair grouping on one side and your dining table and chairs on the other.

If you're tired of the picture-grouping-above-the-sofa look, why not back your sofa with an interesting screen? The screen might be wall papered, mirrored, painted, or fabric-covered.

A screen doesn't have to be a priceless coromandel to be an exciting focal point. To prove it, I recently used an inexpensive plywood screen to perk up a small, dark library. As the room was to be used only at night and the owners wanted a cozy look, I painted the walls a mood-setting hunter green. Bookcases on one wall were painted deep green too. Underfoot was a wall-to-wall ribbed carpet of soft champagne beige, accented with a colorful Moroccan rug of rich red, pumpkin, and green. At right angles to the wall opposite the bookcases I centered two cushy love seats upholstered in heavy basket-weave beige cotton, and for color and excitement I placed the plywood screen, lacquered Chinese red, against the wall. The love seats were piled high with toss cushions covered in a geometric print of pumpkin, Chinese red, hunter green, and chocolate. Tieback draperies of the same print were hung over louvered shutters painted Chinese red.

LATTICEWORK

Latticework is another dramatic and versatile decorating element. What with the greening of America, I'm all for latticework walls and ceilings—you might say I'm on a lattice kick. I'm latticing ceilings these days, and I'm installing lattice on doors and walls. In a home I'm decorating in Bermuda I painted the master-bedroom ceiling azure blue and then installed white lattice strips on the diagonal.

Latticework is easy for the do-it-yourselfer to install, so if you want to give your walls and doors a special look of nature's garden, why not apply lattice to the surfaces? If walls and doors are white, the lattice can be the new young color —leaf green.

A young couple I know decorated their apartment living room in various fresh, bright tones of green with sparkling white accents. They covered one of their green painted walls with white latticework—even latticed the ceiling, too—and hung stainless-steel mixing bowls filled with live greenery from the lattice ceiling and wall. They chose a grass-green carpet along with a love seat and sofa covered in a green-and-white cotton print. Parrot-green occasional chairs and see-through glass-and-chrome tables were perfect in this lighthearted living room.

Occasional Furniture and Accents

An occasional table is a lot more than a place to plop a drink or a cup of coffee. To me, occasional tables are also important accessories that can be used to add color, pattern, and style to a room.

And did you know that there are many ways to make great occasional tables yourself? There are do-it-yourself coffee tables made of simple plywood cubes, as well as skirted tables from tailored to frilly.

To turn a plywood cube into a table, all you have to do is cover it with fabric, mirror tiles, ceramic tiles, sisal, or wallpaper—the covering is up to you. To make a generous-size table using cubes, use four mirrored cubes as "legs" and top with a large square of heavy glass.

When I need an end table in a hurry, I'll tack a plywood round to an inexpensive artist's stool or to an old square end table, and top my construction with a colorful fabric skirt. For a more tailored look in skirting, use lightweight vinyl suede on a square or rectangular end table. Finish the edges with thick braid.

Let's try it on two end tables. Use a rich tobacco-brown vinyl suede, trimmed with tomato-red braid. Walls can be papered in a bookend-design wallcovering of tomato red and sand

beige. Go bright tomato red for trim and use beige sand paint on the ceiling. For carpeting, chocolate-brown sculptured pile would be my choice. Sofa, upholstery, and draperies can be a nubby sand-beige cotton or synthetic.

In front of that sofa, how about a small, round dining table with cut-down legs for another kind of do-it-yourself coffee table. For punch, lacquer the table shiny tomato red.

One of my favorite accent "tables" is actually a large, wood-topped wicker picnic hamper. Try one next to a plump chair in the family room. The hamper can accommodate needlework or mending while the top can easily hold an ashtray, coffee cup, and TV snack.

In a traditional room, I love the look of a miniature chest of drawers used in place of a run-of-the-mill accent table. Or how about a table that's actually nothing more than a stack of handsomely bound books? Scout out those large old leather-bound atlases or record books, stack them up to the desired height, and you have an instant table and conversation piece!

I would like to see that bookstack table used in a den. Choose books bound in rich wine-red and tobacco-brown leathers. Walls and ceiling can be papered in brown butcher paper, with wood trim painted vibrant wine red. For carpeting, I would go wine red, too. Upholster sofa and club chairs in a zigzag stripe of wine, paper-bag brown, and off-white. At windows, natural wood shutters would be my choice.

Please don't leave any chair standing alone, without some sort of table close at hand. You might place a standing lamp table next to an English wing chair. Standing lamps outfitted with circular shelves are favorites of mine, and I use them very often in my decorating work, but there are many other accessories besides the standard table or standing lamp table that can be used next to a chair. Porcelain garden stools make interesting occasional tables, and I've seen them in white, pale green, in fact every color imaginable. Try one decorated with an Oriental motif beside a lounge chair in a traditional living room.

The Chinese have given us black and red

Ideal for a first home is this cheerful living room furnished in fresh, bright tones of green with sparkling white touches. Carpet is grass green, and one of the soft green walls is covered with gay white latticework. The love seat and sofa are covered in a green-and-white cotton print. Occasional chairs are parrot green. Tables are of glass and chrome. Hanging planters filled with fresh greenery are actually stainless-steel mixing bowls.

lacquer taborets, small drumlike stands, to use as end tables beside chairs, and these are particularly pleasing room accessories. The Spanish have given us wrought-iron stands with tile tops of every size and dimension. There are even pedestal-based, round-topped Chinese checkers tables that come in mighty handy as a place for that ashtray and lighter when not utilized for game playing.

I have seen natural wood tables and also natural wicker elephant and kangaroo tables that can be used beside a modern chair or by a wicker chair. You can paint the wicker animal tables to your decorating fancy—white, navy blue, or shocking pink. A client of mine recently purchased an antique clay-colored camel that has a small flat top surface to use as a pull-up table next to a chair in her library—a great accessory for a house in the California desert!

Be original when selecting accessory tables. Try a small old trunk, painted an interesting color, as a pull-table in your library. Or what about a large rock with a smooth top in a modern living room? It may be heavy, but it will add interest to the room. A small nail keg might also be an interesting pull-up accessory in the family room. I would recommend sanding the surface of the barrel and treating it with a stain and sealer.

I like tables that serve a purpose, perhaps more than one purpose. A gateleg table, for example, when folded can be placed behind a sofa where it is perfect for a magazine, a lamp, and an arrangement of flowers. It's great in a small apartment living room, for when dinner hour arrives it can be opened to become a dining table. The card table is also a practical table and can triple in function. Use it for card or game playing. Use it for a luncheon or dinner table. And use it as a desk.

The step table is another of my favorites, particularly when the steps are covered in leather and trimmed with gold or blind tooling. It makes a great end table beside a living-room sofa, particularly so if the steps lift up to reveal extra storage space for home necessities—napkins, coasters, small ashtrays that are only brought out when guests arrive. I am also crazy about nesting tables. These groups of three or four tables are especially handy in the library or family room of an active household. All the tables can be used for snacks when watching TV.

Tables that are for ornamentation only are of little use to me. I have seen many very artistically designed tables of peculiar shapes and sizes on the market that are decorated for look only. For me, tables have to be serviceable; you should be able to use the top surfaces for something. If the table surface is so decorated and so priceless, cover it with a clear glass top that protects without hiding and enables you to use the table for its basic purpose—to do something and hold something.

I did a juggling act one evening at a party and it's an act I hope I never have to repeat! A juggling act is the game party guests play when the coffee table isn't big enough. When the coffee table is skimpy, guests (and family members, too) end up juggling their drinks, cigarettes, and plates (if hors d'oeuvres or buffet supper are served).

Let me say, here and now, that I believe in the big, generous coffee table. As a rule of thumb, the coffee table should be as long as the sofa, and it should be wide as well. There should be enough room for guests to place glasses, cups, plates, and ashtrays.

The top of the table can be of any material you choose; but if you entertain a lot or have children, I would select a material such as glass or laminate that is easy to keep clean and attractive-looking. If you must have a wood coffee table (and I do love the rich look of wood), keep a large supply of coasters right out on the tabletop where people can find them. I never feel welcome in a home where I'm warned, "Don't put your glass down there!" If you serve refreshments, you must expect people to put down their glasses and cups.

If you have no room for a big coffee table, there are alternatives. Use a Moroccan brass tray as a wall hanging; turn it into a table when company comes by placing it on a foldaway base. Look for wood or plastic cubes that can be pushed together at party time. Two heads are better than one, and so are two tables. And who says three's a crowd? Three small tables can make for an exciting coffee table. You'd be surprised how great two or three small, clear acrylic cubes can look in even the most traditional setting. I like to see those sparkling clear cubes sitting on a muted Oriental rug in front of a velvet-upholstered Lawson sofa. In a traditional setting, accessorize the see-through cubes with a small bronze clock, a vase of flowers, and a collection of old china ashtrays. The accessories will tie the modern-looking cubes into your period room.

In a modern geometric-looking setting, choose brightly colored plastic cubes for your coffee table. Flank a blue cube with two reds or two yellows to form a rectangle. Or create a blue-and-red checkerboard square using four cubes.

Groupings, in addition to their eye appeal, offer flexibility. When you need an extra table near that club chair or side chair, just pick up a section of your coffee-table group and place it where it's needed.

For an island room, what about three wicker drums all in a row in front of a wicker sofa cushioned in a bright print of lime green, white, and canary yellow? Or, if you'd rather not go wicker all the way, upholster three small plywood cubes in a padded version of your sofa fabric colors—one lime green, one white, one yellow. Top each table with glass.

In a small room, place together two small, square glass-topped tables with steel legs. The transparent tops will give an open, light feeling, so important in cramped quarters.

A press release on my desk today tells me that rolltop desks are back in fashion. As far as I'm concerned, they've always been in fashion, along with other beautiful desk styles.

I frequently use desks in my decorating work, and I like to select and place a desk so it can serve more than one function. Antique lap desks, for example, are favorites of mine, practical as well as lovely to look at. Placed on a shelf, desk, console table, or coffee table, an old-fashioned lap desk can hold so many odds and ends beautifully. And as I've mentioned, I often place a desk at the end of a sofa where it can double as an end table. The other end of the sofa can be flanked by a skirted table or a traditional lamp table.

Why not turn a corner of your living room into a home office? Choose a small-scale desk that won't overwhelm the rest of your furnishings. In one room the desk was placed near a complementary wall unit that provided additional storage space for books, papers, and supplies. Best of all, both the desk and the wall unit were the kind you can assemble yourself, resulting in a considerable cost saving. The "office" was set off from the rest of the room by a colorful geometric area rug placed in front of the desk.

Put the corners of your home to good use, too. I believe in getting the most out of—or should I say into?—a corner. Of course, corner cabinets provide the simplest answer, and all over the market there are corner cabinets with cupboard bottoms and open-shelved tops in mahogany, walnut, maple—you name the finish. Corner units of shelves alone are also very effective.

In one of my recent decorating projects, I used a pair of handsome English-style mahogany corner cabinets in each corner at the end of a long living room. Between the corner cabinets and in front of a fully draped window, I had ample space for a sofa, two end tables, and a pair of club chairs, but it was those corner cabinets that really made the look of the room. (Corner pieces, by the way, travel from one home to another very easily.)

If you don't want a corner cabinet, there are other things to do with that empty right angle in a living room. You might try sculpture on a pedestal, or hanging baskets filled with greenery. If you're really modern and rather zany, you might want to place an old barber pole in a corner of a living room accessorized with a glass-and-chrome table and red-lacquered bentwood-framed chairs.

There are modern lighting fixtures—cylinders and balls of light—that can serve a corner well. Many of these lighting fixtures come on tension poles that fit snugly between your ceiling and floor. If that isn't original enough for you, you might want to illuminate a corner with an old streetlight. I know someone who did just that with an old gaslight they electrified for use in the foyer of a New England clapboard house. (More about lighting fixtures later.)

Clocks have never been more decorative than they are today. These days you can have a clock that's just right, whatever your taste or budget, from tiny digital clocks in Space Age colors to ceiling-high grandfather clocks in mellow wood cases—the choice is yours.

A beautiful, functional grandfather clock, though a splendid occasional piece, can even be used as a focal point. And that clock needn't be Early American in styling. Today, grandfather clocks are as with it as real live grandfathers.

Table clocks are also favorite accessories of mine and I love browsing in antique and junk shops for unusual old pieces that can be refurbished and used on cocktail tables. My most recent shopping expedition turned up a tiny silver cube clock of the Art Deco period that I plan to use on a glass-and-chrome table in an all-gray bachelor apartment I'm designing.

Stools are the littlest members of the decorative-furnishings family, but they can make a big decorating statement. In the old days, stools were routinely used for seating, but when the more comfortable side chair came into fashion, the backless, armless stool was kicked aside. I think it's time for the stool to make a comeback, especially in today's less-than-generous living quarters.

I like to keep a grouping of three fully upholstered square stools under a long Parsons table. When company comes, the stools can be pulled out to provide extra seating.

Stools, because of their small size, can be a touch of luxury in an otherwise modest room. For instance, there's that eye-catching fabric you admired at $30 a yard. You can't afford to upholster your sofa or even a chair with it, but I bet you could afford to upholster a small stool with it. Who knows? You might really be lucky and pick up a remnant!

Or perhaps you love a certain wild, way-out color or print that you wouldn't dare use on a grand scale. Go ahead and use it on a stool to provide a punchy accent.

If you're an antique lover and can't afford to buy large antique pieces, why not accessorize a pair of reproduction wing chairs with two real antique footstools? Upholster the chairs and the stools in a chocolate-brown-and-white cotton brocade. Paint walls a zingy tangerine and all trim white. Carpeting can be champagne beige. For sofa upholstery, go rich chocolate brown and lavish with toss cushions of tangerine and creamy white. And for extra seating in that room, two square stools with seats covered in tangerine velvet would be my choice.

Ottomans are larger "stools," and are versatile accents for any living room. Have you seen all the super new ottoman styles on the market? The traditional skirted ottomans with soft cushion tops are still with us and always will be, I hope, but there are many other styles around to tempt the decorator, too. There are plasic ottomans molded into delightful curves and covered with soft, stretchy fabrics. There are Parsons-style ottomans with upholstered legs. There are cube ottomans topped with fat pillows.

And speaking of my old favorites, cubes, it's easy to make your own ottoman with a plywood cube or even a sturdy wooden crate as a base. Simply tack layers of thick padding over the cube's top and sides and cover neatly with fabric, using nailheads, tape, or braid to trim the edges. For extra softness, top with a fat upholstered cushion.

Along with new ottoman styles come new ways to decorate with ottomans. People may use an ottoman in a living-room or family-room conversation grouping the way they once used an occasional chair. The ottoman will accommodate an extra guest at a party and can be used as a footrest with a matching armchair when the family is relaxing alone together.

Ottomans can also be kept under tables until extra seating is needed. If you keep two upholstered ottomans under the console table behind your sofa, upholster them to match your living-room upholstery or, for fun, have the ottomans and the table covered in matching vinyl. In a zippy red-white-and-black contemporary room, the table and ottomans could be covered in black patent vinyl and finished with glittery silver nailheads. In a traditional room, you could use tobacco-brown leather or leather-look vinyl and brass nailheads.

Lamps are perhaps the most important accessories in the living room of your home—they are without doubt the most effective and powerful. So be cautious when selecting them. Buy lamps that say something decorative and have some bulk.

In today's world of decorating, just about anything goes for a lamp base. It's amazing what interesting and amusing pieces you can find and convert into lamp bases. You can wire old crockery jugs (I like molasses jugs), or you can have an electrician wire an old tea canister or an old crockery bean pot for an interesting lamp base. Choose lamp bases with some weight. I like plump lamps that sit solidly in place; spindly lamps can tip too easily.

Ninety percent of the rooms in homes across the country have lamps that are too small and underscaled—itsy-bitsy lamps that are just about useless from the decorative standpoint as well as from the standpoint of good lighting. A good height for living-room lamps is 58 inches from the floor to the top of the lampshade, which includes the height of your lamp table, the height of the lamp base, and the height of the lampshade. When planning your sofa/end table/lamp arrangement, the table can be 23 inches high, the lamp bases 20 inches high, and lampshades 15 inches.

For many years I have advocated a personal decorating theory that all lamps in a room should be the same height from the floor; no matter what style lamp you select—Victorian pieces, urns, Chinese vases, big cider jugs, etc.—the lampshade line should be even throughout the room. (Most living rooms require four lamps—two for end tables at the sofa grouping and two others at key points in the room as required for comfort and good lighting distribution.) I also believe that lampshade cords should match the finish of the tables on which the lamps are placed. If tables are walnut, lamp cords should be brown. On white tables, white cords please.

Lamps don't have to match the style and period of the room they grace. Just make sure they harmonize with your decor. If your living room is French, the lamps don't have to be white marble with gilt. If your room is Spanish, you don't have to use Spanish wrought-iron pieces. If you're looking for adaptability, select Chinese vase lamps; they fit in nicely with both traditional and modern looks. For French or English settings, choose porcelain or crystal, or lamps made of wood. For Early American settings, brass lamps are always appropriate, as are lamps with bases of iron, cranberry glass, wood, pottery, and, needless to say, Paul Revere pewter. For rooms with an early-nineteenth-century feeling, gilded bronze Empire-look lamps are just the thing. In modern rooms, most lamps work, particularly antique pieces such as temple jars and native or African figurines. Lamps for modernists to stay away from—anything overly ornamented.

But relying solely on the end-table lamp, the central ceiling fixture, and the floor lamp these days is truly like living in the dark ages. Today, lighting can give you so much more than illumination; it can give your home drama, warmth, excitement!

One lighting breakthrough that I've used in my own home and on many of my decorating jobs is the plant light. Lighting geniuses have managed to isolate those special rays that make plants grow, and have packaged those magic rays in bulbs of various wattages. With plant lights, you can grow a garden of houseplants anywhere in your home—even in windowless rooms! If you want your garden in a dark corner, you can have it just by shining a spotlight from the ceiling.

One friend of mine has created a super window treatment for her city apartment using plant lights. She has installed a ceiling track a few feet from her window to hold two can lamps outfitted with plant lights. Her windows are covered with white louvered shutters, and a variety of beautiful plants hang in front of the shuttered window. With this exciting window treatment, my friend has solved several decorating problems: She has blocked out an unwanted city view; she has created a lush indoor garden in a sunless apartment; and she now has a terrific focal point for her room. All that with just two little bulbs.

For a different lighting treatment in a dark hallway, I like a small floodlight placed on the floor behind a dried-flower arrangement. Arrange the flowers, leaves, feathers, whatever, in one or more baskets, vases, or pots set on the floor. They can stand by themselves or beneath a console table or next to a chair. With the light coming from behind the foliage, the walls of your dark hallway will come to life with a dramatic play of light and shadow.

If you live in a new apartment building, you may be wondering what to do with those ugly horizontal concrete beams just below the ceiling. You're not alone—lots of people ask me for ideas about ways to conceal the unsightly structures.

In your living room, why not create fin-divided recesses under the beam to add three-dimensional flavor? The beam can be covered with painted or stained wood. Within the fin-dividers, which should be stained or painted to match the beam covering, strip lighting can be installed to light up murals applied directly to the walls (between the dividers themselves). And when lighting up something, make certain that something is important. I love important and interesting wall murals, wall sculptures, but I do not believe in lighting up something trivial.

On a recent decorating project in a warm climate, all living room walls were decorated with painted palm trees and flowers on a pale blue background, then washed with small recessed ceiling lights that were installed around the room's outer perimeter. No table lamps were used. For furnishings against the lighted mural walls, floating sofas upholstered in a durable leaf green and melon were selected. Carpeting was pale green, blue, and coffee, and end tables were all white lacquered cubes. For occasional pull-up pieces, ottomans were chosen. No high-back chairs were used in the room so the lighted mural walls could be seen uninterrupted.

Think about proper lighting for *your* special wall decor.

Fin-divided recesses lend a three-dimensional flavor to this living-room wall. Ugly beam is hidden behind wood that matches dividers. Handsome lotus murals, set into divisions, are illuminated with under-soffit strip lighting. Wall of deep-set windows features fiber-glass mesh shades with a pair of handsome fabric-covered screens.

Joanna's fiber-glass Mesh Comfort window shade

Glass in Your Living Room

Glass has been a decorating standard through the ages, especially to protect furniture tops, paintings, and prints, but so much is happening in the glass industry today that it is enjoying greater importance in home decor than ever before. Handsome, thick glass tops on stainless-steel coffee-table bases are appearing everywhere. Glass-topped desks and cigarette tables are here to stay too.

While you see lots of glass-topped furniture with wood bases, wrought-iron bases, bamboo bases, and even with Lucite bases, glass with stainless steel seems to be the newest look. I guess this combination attracts because both glass and stainless steel are reflective, and reflective finishes seem to work well with one another.

Stainless steel and glass can complete an enlightened modern theme for your home with transparent charm, and these pieces work well with period furnishings as well as with contemporary. Heavy upholstered pieces such as chairs and sofas have a lighter look in a room that has glass and stainless-steel furnishings rather than mahogany or walnut wood pieces.

If you are redecorating your living room, try the glass look with your furniture. On a dark-stained parquet floor lay a rug in a pattern that you like in bright green, sunny yellow, and fire-engine red. You can use a stainless-steel-and-glass coffee table on the rug in front of a love seat covered with bright red nylon. (I love a glass coffee table on a printed rug because you can see the carpet design through the tabletop.) Facing the coffee table and love seat, I would recommend a comfortable tufted lounge chair covered in a lustrous royal-blue Naugahyde. I like the light airy look of glass étagères, so against white walls with an 18-inch top border of royal blue, I would suggest two floor-to-ceiling glass étagères for displaying books and accessories. If you have a fireplace, perhaps you will consider sheet mirror on the fireplace wall to complete the glass-look setting.

STAINED GLASS

More and more people these days are seeing the world through rose-colored glasses—and through blue glasses, green glasses, mauve glasses

. . . indeed glasses of almost any color you can name. I'm talking about the stained-glass revival, which began a few years ago when stained glass began moving back into the American home.

I know a few lucky folks who live in old Victorian—and Edwardian—houses that were built with stained-glass windows. And they are lucky. But for those of us who aren't that fortunate, there are other ways to have the stained-glass look.

Some people like just a touch of stained glass, and I have seen many pretty stained-glass mobiles and sculptures as well as Tiffany (or Tiffany-style) lampshades hanging in the homes of America. I like those stained-glass mobiles hung in front of a window among a jungle of hanging plants.

Neighbors of mine went one step further and had an artist friend of theirs create a stained-glass window just for them. The colorful pane of fruit-and-leaf design now graces their new vacation home in upstate New York.

On my antique-hunting expeditions I have come across many a lovely old stained-glass panel. They are most often relics from demolished churches or old homes, and some of them have become part of various decorating jobs of mine.

One of those colorful panels could make a super wall hanging, particularly if lit from behind. Or use one or more old stained-glass panels in place of curtains or shades. Hang one in front of any window where you want to block an undesirable view. Install lights behind the stained-glass panel or let the natural light shine through, if it is adequate.

And have you ever seen a room divider of stained glass? I have—in a one-room London flat. The divider was created from three long, narrow stained-glass panels, suspended from the ceiling on lengths of heavy chain. The stained-glass colors—pale pink, ice blue, mauve, moss green, and goldenrod yellow—inspired the apartment's romantic color scheme: pale pink walls; flowered chintz upholstery of pinks, blues, and greens; and accents of sharp sunny yellow. If your room needs a zippy focal point, think stained glass.

Wicker in the Home

Wicker for all seasons is on the rise! That old porch standby has been rediscovered by everyone who wants to achieve a light, airy, natural look on a budget. And these days the light, natural look is what it's all about.

Wicker today comes in so many shapes and forms that no one has to go without—there's wicker for everyone and for every taste and pocketbook. I've seen Victorian styles; contemporary styles; lacy looks; tailored, closely woven looks; and Oriental looks fit for a potentate.

If your decor is contemporary and you're thinking of purchasing a new end table, club chair, occasional chair, console table—whatever—why not think wicker? Natural wicker blends beautifully with the contemporary look of glass, chrome, molded plastic, and butcher block.

If your decor says Early American, wicker will be right at home. You might add an old-fashioned rocker to your colonial room. Leave that rocker natural, or stain it dark, or paint it a bright happy color—sunshine yellow, fire-engine red, or patriotic navy blue. The choice is yours.

Wicker is still the best way I know to get an indoor summer-garden look that will stay fresh year-round. A pretty garden living room I saw recently was furnished with lacy white wicker chairs, sofa, and tables. The furniture looked super against walls and floors draped in another perennial favorite, patchwork, in deep tones of black, burgundy, and navy with touches of white and sky blue. Upholstery on the sofa and chairs was a poppy print of canary yellow, lipstick red, navy blue, and leafy green on a white background. Accent pillows of patchwork, in the same happy hues, added another summery touch.

And what's a garden without green growing things? I can tell you that pretty wicker room had lots and lots of plants. And for light, there were lamps of wicker—what else?

Living-Room Color

Are you one of those people who has trouble deciding on a color scheme? If so, you are in the majority. I have even heard professional interior decorators confess that they can't make up their minds when it comes to colors for their own homes!

I believe that three-quarters of all color-scheme problems could be solved with a little more planning and less impulse buying. How often a man or woman will say, "I couldn't resist the sale price on that orange chair." Today that orange chair is probably in the attic or spare room. That's where a majority of impulse purchases end up, because they were never matched with existing carpeting, draperies, and upholstery.

The first and most important rule for planning attractive color schemes is to never, never plan a scheme without comparing samples of fabric, paints, wallcoverings, and carpeting to be used. Decorators always match samples, believe me. We never rely on guesswork, and neither should you. Secondly, never, never make a purchase without matching fabric, paint, or carpet swatches carefully. When you can, make those matches right in the room where the fabrics, carpeting, or paint will be used. Test the combination in a variety of lighting situations since colors change as the light changes.

As to combining colors: When in doubt, use a maximum of three colors, one of which is an accent.

Let's illustrate by taking the soft, attractive blend of yellow and blue and adding just a dash of tangy orange-peel orange.

We'll paint living-room walls a soft, warm pineapple yellow and the trim and ceiling white. We'll leave the wood floor bare—or cover all or part of it with a rug of rich royal/navy blue (that's my term for a blue somewhere between brash, bright royal blue and too-somber navy blue). We'll upholster the sofa in a handsome tweed of royal/navy and black (which has been carefully matched to the carpet), then we'll dress up that sofa with toss pillows of canary-yellow and orange-peel silk twill.

Next, using carefully matched fabrics, we'll cover a pair of wood-framed bergère chairs in a floral cotton jacquard of navy and white. For warmth, I would add occasional tables of wood, and Oriental-motif lamps painted in designs of yellow and blue. If another chair is needed, we'll dip into our three-color palette and pull out the yellow silk twill already used for sofa toss pillows.

And there's our charming, foolproof color scheme—rich blue, warm yellow, accents of orange peel and the added contrast of always-right white.

To be completely safe, keep the living room neutral and add color in accent pieces. This

A summer-garden room that will stay fresh all year long is all white wicker and patchwork.

doesn't mean that you should paint everything in sight beige. There are many colors that I consider neutral—that is, colors that blend well with many other colors. Sky blue is a good mixer; so are most members of the beige and brown family, as well as gray or rich terra-cotta. For walls, don't go the timid off-white way. If you want white walls, go white—pure, snow white. It won't look harsh if your room has lots of warm wood about and lots of clear happy color, too.

The key word when choosing color is "clear." Muddy colors and off-colors are decorating enemy number one in my book. What is attractive about mud?

As for dark walls—walls painted burgundy, navy, chocolate, forest green, eggplant—I love them, and, as I pointed out in Chapter 1 on entryways, I don't believe they should be relegated to large rooms. I have successfully decorated many a small room with dark walls and with dark upholstery, too.

Still, every spring I find myself musing on the renewing effects that clear pastel colors can have in the home.

If you shy away from pastels because you foresee upkeep problems, let me tell you that easy-care pastel decorating is a fact, what with washable, drip-dry fabrics for curtains and cushions; wipeable vinyls for upholstery; protective fabric finishes; and soil-hiding carpets. With all those easy-care features readily available, you can use pastels in every room of the house without a care.

If you want to give your living room a pastel refresher, take a few hints from a springtime room I saw recently. Walls were painted a soft, pale celadon green, and the room was carpeted in pale sand-beige plush, protected in heavy-use areas by a lacy sisal mat.

At the other extreme from those who unnecessarily shy away from pastels are people moving to Florida, who suddenly develop an aversion to anything dark—particularly dark wood. They will paint lovely mahogany furniture white, yellow, green—any light color you can think of—simply because they've heard that dark wood is taboo in Florida. I have seen some beautiful old and cherished furniture ruined this way, and for no reason.

Not that I don't advocate light, cheery colors for the tropics—I do. The many tropical homes and hotels I've worked on feature pastels and sunny yellows. But why not use that mahogany dining-room set in a yellow-green-and-melon color scheme? Why not use that walnut bedroom set with a green-and-pink color scheme? Why not take those antique occasional tables to Florida

Springtime is captured alive in a pastel living room. And that springtime look is kept alive on upholstered furniture and on draperies through the use of fabric protector.

Broyhill upholstered furnitu
Scotchguard fabric protecto

Dark wood for end tables and tall shutters contrast with airy wicker and "Florida" greens and yellows on walls and upholstery for chairs and sofa bed.

and use them in a tropical scheme? I say, do it. I, for one, enjoy the contrast of dark wood against those light, bright colors.

If you're planning a southward migration soon, and will be redecorating, here's a living-room scheme that combines the best of both worlds—the dark, warm woods we usually associate with the North, and the light colors and wicker furniture of the South.

Three walls and ceiling are painted dewy grass green, punctuated by a wide cove of sunny yellow. The fourth wall is papered in a cool

floral splash of sunny yellow, leafy green, and sky blue. Matching fabric is used on a sofa bed with plump tufted back and arms. The floor of pale vinyl "boards" is resistant to sand and sea-water. Best of all, it can be cleaned with a damp mop. (Who doesn't appreciate easy upkeep when tropical skies and beaches beckon?) The furniture is a comfortable mix of North and South— Louis XIV and XV chairs upholstered in sea-foam green and yellow; two antique end tables of mellow wood; and Florida wicker bookcases and cocktail table. Floor-to-ceiling shutters of dark wood at windows balance the light, bright upholstery and the airy window treatment of white sheers.

While most people these days want rooms that are light and bright, there are instances where more intense, dramatic colors work better. For instance, in rooms used primarily at night. It's not a must, of course, but a dramatic nighttime scheme has a warmth and coziness that I like. And these days, when so many rooms are used more at night than during the workday, this type of scheme makes sense.

My friend, fashion designer Bill Tice, has a vibrant nighttime scheme in his living room. Bill is at his office all day and uses his apartment primarily at night, so he chose a scheme that would work well at night.

Bill started by painting walls a tangy orangey-watermelon color. "The painters couldn't get the right shade, so I finally cut open a watermelon and said, 'Copy that,'" Bill told me.

There was another motive for the color choice: Bill is a firm believer in the theory that color affects mood. Orange, he says, is an energy color. And couldn't we all use a little energy after a long, hard day at work?

Against this vivid wall color, Bill has used lots of pretty pale blues. Floor-length taffeta draperies are pale blue strié, hung over lime-green curtains. The sofa is an Oriental print of blues, oranges, and white. Club chairs are covered in a powder-blue-and-white cotton tapestry, and there's powder blue and white on the floor, too —in an Oriental-design area rug.

Textures Make a Difference

When you think of your home's decor, you probably think first of the furniture styles and colors. Most people do. But what about the textures?

Interesting textures—in fabrics, carpets, wall-coverings—can really make an exciting decorating difference. And texture comes in so many easy-to-use forms these days. For walls, there's stucco wallboard, sand paint, grass cloths, cork, suedecloths, foils, wet-look vinyls, and flocking. For floors, there's carpet texture galore: velvety plushes, ribbed corduroy, rugged handwoven looks, smooth -indoor-outdoor, and nubby sisal matting.

Upholstery fabrics today offer a great range of terrific textures including the newest look inspired by the distant past. I'm talking about the booming popularity of rustic handwoven looks for upholstery. These fabrics are being imported from all over the world, with Ireland, Haiti, and India leading the way.

In days gone by, when decorating rules were rarely broken, smooth textures were the rule for elegant interiors, while rough textures were relegated to rustic interiors. Today, rules are made to be broken, so we're seeing lots of textural contrast in interiors.

A living room I decorated recently is a good example. In that room, done in an elegantly natural manner, I played the sheen of lacquer against the roughness of sisal carpeting, suede-cloth, and nubby cotton upholstery. Walls were painted fawn beige, with trim and ceiling of pale ivory. For sofa upholstery, I chose rugged suede-cloth in a fawn beige to match walls. Chairs were slipcovered in rough white Haitian cotton. The cotton was used for draperies, too. Smooth-as-glass lacquer in sand beige was featured on occasional tables. Green plants were housed in rough woven baskets in shades ranging from nut brown to pale straw.

The room, you will note, has almost no bright color in it. Instead, eye appeal comes from the variety and contrast of textures used.

If your living room has a preponderance of rough textures, give another dimension with shine. Have you ever noticed how a polished floor, a mirrored wall, or gleaming lacquered furniture gives a room something extraspecial?

Whether your room is traditional or up-to-the-minute contemporary, it can benefit from shine. And these days shine comes in so many exciting forms: shiny foil papers for walls; shiny finishes for floors and furniture; shiny chrome for accents, accessories, tables. And have you seen the latest? I'm talking about the great revival of polished-steel furniture with its muted shine.

If your living room needs a pick-me-up, try shine. Strip the wood floor and stain it deep ebony. Keep it shining with regular applications of paste or liquid wax and frequent vacuuming (a dirt buildup scratches and dulls floors).

Shine up walls with a wallcovering of shiny brown tortoise patent vinyl. Against that slick dark background, try the drama of a cushy sofa

In this large living room modulation pieces, which form a sectional sofa, are covered in oatmeal tweed. The grouping is spacious and gracious against a dramatic background of a sweeping coppery supergraphic wallcovering.

slipcovered in off-white and crowded with toss cushions in prints of wine red, poppy red, ebony, chocolate, and butterscotch. Choose one of those prints and use it for upholstery on club chairs. Occasional chairs can be upholstered in poppy-red patent vinyl. For lamps, go shiny again—choose brass-trimmed polished steel on end tables lacquered poppy red.

Shine at windows? Try mirror-tiling the window reveals. Remember, a little shine goes a long way: a big brass bowl, a gold-framed mirror, a collection of shimmery silver-framed photos on an end table may be all the shine you need or want. Just make sure there's shine somewhere in every room of the house.

Summery Schemes

In the spring my garden is abloom with hyacinths, tulips, crocuses, and bluebells. And so is the interior of the Varney home. This is the time of year when my wife and I do an all-out spring cleaning and freshening of our city apartment and our little house in the country. The windows are thrown open, cushions are aired, floral slipcovers come out of storage, and heavy draperies are off to the dry cleaners and on to storage.

Ah, those beautiful spring flowers do inspire me! Think of ways to freshen up your living room in the springtime look. Slipcover the sofa in a pretty tulip print of reds, pinks, yellows, and greens on a white background. And what about making some zippered cases for the sofa throw pillows in pretty tulip colors—pink, red, yellow, lavender, white?

Slipcover club chairs, too, with a springy green-and-white striped fabric. Take down the overdraperies and send them to the dry cleaner, then pack them away until fall. Leave the white undercurtains up. In place of the overdraperies, hang a pretty valance of the tulip print, lined in spring-green cotton. And when spring-cleaning, consider new white silk lampshades as a seasonal replacement for the darker ones you may have now.

Our neighbors in the country were one step ahead of us. When we dropped in on them one weekend, we found their spring transformation had been completed. I must describe their living room because to me it epitomizes the fresh springtime feeling I love to live with right through the summer.

Walls are country white stucco and so is the ceiling, which is crossed with thick hand-hewn wood beams. The wide-plank floor, covered with rugs during the ski season, is bared and polished for spring and summer living.

At windows, airy tieback curtains of antique-blue-and-white toile frame a garden view. The sofa is slipcovered in a spring-garden floral of hyacinth blue, wood violet, and leaf green on a white ground. A club chair is dressed for spring in nubby white cotton.

Springtime at my neighbors' place, and in the Varney household, also means bringing in armloads of forsythia, tulips, daffodils, and greens from the outdoors to create bouquets for mantel, coffee table, and end tables.

But not everyone is an avid flower gardener, nor is the flower-garden decorating approach for everyone. Perhaps you're a hiker and springtime reminds you of nature walks and of woodsy sights and colors. Would you like to bring a bit of the spring wood into your home? Here's how I would do it in a living room.

Start with walls painted white and paint the ceiling a soft, pale yellow. Slipcover sofa in fir-tree green and strew with cushions of leaf green, pale lemon yellow, and sky blue. Cover club chairs in a variegated stripe of bright spring green and white.

Underfoot, the natural look of bare wood or terra-cotta vinyl tiles would be my choice. At windows, hang simple curtains of glazed cotton printed with leaves and ferns in natural greens, yellows, and browns—all on a white ground. For privacy and more of the woodsy look, I would install natural bamboo blinds under those curtains.

Decorate the white walls with prints of wildflowers and leaves. Look for old botanical prints in secondhand bookstores and print shops.

Summer fruits are special favorites of mine, and here's a summer fruit salad I wish I could share with everyone! There were plump red strawberries, fresh golden pineapple wedges, and luscious blueberries in my salad, all nestled in a bowl of pure, sparkling white.

Those summer fruits looked so tempting I hated to eat them. If you've ever had that feeling about a lovely-to-look-at fruit salad, here's one that's for looking only.

I recently designed a garden-fresh living room around two convertible sofas done up in a print of the biggest strawberries around—yellow blossoms and all. The plump strawberry sofas face each other across a white wicker coffee table. Walls are painted grass green, overlaid with outdoorsy white trellis created from inexpensive lath strips. A nylon carpet echoes the green walls.

Green salads are also an important part of the Varney family diet, particularly during the hot summer months when local gardens are bursting with greens. And what greater decorating inspiration can one find in those delectable greens?— the dark, cool green of spinach; the frosty green of iceberg lettuce; the yellow green of endive.

I have a friend who loves the "salad greens" so much, she has used them throughout her small

Big strawberries make a positive statement on these plump sofas. Who said you can't use big prints? They are wrong.

apartment. The look is cool and breezy even on the hottest August days.

In the living room there's a trellis-patterned carpet of various greens on a creamy white ground, bordered in deep spinach green. Her walls are painted fresh, frosty white.

Spinach green is again the choice for a sofa, crowded with pillows ranging in color from misty iceberg to endive yellow to the fresh bright green color of crinkly chicory.

Chairs are upholstered in a flame stitch of endive yellow and white, and at the windows my friend has hung louvered shutters painted spinach green.

For contrast with all those summery greens there are snappy accents of radish red and carrot orange in picture frames, ashtrays, and floral-patterned lamp bases.

Summer stripes. The pencil-thin stripes of a baseball uniform. The colorful stripes of a beach umbrella. The wide candy stripes of an awning.

Let's use summer stripes all over the living

room—with prints, with solids, you name it. I call the stripe the decorating common denominator, for its ability to mix beautifully with other patterns and with every decorating period.

Stripe the walls in a wide, wide awning-stripe wallcovering of sky blue and white. For fun, take your paintbrush and continue those sky blue stripes across a white-painted wood floor! Color the ceiling sky blue.

Furnish with a mix of wicker, wood, and molded plastic—all white, of course, and all slip-covered in a field-of-daisies print of white, yellow, and grass green on a sky-blue ground.

Summer is vacation time; travel time. But if you're not journeying to foreign shores, there's no need to feel left out of things—just add dashes of foreign excitement to your decorating.

Add the flavor of a tropical paradise with a giant wicker ceiling fan or peacock chair. And how about draping your sofa in a summer sarong of cotton printed with jungle birds and flowers?

Add the spice of Africa with colorful woven baskets. Use a giant lidded basket for storage in place of a sofa end table. Use small flat baskets to brighten a white wall. Use sets of nesting baskets everywhere; they're great for holding all those odds and ends that always seem to need a "home."

Add the grace and mystery of the Orient to a contemporary or traditional room with a shoji-screen window treatment, or a nest of black-lacquered tables. Let Oriental whimsy take over with a ceiling or wall arrangement of colorful Chinese kites or a giant Japanese paper umbrella.

If you've been dreaming of a trip to France, visit the land of romance via provincial fabrics—those charming, small-scale prints. Or let your room speak French via a provincial rush-seated bench or a wall grouping of French posters. My favorites are the French travel posters that use the works of French artists to convey that country's charms.

Pattern-on-Pattern

If your little world is looking drab, do as Gloria Vanderbilt does and add a profusion of colors and patterns. When I dropped by Gloria's New York studio recently, it was a gray, rainy day outside, but inside Gloria's world, all was sunshine.

Gloria, as you know, is a designer of everything from fabrics to sheets to china and glassware. Her most recent venture is into the world of wallcoverings à la Gloria for James Seeman Studios.

Gloria's philosophy is one I agree with again and again: "It can be a drab, sad world, so surrounding yourself with things that are joyous is important."

Her interpretation of the joyous look is based on two elements: color and pattern-on-pattern. In her studio, for instance, I sat on a deep sofa upholstered in a ribbon-and-flower chintz of pastels and scarlet on a black background. Piled high on that sofa were soft pillows covered in a sunny abstract print of hot pink, lemon yellow, sky blue—what I call Mediterranean colors.

Gloria is not afraid of combinations many people would shy from, and she would love to bring the whole world around to her way of seeing things. As she says, "People are scared of their own taste, which is a shame. If you can't show your taste in your own home, where can you show it?"

Gloria's home is certainly a reflection of her tastes. Her living room is a happy blend of pastel patchwork walls and tulip-strewn upholstery.

If you, like Gloria, "love being surrounded with organized clutter," and you have the kind of personality—like Gloria's—that's at its best when doing ten things at once, all beautifully, then the "Gloria look" is for you.

To achieve it, follow her lead and paper living-room walls in a pale patchwork print (a hint of pattern is all you need). Then find a floral print and buy it on three different background colors —black, scarlet, and yellow. Use one color for the sofa, one for a chair, and the third color for a second chair or for occasional chairs. Be bold and pattern the floor, too, with a geometric-patterned carpet of yellow and white. And have yet another geometric print on a skirted end table.

You'll find more suggestions for the use of pattern-on-pattern in Chapter 3 on bedrooms.

Summer, fall, winter, and spring are slipcover seasons. Think about slipcovers in happy-colored chintzes, cottons, and linens.

Slipcovers serve a dual purpose: They give a warm-weather lift to your room and they protect your upholstery. And speaking practically, that's important in summer when perspiration, beach sand, and the patter of little bare feet all conspire against your furniture.

Whether you make slipcovers yourself (this is for experienced seamstresses only, please!) or you have them custom-made, fit is the all-important word. Even the most beautiful slipcover fabric will do nothing for a room if it hangs in baggy wrinkles. Choosing the right fabric will help with the fit. Stick to firm, closely woven, lightweight fabrics that hold their shape, or use a stretch-knit that will hug your upholstered pieces without a wrinkle. Avoid slippery fabrics like silk that will slither and slide and spoil the fit. As for colors and patterns, the choice is endless, but, of course, the colors should be clear and bright.

You can bring a wintry living room to life with the addition of slipcovers. For the sofa, how about a geometric-print patchwork-design cotton of emerald green and canary yellow? Above the blinds, hang a valance of the patchwork print, and add a pretty skirt to one end table in a calico print of the tiniest green and yellow buds on a white background. Trim the skirt, lattice-fashion, with emerald-green and canary-yellow ribbons.

And on that skirted end table, I'd like to see a cluster of three or four small white and yellow wicker baskets with all handles, filled with leafy green plants.

I'm sure you've run across a beauty checklist in a fashion magazine. I believe in checklists and I certainly believe in beauty, so I thought why not a beauty checklist for the home?

The autumn season—between summer vacation time and upcoming holidays—is a good time to go over your living room with a beauty checklist, looking for those places that need a facelift.

Check your living room against my beauty checklist:

Walls—Take care of those fingerprints and sooty spots now. I hope your walls are painted with washable paint! If not, perhaps the cool snap in the air will inspire you to take up paintbrush and roller and give the living room a color lift. Try something different—apricot walls, perhaps.

Wood floors—There should be nothing here but shine, shine, shine—the better to reflect the glow of holiday candlelight.

Carpet—No bald spots or stains, I hope. But if the inevitable wear and tear has taken its toll, try covering the worst spots with pretty little scatter rugs. I like fluffy fur, Orientals, and pale dhurries from the Middle East.

Upholstery—I hope yours has been getting a rest under summer slipcovers. If not, perhaps it's time for a full-scale professional cleaning.

Colors—Drab colors, if they're still around, must go or be brightened with accessories. If reupholstering or slipcovering is part of your fall beauty treatment, choose something in one of the new soft, pretty tones: pale shell pink, mauve, apricot, or dove gray.

Accessories—Add a few with a new look; retire a few tired old friends to the attic for a rest. I believe that accessories should be rotated. After all, who wants to look at the same vase or ashtray month after month. Not I! My favorite accessories are woven wicker baskets in natural tones and bright colors; things personal, such as family photos in interesting frames, handmade needlepoint cushions, children's drawings, framed and hung.

Using Fashion Fabrics in the Living Room

Where do you shop for upholstery and drapery fabrics? Most people head for the upholstery-fabric department, naturally. But did you know that many decorators look first in shops specializing in fabrics for apparel?

If you think that stretch-knits, wool "suiting," gabardine, and the like are for clothing only, think again. I have been using those fabrics for years in my decorating work.

An apartment I designed recently featured fine creamy white wool gabardine for chair upholstery. Sofas were upholstered in a gabardine of rich chocolate brown, frosted with a scattering of white cotton Turkish corner pillows. Walls were covered in shiny tortoise vinyl. And for carpeting I chose nubby off-white wool.

Those stretch-knit fabrics that are used almost universally for everything from menswear to women's evening gowns are rarely seen in upholstery-fabric shops. I buy them in dress shops and use them to reupholster chairs—particularly the contemporary styles that require tight-fitting covers. If you plan on doing your own reup-holstering or slipcovering, leave the tailored fabrics to the experts and consider using knits. As I mentioned earlier, you'll find knits easier to fit than nonstretch fabrics, and good fit is the difference between a professional-looking slip-cover and an amateur job.

As for those soft, matte-finish nylon jerseys that so many fashion designers are wild about these days, I use them for table skirts, trimmed around the bottom with jumbo welting, because I love the way the jersey falls into soft folds and swirls.

Gray flannel, once used exclusively for suits and slacks, is one of the superstars of today's decorating scene. Gray flannel for upholstery, gray flannel for walls, gray flannel for period rooms, gray flannel for contemporary settings, for bedrooms, for dens, for living rooms. The popularity of gray flannel doesn't surprise me. It is, after all, one of those fabulous neutrals that goes with anything and everything.

Use reserved, conservative gray flannel for a living room that is anything but! If your furniture is French Provincial, how about gray flannel upholstery instead of the usual brocade or velvet? Strip the arms of that French Provincial sofa, and the arms, legs, and backs of those bergère chairs. Upholster them all in charcoal-gray flannel. Light, natural wood against gray is a look I like.

Paint walls in your living room a rich egg-yolk yellow and all wood trim and ceiling white. For toss pillows on the gray flannel sofa, go goldenrod yellow and Siamese pink! Draperies can be golden yellow silk tiebacks lined in Siamese pink, and hang them over filmy white sheers. Skirt one end table in a large-scale black-and-white floral cotton brocade. Your second sofa end table and your coffee table can be clear Lucite cubes. For end-table lamps, my choice would be Lucite again, shaded in white. Underfoot, how about an Oriental-style accent rug of yellow, black, white, and rich gray?

Crewel is the oldest form of embroidery known, but that doesn't stop it from being one of today's most popular crafts, and also one of the most popular decorative fabrics. I know many people who are stitching away at crewelwork that they will use for pillows, pictures, and even upholstery

(ambitious!). And I know people who are buying ready-made crewel fabrics for draperies, upholstery, bedspreads, you name it.

Crewel, as we know it, developed in England between the sixteenth and eighteenth centuries. The word "crewel" means two-ply yarn, and technically crewel is any embroidery done in wool on any kind of fabric. The crewel we are most familiar with is done on cotton or linen.

In the early days of America, hand-done crewel work on linen or cotton was popular for decorating bedrooms and living rooms. Go see the excellent examples of crewel bedspreads and bed hangings at the Winterthur Museum in Delaware and at Williamsburg, Virginia.

I like crewel on wing chairs, on footstools, at windows. I like crewel in traditional settings, and I enjoy seeing a touch of crewel in contemporary rooms as well.

Plan a cozy living room around a conversation grouping of two love seats covered in a crewel fabric of green, blue, dusty pink, burgundy, gold, and brown on a creamy background. Paint walls a warm burgundy and all trim cream. Leave floors bare except for a fluffy ivory area rug in front of the love seats. Cover comfy club chairs in creamy white (I would recommend well-fitted slipcovers for easy cleaning). If there's a long sofa in the room, cover it in the dusty pink of the crewelwork, and make sure there are lots of cushy toss pillows in solid burgundy and in the crewel fabric, too. At your windows, hang ivory draperies under a crewel valance, and use the crewel for tiebacks too. For a coffee table, my choice would be two clear acrylic cubes sitting on that fluffy area rug. End tables might be Indian brass.

I have always been a fan of cotton print fabrics, so I'm pleased that cotton prints—florals, geometrics, batiks, and stripes—are no longer being relegated to the summer slipcover market. Cotton florals with glazed or matte finishes are all over the market these days, especially on plump, pillowy sofas and club chairs. Many of the happy prints I've seen recently have been trimmed with solid-color welting—a yellow-and-blue print with blue welting, or a blue-and-red print with red welting.

If you're in the market for living-room furniture that's both cheerful and sophisticated, shop for chairs and sofas upholstered in a quilted Oriental cotton print of jungle green and wine red. Paint walls champagne beige and choose a carpet in wine red. Hang wine-red draperies at windows. For chairs, my choice would be a pair of the new armless chairs with plump cushions, upholstered in a small-scale geometric print of jungle green, wine and sand beige.

I recently upholstered a pair of armless multi-pillow chairs in a fun variety of cotton stripes. I used emerald-green-and-white tenting stripes for the chair backs and bases, and stripes of pink and white for pillow number one; stripes of yellow and white for pillow number two; and the

emerald-green-and-white stripe for the topmost pillow. It's a fun look and one I like to mix with floral prints.

For those who love things ethnic and colorful, try batik. There's real batik, as well as batik-influenced prints, and they know no season. In the room shown, batik-look upholstery in rich fall tones of gold, pumpkin, and beige was used. It looks right in season in a cozy country room furnished with country French chairs and sofa and graceful Queen Anne accent tables. The fabric's subtle diamond-patterned background is picked up by the beige and brown diamond-patterned wallcovering, and the fabric's russet

A cozy, country French living room features cotton print upholstery on country French sofa and chairs, and Queen Anne–styled accent pieces.

rend Line's country French sofa and chairs

Peters-Revington Queen Anne–style tables

and pumpkin-colored butterflies and flowers are reflected in the crackling orange flames of a cozy fire.

When summer comes again, the upholstery fabric of cool cotton will look as fresh as can be —no slipcovers needed.

Gingham is perhaps the most popular and versatile of all prints. It goes everywhere—there are gingham-covered club chairs with shirred gingham skirts, gingham-covered sofas, and now even gingham wallpapers, gingham lampshades, and gingham window blinds.

Gingham *is* a great print. It is not solely for the children's playroom, and you can take my word for that. A green-and-white gingham check would be mighty smart upholstery in a living room that features a happy flower print at the windows, particularly if the print features pink and red roses entwined with green leaves on a white background. This combination would look fine with either white, green, chocolate, or red walls.

Some friends of mine, Karen and Hugh La-Motte, mixed all colors of gingham in their country living room. They chose a pink-and-white check for the sofa and lavished it with gingham checkered pillows in yellow and white, green and white, and blue and white, all with ruffled borders. A white fur rug was used on terra-cotta tile flooring, and walls were white-washed wood-grained paneling.

In your own home, try windowpane checks, houndstooth checks, tattersall checks, and gingham checks. If you look around your home and can't check off any of them, you're missing a good decorating bet. The check is one of those do-everything decorating designs I can't live without.

In formal traditional rooms, I love the look of taffeta tattersall checks for upholstery on occasional chairs. I like to use a tattersall checked taffeta on the frames of bergère chairs with cushions upholstered in a floral print. Or I may choose a pretty pastel tattersall taffeta to line a scalloped white linen bed canopy.

Houndstooth checks say sport to me. I love chocolate-and-white houndstooth upholstered chairs in a wood-paneled living room, or a snappy apple-green-and-white houndstooth check for a casual, airy room with poppy-red carpeting and lemon-yellow accessories.

Gingham checks say country casual. And isn't that the look everyone wants these days, even if that "country cottage" is really a city apartment?

For the one-room studio apartment dweller who dreams of greener pastures, here's a fresh green and white scheme to try: Walls are fresh country white—the color of frost. Trim is white, too. For a happy surprise, I would paint doors a deep, rich, shiny forest green. And make sure those doors have shiny brass knobs. Upholster a sofa bed and two wood-framed easy chairs in a bold gingham check of forest green and off-white. Carpet in beige sisal matting or sand-beige shag, and keep all wood furniture in the room light, light, light—one-room living calls for airiness.

No matter what period of decoration you are planning for your home, velvet is a good bet. There are all kinds of velvets—rayon velvets, silk velvets, striped velvets, cut-velvet patterns of roses on a white background, and even polka-dot velvets. Velvets are for the budget-minded, too. There are many inexpensive varieties on the market, and these are flame-retardant and even stainproof.

Velvet is admired by many people for its soft quality. It is a favorite of young and old, the traditionalist as well as the modernist. Many modern furnished apartments use velvet for the sofa covering or for drapery, and I think everyone will agree that velvet is very, very right in a French-inspired salon, a Spanish room, or on wing chairs in an English-style room.

When you want a majestic look, think velvet. In a traditional living room with soft champagne walls, hang overdraperies of champagne velvet, lined in a shrimp color. Upholster your sofa in champagne velvet too, and accent it with lemon-peel-yellow and shrimp-colored pillows. For club chairs, my choice would be lemon-peel moiré, again for the soft look, and I would like champagne-velvet cut-pile carpet.

And what about planning a modern living room with velvet walls? Velvet has been laminated to strippable paper these days and can be put up just like ordinary wallpapers. Cover your walls with mint-green velvet, and paint woodwork rich beaver brown. For upholstery on a stainless-steel-framed sofa, choose a brown and white geometric cut-velvet design. For lounge chairs choose topaz Naugahyde. Lamps of clustered balls topped with

Gray is a popular contemporary color. This room, on the Avenue Foch in Paris, uses blue-and-white Chinese lamps and ashtrays as color-accent appointments.

When planning window decor in rooms with a view, keep the view as open as possible. Outside lighting on plant beds is important for the right look.

The best arrangement at the fireplace is this one with sofa and club chairs. Coffee tables here are red coramandels.

In this living room the Zuber decorated screen is the focal point. Turkish-cornered hassocks with green leather-covered table are used when additional conversation seating is needed.

The rainbow is the color story of this living room designed by my friends, Richard Ohrbach and Lynn Jacobson. See what you can do if you're daring!

The L-shaped sofa is still a favorite with the modernists. A flood-lighted wall gives a dramatic effect.

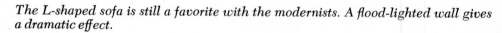

white linen shades on each would be perfect on Parsons-style tables lacquered topaz. Choose white vertical blinds for the window treatment.

I like the look of velvet that is slightly worn, believe it not. In my library I have a pair of ten-year-old round-back club chairs covered in a rich copper velvet. While they are a bit worn, they look good to me!

As I mentioned earlier, the totally upholstered look is big; furniture arms, legs, and feet are getting the padded treatment.

I like the softening effect of all-over upholstery in today's boxlike rooms. A modern living room I saw recently was all soft curves and inviting cushions thanks to total upholstery on chairs and a sectional sofa. All the upholstered pieces had been covered in a snappy fern-and-flower pattern of parrot green and poppy red with touches of sunny yellow, royal blue, and sparkling white.

The upholstered look was even carried over to a console table and bench. And the console-table *wall* was upholstered too, to match the sofas, chairs, and table. Underfoot, a solar-orange tie-dyed carpet added a further dimension of comfort.

Today you can buy synthetic upholstery fabrics that feel as nubby as real wool; as soft as real fur; as sleek as genuine leather; as velvety as suede. And the synthetics have the advantages of easy care and a price tag that's generally lower than that of the real thing.

Not that I'm downgrading the real thing. I love real 100-percent wools, cottons, and leathers and use them often in my work. Leather is a decorating classic that never goes out of style. Real leather (or a good fake) for upholstery is

"Nordic Splendor" carpet from Lees

Selig sofa

The all-over upholstered look on sofa, chairs, console table, and bench, plus a rich, tie-dyed carpet, softens the lines of a boxy modern room.

at home in any decor. What man doesn't love a comfy club chair upholstered in rich brown leather? I own one, and it's the first place I head when I arrive home from the office. And what homemaker doesn't appreciate the practical features of leather—particularly its long wear?

Today, leather has gone all the way. I've made leather-covered Parsons tables, leather-covered console tables, leather-covered chests of drawers. I've even upholstered chair legs in leather to match chair upholstery!

When purchasing a sofa, consider a tufted chesterfield model in leather. A room I'm designing right now will have two golden-yellow tufted leather love seats. Draperies in the room will be a large-scale floral print of deep goldenrod yellow, royal blue, mint green, burnt orange, and pink. Walls will be paneled in rich wood. For carpeting, emerald-green plush was my choice. Club chairs in the room will be burnt orange, and side chairs are to be upholstered in a ribbed fabric of royal-blue-and-white stripes.

Leather-top desks are also a favorite of mine, and the leather top doesn't have to be the usual brown or beige or green. It can be pale pink, white, yellow, pale blue!

Brightening the Drab Living Room

Many, many readers write to ask me how to brighten their drab rooms. One way *not* to brighten drab rooms is by introducing only one spot of color or bold print.

In my experience as a decorator, I've discovered that people want color and pattern, but they're also afraid of it. So they take half measures and buy just one brightly colored chair, or paper just one wall in a bold print, or hang just one big, bright poster. But take it from me, trying to enliven a boring room with only one spot of color will make the rest of the room seem even more drab in contrast.

I recently visited a home where the hostess complained that her emerald-green sofa stuck out like a sore thumb—and she was right. She had tried to brighten her room by buying a beautiful, bright emerald-green sofa, but, alas, contrasted with her unadorned white walls and dark wood furniture, her sofa looked like a brilliant tropical fish in a tank full of dreary gray guppies!

The cure for her "sore thumb," I told her, was to balance that bright sofa with more bright color elsewhere in, or near, the room. I suggested painting the hallways on either side of the room the same emerald green as the sofa. Furthermore, since my hostess liked cranberry red, I told her to buy a cushy armchair in that color and to strew that emerald-green sofa with toss cushions of cranberry red. For her dark-stained floors, I recommended a bright Oriental carpet of emerald, cranberry, and shades of tan and beige.

Color alone isn't always the whole answer, however.

"If you got it, flaunt it!" was a popular expression a few years ago. But what do you do when you haven't "got it"? My answer as a decorator is "camouflage it." Good decorating, in my experience, often depends as much on playing down the unattractive as it does on "flaunting" the beautiful. If you've ever seen a beautifully furnished apartment with peeling walls, you know what I mean.

A wood floor is beautiful to behold, when it's in good condition. But a stained, splintery floor should never be flaunted. It should definitely be camouflaged with carpeting, vinyl tile, or area rugs.

Many old apartments and homes are prime candidates for the camouflage treatment. Peeling walls, unsightly radiators, and more are often the lot of the apartment dweller.

Russ Elliott, a New York artist and friend of mine, had all those problems in his one-room studio apartment. And being an artist, Russ met those problems head-on, using all the camouflage tricks he could muster.

Cracked old walls are now concealed behind coffee-brown wood paneling. Protruding cornices and beams fade into the background because they are painted the same rich brown.

After tackling the walls, Russ went to work on the old floors. He covered them with a handsome earth-toned cushion vinyl in an eye-catching octagonal print.

At windows, camouflaging an unattractive view and maintaining privacy were Russ's requirements. He got them both, plus the light he needs for his work, by installing fiber-glass mesh shades. They block the view and prying neighborly eyes, but let the light shine through. He also conceals an ugly window air conditioner behind a big bushy fern when it's not in use.

To camouflage all the clutter that an artist must have for his work, Russ built an L-shaped banquette arrangement in a corner, with storage drawers below and seating up above. The seating area actually does triple duty: It's a sofa during the day, a bed at night, and, with the addition of a table, can be used at mealtimes, too.

With a little ingenuity, you can camouflage beams, radiators, steam pipes, awkwardly placed windows, doors—whatever your living room's flaws happen to be—and often the treatment you choose will turn out to be not just a cover-up but a positive asset to your decor.

The Fiber Family

Have you made the acquaintance of the fiber family? If not, you should. The fiber family—sisal, tatami, wicker—is a big name in decorating these days and is being invited into some of the most elegant homes.

The tatami branch of the family, as the name implies, hails from Japan. There, tatami mats are used to cover the floors since that's where most of the Japanese do their sitting, sleeping, and lounging. You can use tatami on the floor if you choose, or on walls for a crunchy, natural look that is also a great way to hide broken or cracked plaster.

The sisal branch of the fiber family is also often found on the floor, as you know. There are sisal mats in every size, from doormat proportions all the way up to wall-to-wall carpeting. Sisal is also being used on furniture. I have seen it stretched over plywood cubes to make super-looking occasional tables.

The hardiest and most popular member of the fiber family is wicker. No longer reserved for porch chairs and sofas only, today there are wicker étagères, wicker desks, wicker wall units, wicker beds, wicker chests, and wicker lamps.

It wouldn't be at all difficult to decorate a whole living room, ceiling to floor, with members of the fiber family. However, I prefer mixing them with other items. An attractively casual living room, for instance, might feature tatami walls lacquered vivid bittersweet. The floor could be covered with natural hay-colored sisal. Rather than go fiber for furniture, I would choose the clean lines of Parsons-style occasional tables and the cushy comfort of a beige-upholstered sofa.

Additional seating could be provided by an armless chair and matching ottoman upholstered in rich swirls of chocolate brown and black. And for accessories? Why, I would choose baskets, of course. Covered ones for storage and the lidless variety for holding green plants.

What's newsworthy about something that's been around for centuries? When that something is linen, the answer is "plenty."

Linen, as you may know, has been around since the beginning of recorded history and probably before. The Egyptians of old raised flax and used it for everything from clothing to shrouds for their mummies. Most linen now comes from Belgium and it has been around the home for centuries.

What's new about linen is the many new ways it is being used in the home. Pure linen for vertical blinds is very much in. And pure linen wallcoverings in fabrics and specially prepared forms are in, too. The new wallcoverings don't stop with woven looks; I have seen wallcoverings created from individual Belgian-linen fibers glued in interesting patterns to paper backings. And those nubby wallcoverings, in flaxen tones, are perfect backdrops for the natural look.

For handy do-it-yourselfers, I recommend stapling linen fabric right to the wall. You don't even need padding. I picture those natural linen walls in a formal, yet comfortable, room, furnished with French bergère chairs and deep cushy sofas, all upholstered in rich coral-colored linen. Doors and trim can be painted glossy black. For draperies, beige natural linen to match walls would be my choice, lined in coral fabric. Underfoot, I see a delicately tinted Oriental rug in shades of pale blue, coral, and ivory.

Cleaning Belgian linen is not as difficult as you might think. Because it is a natural, it is antistatic, which means it repels dust. To clean linen-covered walls, all you do is vacuum twice a year. Spots can be removed by sponging with a solution of mild detergent and water.

Faking It

The fake look in decorating is big these days, what with the worldwide effort to save natural resources and endangered wildlife. But the fake

"Tempo" Hide-A-Bed sofa by Simm

The fiber family—the natural fiber products—puts on a strong showing in a room with tatami-covered walls and a stretch of sisal on the floor, a natural backdrop for the sitting and sleeping comfort of a sofa bed.

look in decorating is nothing new, you know. Fake lizard, fake fur, fake gemstones, fake wood, fake marble, fake tortoise have always been available.

The French, who call fake finishes for furniture and walls *faux,* have decorated the "fake way" for centuries. And I don't have to tell you that if the French love the *faux* look, it must be elegant.

Faux finishes can be achieved in a number of ways. The most elegant method is with paint. There are still old-world craftsmen who can paint a wall or a piece of furniture to look like precious marble, fine wood, or rare gemstones. But if you

are handy with a brush yourself, it is possible to create some of the simpler finishes by following instructions in one of the books on finishing available in the library or in your local bookstore.

A gracious living room I saw recently featured a mantel painted in *faux marbre*—fake marble. That mantel certainly proved one decorating point: *Faux* finishes are a great way to create an interesting focal point, or to turn an undistinguished room feature or piece of furniture into a treasured conversation piece.

Flanking the room's super *faux marbre* mantel were a sofa upholstered in a nubby oatmeal tweed and a wing chair covered in an abstract print of raspberry red, teal blue, leaf green, and warm beige on a creamy white ground. The same print was also used for luxurious tieback draperies, hung over white louvered shutters. Another *faux* touch was a comfy armchair upholstered in beige and white zebra-print fabric. Pulling the whole look together was a warm carpet in ringing red. Touches of gleaming brass —in lamps, a mantel clock, and a mirror frame— added to the room's appeal.

Ways to Warm the Home

I love the warm look all over the home—brass lamps on the end tables; warm, lighted, real candles on the dining table; hurricane lamps lighted by kerosene; and, of course, a burning log fire in the family room, dining room, living room, or master bedroom.

Lucky are those people who have fireplaces all over the house, not only for the practical warmth during the winter, but also for the coziness it

An elegant faux marbre *mantel and a ringing red carpet are the focal points of a gracious, traditional living room.*

"Bright Dream" carpet from Burlington House

gives to a home. If you have a living-room fire-place, don't forget to light it, and keep your fire-place accessorized with shiny brass andirons and brass log baskets. Of course, I like wicker log baskets and black metal pieces, too.

The warm look means getting rid of starkness. A fabric tapestry can bring a comfortable and happy note to the wall above your sofa. You'll find a tapestry far more warming on the wall as opposed to a large mirror, or you may want to hang a large geometric abstract with warm and happy colors on your living room sofa wall.

In the living room, cushy large pillows on the sofas, or tossed on the club chairs or piled up on the floor, always give a warm look. Choose pillows that are plump and that have Turkish corners. And pick pillows in warm colors—golds, oranges, reds, yellows, russets. The oranges and reds can give a toasty look to a blue-green upholstered sofa.

Here are some other ways to banish the stark look and bring warmth to your living room.

HANDCRAFTS

For some reason, things that look handmade have a warmer, friendlier look than their machine-made counterparts. Handcrafts are thus important accessories, whether from Africa, pioneer America, Europe, Asia, or South America.

Handmades are very much a part of today's eclectic look. Those rustic, primitive handmades work well with things sleek and modern. And of course they look super with today's natural-look furnishings.

In the living room, a dramatic black-and-white scheme is softened with the liberal use of hand-mades and with a rich brown carpet. A white textured sofa sports a collection of brown, beige, and white handwoven pillows. Plants are decoratively displayed in baskets. And as a focal point, a black-lacquered wall holds an arrangement of contemporary fiber sculpture and more of those great African and Asian baskets. To complete the mix-and-match look, there's a cut-down an-

tique dining table in front of the sofa and a window treatment of white vertical blinds.

AREA RUGS

The wall-to-wall carpet is losing ground to the smaller, more versatile area rug. Not only does its colorful pattern lend warmth to stark expanses, but today's mobile American family is discovering that the area rug is much more practical in terms of versatility. It can be picked up and moved, and then moved again—from room to room and from home to home. The area rug from the city living room may eventually find its way to the country house. The area rug from the rambling homestead may find a new home in the retirement apartment.

Area rugs, of course, are perfect choices for conversation groupings, since they set off and help define special groupings. And they're even climbing the walls these days. For a toasty look, with the hearth as the focal point, you might choose two area rugs—rya in toast, brown, beige, and gold for the floor, and a bright woven Indian look with fringe in persimmon, yellow, brown, and beige for the wall. Lay the rya on a walnut-stained wood floor and arrange furniture facing the rug. To carry out the warm look, upholster the loveseat in a glowing tangerine velvet, and choose a brown tweed texture for chairs.

Because of their small size, area rugs are easily made up by do-it-yourselfers. A client of mine sewed black and white 24-inch squares of cotton carpet remnants into a beautiful wall hanging for her living room. It looked terrific with her white wicker furniture, black-and-white print slipcovers, black slate floor, and black-and-white-print floor pillows.

ART

Art in the home adds a lot of pleasure and relieves the starkness of bare walls. Use paintings, prints, tapestries, and drawings, but hang only the

In the living room shown, a dramatic black-and-white scheme is softened with the liberal use of handmades and with a rich brown nylon carpet.

things you really like. I am not a believer in the theory that paintings should always relate color-wise to a room's color scheme. Beautiful land-scapes and most paintings in general work with every decorating scheme. Those that don't can be brought into harmony through matting and framing.

While in Hawaii I visited the home of the famous artist Margaret Keane, who has built international fame for herself by painting eyes, which she believes are the windows of the soul. Margaret, a petite blonde who comes from Nash-ville, Tennessee, told me that she started painting while in grammar school when she would scribble eyes on the back of her school pads.

Margaret Keane's own home, where she has her studio, is situated in the hills in the Kahala section on the island of Oahu, and from her ter-race one can see all of Honolulu. It is a spacious and open ranch house where the outside has been brought into the decorating. There are island wicker furnishings on a deep blue-green shag carpet—the coloring of the carpet is much the same blue-green as the Pacific Ocean—and the white walls in her living room are covered with her own paintings as well as those of other artists and friends.

One of the most fascinating do-it-yourself deco-rating ideas I have seen recently is Margaret Keane's large round glass-top cocktail table. Under the glass top, the surface of the table is covered with a collage of her own paintings of faces. The Keane faces in the center are small and graduate to large faces at the table's per-imeter so that the table is a circle of faces—all with startling eyes. If you have a special favorite collection of pictures, pressed flowers, or any-thing flat, why not consider decorating your coffee table with some Keane imagination? All you require is a clear glass top to set on the table surface. The glass will keep everything in place and serve as protection, too.

Art for your walls can be costly if you're thinking in terms of original paintings by recognized artists, and many people settle for reproductions. However, I talked with some art consultants and they believe that one of the best buys in art today is the original print, such as the lithograph or etching. An original print is produced in limited quantities from a plate created by the artist. I strongly recommend buying these prints instead of purchasing reproductions of famous paintings.

Posters are a colorful and inexpensive way to decorate large wall areas, and some posters may become valuable in the future. When I stopped by one of the galleries, for instance, I saw an exhibit of turn-of-the-century posters. Those posters, may I remind you, were next-to-worthless advertisements when they were created. Today, they are costly works of art!

Whatever you choose to hang on your walls, make sure you hang them effectively. A most common error is hanging pictures too high. Pic-tures should be hung just below eye level of an average-size person, just as they are in galleries and museums.

If you have a small picture, don't leave it stranded all by itself on a big open wall, hang it with other pictures or over a piece of furniture. Pictures hung over sofas and chairs should be placed just high enough so that people leaning back don't hit their heads against the frame.

I like to hang picture groupings in an irregular pattern. And, boy, do I dislike the row approach to picture hanging—everything in a straight line at the same height and in the same style of frame railroaded on walls above the sofa! I'm not much for hanging a pair of paintings over the sofa either; one painting on the wall to the left over the sofa would be fine with me, and perhaps on the wall to the right side a bracket holding an attractive plant.

Why, oh, why does everyone think a picture has to be centered over a fireplace? It doesn't have to be, you know. Hang your picture on the wall over the fireplace to the left, and perhaps use a pair of candlesticks on the right side of the mantel. This arrangement will give your fireplace a good look.

When hanging pictures, photos, or whatever you like on the walls, get the right tools, and be

Area rugs warm the floor and climb the walls of a cozy living room with hearth. The shag rya-type rug and woven wall hanging/area rug lead all eyes to the fireplace.

Phyllis Morris—designed benches

Decorate your walls with the things you like. In this living room a painting looks out over the setting and is balanced with a yellow-and-white daisy oil and a small carved-wood head. Tufted velvet benches find a home under the coffee table and add greatly to the conversation grouping when needed for sitting.

Margaret Keane painting

certain to buy picture hooks of the right size to support hangings. If you're concerned about big pictures tipping or flopping from one center hook attached to the wire on the back of the picture frame, use two hooks several inches apart to better support the weight. As for those "decorative" hooks that are supposed to show on the walls along with the pictures, I dislike them. In my opinion, picture hooks should never, but never, show.

The botanical look is big on the decorating scene today. All about the market there are botanical prints that can be framed and hung on walls. And there are botanical-print fabrics for curtains to be hung in the living room, dining room, bedroom, kitchen, or bath.

Recently I saw a charming room in which white-framed botanical prints were hung on bright melon walls. A profusion of interesting plants filled white shelving in window areas, which had been covered with translucent acrylic panels to hide an unpleasant view. The sunny colors in the room featured golden yellow subtly patterned shag carpet of spun nylon. Handsome white casual furniture was enhanced with lemon-and-lime striped fabric.

Botanical prints are hung on the walls of this room styled with bright melon painted walls, white trim, and golden yellow subtly patterned shag carpet of spun nylon. Windows hiding an unpleasant view with translucent acrylic panels have been oufitted with white shelving filled with a profusion of live plants.

Why not hang a grouping of old botanical drawings on the wall above a sofa? A friend covered a folding screen with botanical prints taken from old college books, gluing the pages to the plywood screen. Some people paint leaves and plants directly on lampshades.

FLOWERS AND PLANTS

I think greenery or flowers should be on the decorating list for every living room. I have checked into many, many hotels throughout the world, and some have been mighty dull and dreary, but when a vase or two of flowers had been placed about, everything looked brighter A vase filled with flowers seems to take the center spotlight, new life and beauty enter the room.

Filling vases with flowers takes little effort and can give loads of eye appeal in your home. If cut flowers are too expensive for your budget, fill vases with greenery—rhododendron, laurel, huckleberry, or pine—which will last for several days and even weeks. I have found when rhododendron leaves start to fade, a quick shower in the family bath will revive them almost instantly.

When entertaining time comes around for one friend, she says, "I'll just fill the room with lovely bouquets of flowers in large, clear glass vases, and the room will look beautiful."

She's right. I like flowers best when they are displayed in clear glass vases, because the clear glass doesn't compete with the beauty of the greenery or flowers. You don't have to buy large, expensive glass vases—there are many inexpensive pieces on the market that will do the decorative job very well—but I do think it's best to buy glass vases in pairs; a pair of flower-filled vases will look so attractive placed gracefully on a pair of console tables in the living room or dining room.

I also like plants in clay pots, wicker or straw baskets, shiny brass urns, or white porcelain. I prefer that clay pots be left natural terra-cotta, but if you want painted pots, make them white. I've personally never liked pots painted green, royal blue, or pink. If you like colored pots, buy decorative cachepots and set the ordinary pots inside.

Think of flowers and plants as part of the overall decor and place them where they look best. A basketful of yellow and white daisies can say a lot on the coffee table in a living room decorated with sky-blue walls, emerald-green sofa upholstery, and yellow-and-white-striped club chairs. Bright red geranium plants will look best on the sill of a window that has white organdy crisscross curtains. Make flowers and plants work day and night. Don't leave a flower arrangement in a corner that gets no light at night—it will never be seen. Place a vase of flowers on a table where the lamplight will reflect their beauty.

DETAILS THAT CAN WARM UP A ROOM

Are you a detail person? A successful banker I know is one. In fact, he told me recently that the secret of his success is "attention to detail."

I believe that decorating success also requires attention to detail. I have personally spent days—sometimes weeks—searching for just the right trim for a set of draperies, or just the right fabric to cover a footstool. The fact that the drapery trim is only a tiny part of the room's decor does not make it any the less important than the wall color or upholstery fabric.

Today people who care about detail are using trimmings all over the home—on curtains, sofas, club chairs, window shades, wastebaskets, library bookshelves, and evon on picture frames.

I love trims on drapery and always use them in my decorating work. Visualize a living room with white walls. At the windows hang white draperies with borders of royal-blue, yellow, and emerald-green grosgrain ribbon trim. Valances over the draperies are sunny yellow, lined in emerald green. The floor features an area rug of bright emerald green with a sunny yellow border. Sofas are covered in a white-navy-and-yellow tweed accented with navy and emerald-green throw pillows. Club chairs are slipcovered with white linen edged with sunny yellow welting.

I love sofas that have a gimp trim of a contrasting color. If you are a royal-blue enthusiast, why not use an exciting royal- silver-and-white braid around the panels of a royal-blue velvet sofa? You can also use it to trim the window shades or the overdrapery.

Trims go in every room of your home. I love bedspreads trimmed with braid or contrasting welting. And if you want kitchen curtains that really sparkle, why not trim white curtains with

It's time for trimming, and with trim you can do most anything. This living room with gray slate flooring features a modern stainless-steel sofa covered with royal-blue velvet, trimmed with a royal-blue, silver, and white braid. The same braid is used on folding white screen panels at the windows. Zebra rug under glass coffee table with stainless-steel base is a striking contemporary note.

a bright red, apple-green, and black ball fringe? If you are more conservative, trim yellow café curtains with chocolate brown side and bottom borders.

Some friends of mine created panels for their beige walls simply by using a red-brown-and-white braid. The braid was pasted to the walls with glue.

I notice detail as soon as I walk into a room, and one of my pet peeves is the ordinary doorknob. It is a detail that often ruins the appearance of an otherwise lovely room. The ordinary doorknob is the stark chrome-plated or brass-plated doorknob that is standard in many newly built homes, and in my opinion should be replaced. There are many pretty and inexpensive doorknobs on the market—doorknobs of metal and doorknobs of china. I have also known people to replace their ordinary doorknobs with antique doorknobs of solid brass, china, or wood, which can often be salvaged from doors in buildings that are being torn down.

COLLECTIONS AS ACCESSORIES

Have you ever been charmed by a group of objects on someone's coffee table? I was fascinated recently by a collection of antique smoking pipes—meerschaums and such—in the home of a lawyer friend named Bill. The old pipes, none of which cost more than a few dollars, were displayed in racks on a shelf, and some were laid out on the coffee table where fascinated guests, like myself, could study their antique beauty.

Just as a person's hobbies make him more interesting, accessories that reveal a person's interests make his home more human, warmer, more interesting. The ones I enjoy most are those that are useful, like Bill's pipes. But I also enjoy the collections of minerals, shells, and other natural wonders, which have become popular of late. From my point of view nothing accessorizes today's natural-looking rooms as appropriately as artifacts of Mother Nature.

I recently saw a super display of such objects in a young collector's apartment. To create a suitable showcase for his geode collection, this young man built an L-shaped false wall of gypsum board about six inches in front of the room's real wall. One long L-shaped niche and several smaller niches were cut into the false wall. The shelves, lighted from behind, were built into the niches to hold the colorful geode collection. To finish the false wall, a soft beige linenlike wallcovering was used, which blended beautifully with the beige-and-white geometric upholstery of the cushiony sectional sofa. A corded velvet armchair and ottoman in sand beige and a thick sandy shag carpet completed the attractive natural look.

Seashell collections are also fascinating, and their beauty has inspired many delightful shell-print fabrics and wallpapers on the market today as well as shell-design accessories.

Shells can be useful as well as decorative. We've all seen seashells used as ashtrays, but have you seen the mirrors with shell frames, and also the shell picture frames? I have seen tables of see-through plastic that revealed seashells and handsome greenery. And recently I have found on the market shell-base lamps made with white plaster or with actual shells. One of my friends filled a clear glass cylinder with shells to make an unusual lamp base.

I recently decorated a living room around a sea-shell print—white conch shells on a navy-blue background. Walls were painted white, and the shell-print fabric hung at the windows. The fabric was also used on club chairs that flanked a light-blue-and-white tweed sofa. Carpeting was light blue. On navy-blue lacquered tables I placed white plaster shell lamps with white shades. The coffee table was white lacquer and had a virtrine glass showcase top. Under the glass of the vitrine top were shells of all sizes and shapes displayed on a sand base.

Many people collect seashells, and the do-it-yourselfers can decorate their own picture frames, mirrors, ashtrays, etc., with their collections of shells. Small shells can be used to hold cigarettes, too. I have also seen shell wall sconces—electrified, of course—and there are chandeliers made with shells, too—conch shells and Capiz shells. I love Capiz shells and have used pearly Capiz-shell disks for chandelier fittings on many of my decorating projects.

Of course, you can find silverplated or gold-plated shells, as well as shells made of metal or porcelain, in gift departments of leading stores all over the country.

Tortoiseshell, according to Webster's dictionary, is that "mottled horny substance of the shell of some turtles used in inlaying and in making various ornamental articles." Webster's is a bit behind the times, I think. Today, Webster's might define tortoiseshell as that "mottled horny substance of the shell of some turtles *formerly* used in making various ornamental articles."

Why the "formerly"? Because today turtles are being protected—we don't want them to become extinct—so real tortoiseshell ornaments are no longer being made. But tortoise fans needn't deprive themselves. Thanks to modern technology, skilled artisans, and antique collectibles, the tortoiseshell look will never be extinct. There are still many beautiful antique tortoiseshell ornaments around, and they have increased in value considerably. If you're lucky enough to have amassed a collection, by all means display it. But even a few pieces can be effective. A tortoiseshell picture frame, a pair of tortoiseshell bookends,

A collection of colorful geodes stands out against a soft neutral background provided by the sand-beige upholstery on armchair, ottoman, and sofa.

and a tortoiseshell cigarette box that graces the coffee table in my living room are all valued treasures in my home.

And if you want more than touches of tortoise, you can have as much of it as you want, thanks to man-made reproductions of this natural wonder. William Weaver, a friend of mine who is a great craftsman, creates painted tortoiseshell finishes on tables, chairs, cubes—you name it. At this moment, I'm having the top of an old Queen Anne table finished in the tortoise look. The table will be used with Queen Anne chairs that have chocolate-brown lacquered frames, and seats covered in vibrant emerald green.

Tortoise-design upholstery fabrics and wallcoverings can also warm up a room. For tortoise lovers, here's a look that's sure to please. Cover walls with tortoise vinyl wallcovering, paint woodwork and doors white, and finish ceiling in reflective gold-leaf paint. Hang tomato-red draperies and valances over white or silvery narrow-slat blinds. For upholstery, choose a print of beige, pale blue, and white on a tomato-red background. Club chairs can be covered in a beige-and-champagne textured fabric. Shiny brass lamps on black-lacquered end tables would be my lighting choice. Paint coffee table tortoise-shell, and accessorize with a red-lacquered Chinese melon box and clear crystal ball. And who said candlesticks are only for the mantel? I would like to see a few wooden candlesticks, topped with white tapers, added to this coffee-table grouping.

MIRRORS IN THE LIVING ROOM

While mirror is not usually thought of as warm, it can be, because it can double the effects of such "warming" elements as fireplaces, candles, paintings, sunny garden views, etc. And the mirror is the image of today. Have you noticed how the decorative use of mirrors has boomed lately? I have. You see mirrored walls, mirrored ceilings, mirrored furniture, mirrored window-frames—the list is endless.

Even conventional framed mirrors make terrific wall accessories, particularly when a sizable painting is financially out of reach. If that sofa or mantel wall is missing a vital something, scout the secondhand shops, garage sales, and antique shops in your area for a decorative frame to fill with a mirror.

To get even more mileage out of mirrors, try mirroring an entire wall. Mirrored walls are associated with slick, modern interiors, but I like the look of a mirrored wall just as much in traditional rooms. They add the excitement of today to a setting of antiques, warm wood, and rich upholstery.

In a traditional living room I did recently, inexpensive, ready-cut mirror tile provided a glittering backdrop for a charcoal-gray tuxedo-style sofa. The unmirrored walls were covered in the charcoal-gray sofa fabric, and wood trim and ceiling were white. Cushy armchairs and an antique wing chair were upholstered in an English chintz of goldenrod yellow, lemon yellow, dove gray, and white. The wall-to-wall carpet was charcoal gray, and sofa toss cushions were vibrant goldenrod and white. The windows were flanked by tall, two-panel mirrored screens to reflect the garden view beyond. For privacy there were fold-away Roman shades in goldenrod yellow.

With all these ways of warming up a room, there's no reason to huddle up in a living room that leaves you cold!

Periods and Styles

The word "tradition" has returned to the decorating vocabulary. But what does it mean? One lady I know said, "I love traditional decorating, but how can I keep it looking fresh and new?" The simple answer is that traditional doesn't necessarily mean old-fashioned.

A traditional living room, furnished with classic roll-arm sofa, love seat, and chair/ottoman combination, might be brought up to date by taking a bright new tack with colors and fabrics. A quilted cotton/linen print of orange day lilies on a yellow ground has all the pep of today's colors as well as the gentle charm of another era. And the subdued traditional look of wood paneling and occasional tables might be offset by dressing the window with nothing but green plants.

As a decorator I am always 100 percent tradition-conscious. I have always believed that even the most avant garde decorator must study and learn from the past.

EIGHTEENTH-CENTURY ENGLISH

When I travel back to the decorative past, my favorite stopping place is eighteenth-century England—the great heyday of English design. Those were the days of the Queen Anne look, the days of cabinetmakers Chippendale and Hepplewhite. It's a look and style that will never be out of date, because it is so adaptable. The English look can be formal or casual. And a blend of English styles with other periods will always work. I love the look of stately Queen Anne chairs pulled up to a contemporary glass-topped table. And I love the look of leather-covered English wing chairs in a contemporary living room.

If you're a purist who loves a formal look, go English all the way. Make the focal point of your English room a curvaceous camelback sofa upholstered in a luxurious hunter-green leatherlike material. On a comfy wing chair and on seats of Queen Anne occasional chairs for the game table, the same material may be used. Walls can be

"Granada" Naugahyde upholstery

The look of eighteenth-century England is interpreted for today with traditionally styled furniture upholstered in rich leatherlike material.

painted soft, soft lemon yellow with moldings painted mustard, and underfoot a lively floral rug with Oriental overtones in shades of mustard, rust, and greens on a cream background would be super choice. The eighteenth-century English were mad for things Oriental, you know.

AMERICAN COLONIAL

The American Colonial style of decorating and furnishing dates back to the years 1700–1781.

In 1700 American cabinetmakers left the coarser Early American styles and began to adapt British Georgian, Queen Anne, and Chippendale designs.

I love American Colonial furniture with its graceful Windsor chairs, its polished spindle-back wooden chairs, and its blockfront furniture in walnut, mahogany, and sometimes maple and pine. The city folk who decorated with American Colonial furniture combined it with brass andirons and other polished brass accessories. Clocks and large handsome mirrors were also popular

Stratford's roll-arm sofa, love seat, chair/ottoman

Peters-Revington's "Bucks County" table

A traditional living room, furnished with roll-arm sofa, love seat, and chair/ottoman combination and with occasional tables, looks right at home with its bare window treatment and lively yellow-and-orange color scheme.

accessories, as were porcelains. Walls were cream-colored or sometimes done in tones of blue-grays, browns, reds, mustard golds. And for upholsteries, the American Colonist used muslins and chintzes in the country, damasks and brocades in the city. Leather-covered furniture was very popular in 1700–1781, and it still is. You can also be certain that a graceful wing chair covered in green or red velvet would have found its way into the American Colonialist's home.

For an American Colonial living room, walls can either be paneled, painted, or papered—take

your choice. If you plan around the look, why not paint your living-room walls blue-gray with cream-colored trim. If your American Colonial living room is in the city, use French or Oriental rugs on the floor. If it is in the country, braided or hooked Early American rugs will do. In a city living room with blue-gray walls and cream trim, my preference would be an Oriental rug of reds, creams, and light browns. A wing chair covered in ruby red leather would be just the thing to flank that wood-manteled fireplace outfitted with brass firedogs.

FEDERAL

Did you know that the American Revolution, fought for political change, also brought about changes in the look of the American home?

The Revolution, you see, caused trendsetters of that time to turn away from those eighteenth-century British influences and seek a look that would be more in keeping with the new political climate. It was Thomas Jefferson who suggested that America model her architecture and interior design on Ancient Greece—a great democracy of an earlier age. The result—the Federal period —is seen in the architecture of government buildings and in the interiors of the homes of the day.

The Federal period is characterized by classical motifs, of course. Mantels and doorways were often topped with Greek-style pediments. Furniture designs were graceful and elegant—in fact, everything about the Federal period was elegant.

It's a great look, and if it appeals to you, why not let the Federal period be your inspiration?

Start by painting living-room walls rich chocolate brown. For moldings and pediment trim for bookcases or mantels, dark-stained polished wood would be my choice. A tweed carpet of browns and bronzes would be practical as well as handsome. And to match those chocolate-brown walls, how about a pair of velvet-covered wing chairs with gold nailhead trim? Bring your Federal-style room into the twentieth century by adding a Plexiglas coffee table and a comfy sofa upholstered in warm wine-red leather or fabric. Go wine red for swag and jabot draperies, too, hung over wide-slat wooden venetian blinds. And for the perfect finishing touch, choose accessories and lamps of gleaming brass.

VICTORIAN

I had thought, because of the Victorian scale of things and the smallish size of today's living spaces, that Victoriana would stay out of fashion. But those big chests and chairs are coming back into style. If you're one of those who fancy Victoriana and you live in a smallish home or apartment, allow me to offer just one word of advice: Take it slow and easy. If you don't, the day may come when there may be room for a few more pieces of furniture but not for people.

The Victorian period in America and in England was not known for good color or for much color appreciation. The Victorians did manage to produce some interesting designs and floral patterns for chintz fabrics, but the colors of the chintz were hardly ones from an English country garden on a sunny day. Truly authentic Victorian colorations, even in the chintz, were austere and, to me, depressing—dark browns, cocoas, tans, many tones of dark and bottle green, many violet tones.

If you are planning an authentic Victorian living room, color walls an off-beige and leave woodwork and doors deep-stained walnut brown. Draperies to hang from brown wooden rings can be brown velvet, fringed in deep cocoa. For sofa upholstery pick a large-scale floral chintz in browns, bottle green, and near-violet tones. Cover Victorian chairs in brown velvet. Marble-topped, wood-base end tables and coffee table in the Victorian manner should be used to keep to authenticity.

For a Victorian look that's brighter and more up-to-date, I'd suggest this color scheme: With champagne-colored walls and deep brown woodwork, use jonquil-yellow velvet draperies, lined in cantaloupe and trimmed with brown braid. For the Victorian sofa, pick a floral chintz of melon, yellow, and emerald green on a chocolate-brown background. Use cantaloupe velvet on Victorian memorabilia—and spot your living room with baskets of fresh-looking silk flowers.

FRENCH PROVINCIAL

French country furniture is one of those classic looks that remain in favor because they're so adaptable. For instance, I enjoy mixing French country pieces with today's popular natural look. The effect is as informal as today and as elegant as the court of Louis XVI!

Try this scheme in a French country living room and you'll see what I mean. Paper walls in a small-scale geometric of wheat beige, chocolate brown, and off-white. Paint trim and ceiling creamy white. Upholster your French bergère chairs in café-au-lait suedecloth, and your sofa in off-white linen trimmed with fawn-color braid. Pile the sofa with toss cushions of wheat beige, café-au-lait, and chocolate brown. At windows, I would choose tieback curtains of off-white, lined in café-au-lait. Sound super so far? There's more!

Instead of carpeting, cover the floor with beige sisal matting. Accessorize the window area with copper planters and baskets filled with green plants and dried baby's breath. Copper accessories and baskets are very much a part of the French country scene—and of the natural look, too.

LOUIS XVI

If you like the French flavor but find French Provincial a bit rustic for your taste, the more formal Louis XVI style may be for you. Louis XVI, who reigned from 1774 to 1793, was partial to beautiful woods—satinwood, rosewood, beech, walnut, and even mahogany. He liked simple legs, often tapered and fluted, on tables and chairs, but favored tables and desks with handsome motifs—sometimes lyres, torches, garlands, or oak-leaf details. He also liked decorative panels on the walls, and he was a wallpaper enthusiast. His drawing rooms most often had fabric-covered walls on which handsome gilt carved mirrors were hung.

For flooring in a Louis XVI–style room, parquet floors covered with Oriental or French rugs would be the best look. And to be most proper in your Louis XVI decorating, choose silk, taffeta, satin, or fine cotton for wall-coverings, draperies and/or upholstery. If fine cotton is your choice, select a striped floral design or feathered pattern. The colors for Louis XVI decor are either pale or strong-toned.

I love a Louis XVI–style living room, and one of the most charming that I have seen recently had walls covered with a soft blue damask scroll design on a champagne background. The parquet floor was decorated with a French area rug repeating the soft blue and champagne of the walls. Champagne sheer curtains were hung at French doors. Louis XVI chairs upholstered in French blue silk graced the sides of a Louis XV-style mantel of white marble. A love seat also covered in French blue silk, as beautiful from the back as the front, was used freestanding opposite the fireplace grouping. A crystal chandelier was the finishing touch in the serenely elegant room.

JACOBEAN

Jacobean furniture is having a big revival. The style is part of Early English Renaissance (1500–1660), sometimes called the age of oak, but, if you like to be historically accurate, the actual period of its existence was from 1603 to 1649 under the reigns of the English kings James I and Charles I. The style includes some Gothic elements and is Flemish-influenced.

Jacobeans often used diamond shapes, hexagons, double rectangles, crosses, and other geometric forms on woodwork paneling, and they also liked diamond-shaped glass set into windows. For furniture, they favored Bible boxes, gateleg tables, and wainscot chairs, using carved oak turnings for the feet and legs. Those straight-backed Jacobean chairs may look uncomfortable, but, believe me, they aren't, especially with a soft cushion pad on the seat.

And if you think that the country-squire days of Jacobean have gone the same way as the coach and four, you are wrong. For the twentieth-century city dweller there are sturdy oak Jacobean pieces that are right with the time, and they're suitable even for small-scale living areas because furniture manufacturers have scaled down the pieces to today's room sizes and ceiling heights.

Why not try a Jacobean cabinet-and-desk combination in your living room? You'll find it functional and practical since you can store your books or show off your accessories, plates, ginger jars behind the mullioned glass doors in the upper portion, and put things you don't use constantly in the lower section, behind the oak doors.

For your Jacobean living room, choose warm colors for upholstery and curtains—beiges, soft creams, light blues, russets, golds, and mochas. All these colors are right in the Jacobean spirit of things.

MEDITERRANEAN

Did you know that the look we call Mediterranean is actually of African origin? That's right —it was the Moors, natives of North Africa, who

This serenely elegant living room features Louis XVI chairs in French blue silk on either side of a Louis XV mantel of white marble. French-blue silk love seat, as beautiful from the back as the front, is used freestanding opposite the fireplace.

Jacobean-style cabinet-desk unit on the far wall of this multipurpose room has been designed for today's living. Three pieces assembled together form the unit.

introduced to Spain and Portugal the features we associate with the Mediterranean look.

The Moors were Moslems. And since Moslem law forbids the use of animal or human forms in design, Moorish craftsmen came to develop elaborate geometric patterns which have become the hallmark of Spanish tiles, Spanish carvings, you name it.

The look the Moors inspired was definitely a rustic one. Moorish rooms contained little furniture, and what there was was rough and rugged. Chairs were rush-seated; mattresses were placed directly on the floor; walls were of rough plaster. As a carry-over from their nomadic past, they had rugs everywhere, in rich patterns and geometric designs. There were rugs on floors, on walls, and on built-in benches used for seating.

If you already have Mediterranean furniture in your home, here's a Moorish-style living-room scheme you can try. Upholster your sofa in a rough-textured stripe of magenta, royal purple, scarlet, and pumpkin. I would like that colorful sofa placed against a white stucco wall. (The look of stucco is easy to achieve these days with commercially available textured paints.) Underfoot, how about a Moroccan rug in your sofa colors with strong dashes of white? Club chairs can be upholstered in palm-green suedecloth. For lamps, brass or copper would be my choice. And how about brass tray tables to really put your room in the Moorish mood? For draperies, go palm green. And hang those draperies over dark-stained bamboo roller blinds.

EGYPTIAN

Egyptian and Middle Eastern styles are on my mind these days. The reason is the Ibis—a new Egyptian–Middle Eastern restaurant for which I have designed the interiors.

Does Egypt sound exotic and far away to you? It isn't, as far as decorating is concerned. Many of the everyday decorating motifs you see around got their start way back when in the land of the Pharaohs.

For instance, did you know that the ancient Egyptians were the first to veneer furniture? And where would we be today without veneers? They are now an integral part of all our furniture.

The sphinx, also an Egyptian legacy, is carved on many pieces of European-designed furniture, particularly furniture of the French Empire period. After Napoleon visited Egypt, French cabinetmakers, fired up with patriotism, honored him and indulged their newfound interest in Egypt by decorating their furniture with lion's paws, lotus blossoms, and, of course, the sphinx.

Egypt is also the land of palm trees and shifting sands. It's from those shifting sands that I took my inspiration for the interiors of the Ibis. I used that neutral sand color everywhere: The walls are painted with large murals in various shades of sand, and underfoot there's a tweedy sand-colored carpet. Banquettes are upholstered in sand-beige fabric, and so is a French Empire love seat, sphinx carvings and all, that I used at the entrance. For privacy between banquettes there are sand-beige draperies tied back in brown. And for accents I used all the soft desert colors—Nile blue, desert rose, and warm gold.

If the Ibis scheme sounds good to you, try it in your living room. Start with walls papered in sand-beige grass cloth, and paint trim rich chocolate brown. Carpet in thick sand-beige shag and upholster your sofa in sand, welted in chocolate and accented with pillows of Nile blue, pale desert rose, and chocolate. At right angles to that sofa, I picture two cross-legged chairs with leather seats. (You've seen those chairs, I'm sure, but did you know that they originated centuries ago in ancient Egypt?) At windows, hang simple panels of beige fabric trimmed with flat chocolate-brown tape and tied back with brown tasseled cord. Flank your sofa with Parsons tables lacquered Nile blue, and in front of that sofa a coffee table of brown smoked glass would be my choice. More Egyptian touches: giant palms in raffia baskets and a collection of crystal and onyx obelisks.

AMERICAN INDIAN

The American Indian look in decorating has been a favorite for years. Lots of folks like the warm Indian colors—bark brown, corn yellow, tepee beige, arrowhead gray, mixed with all the headdress-feather reds, browns, oranges, blues, and white.

I love the Indian colors, and I must admit I am very partial to the Indian blanket design. The Navajo rugs truly excite me, and in a modern room that I am now decorating, the center of attraction will be a large Navajo rug in shades of blue, wheat, and brown. The rug will hang on a long, high living-room end wall above a credenza that is being covered in leather and trimmed with brass nailheads. An antique clay Indian water bowl will sit on the credenza directly in front of the wall-hung rug.

When decorating with Indian colors and patterns, think about using them in the modern mix. Why not cover living-room walls in deep bark-brown suede fabric or brown velvetlike nylon carpeting? For flooring, use the same brown carpeting topped with an area rug in an Indian design of an arrowhead pattern of terra-cotta, stone gray, and coffee brown mixed with black. With the bark-brown background, choose modern white furniture. White-framed chairs can be covered in a rich russet corduroy. At windows hang draperies of a flame-resistant modacrylic fiber in a stripe pattern of black, rust, and tepee beige. For extra seating, why not build a tepee pillow ledge or seat on one side of the living room? The seat can be some 16 inches high by 24 inches deep, constructed of plywood and covered with the brown carpeting. Pillows can be covered in an Indian design of brown, corn yellow, blue, and terra-cotta on a wheat background.

The popular Indian look is reflected in this living room with walls and floor covered in brown velvetlike nylon carpet. Area rug is of Indian design in terra-cotta, stone gray, and coffee brown mixed with black. Pillow seating features Navajo print of bark brown, corn yellow, pale blue, and white. Striped draperies in black, rust, and tepee beige are of flame-resistant modacrylic fiber. White-framed furniture is covered in deep russet.

Collecting Indian artifacts is a pastime of mine, and for wall decoration in my library I have a collection of mounted Indian arrowheads of all different sizes and shapes. The arrowheads have been wired to terra-cotta-colored fabric-covered panels, against which the gray stone arrowheads show up beautifully.

Art Deco

The latest decorative style to stage a comeback is Art Deco, the style that flourished in the 1920s

and 1930s. Art Deco was streamlined, elegant design. Deco designers were in love with the sleek, the silvery—and with movement; speeding trains and planes were an inspiration to Deco designers who translated motion into streaming lines—cut into stainless steel and aluminum, etched into mirrors, and carved into wood and Bakelite. Art Deco also loved bubbles—you see them everywhere in Deco pieces: bubbles etched on mirrors, bubble-shaped vases and chinaware. The movement borrowed from the past, too—from the Egyptians and Babylonians who contributed the ziggurat shape of their stepped pyramid temples. (King Tut's tomb was the talk of the twenties, you know.) A passion for architectural shapes gave rise to cabinets and chests that took their shapes from buildings, giving them a characteristic square form.

An Art Deco living room might start with a large-scale floral-print fabric in greens and coral on a creamy background. The fabric print might be an inspiration for a custom-made carpet or for a stenciled floor, in which the print could be blown up to an even larger size. If you've ever been to New York's Rockefeller Center, then you know that Art Deco designers did things on a grand scale. Let the big, bold print spill over onto window shades, too. The big print should take center stage, so furnish the room with glass, chrome, and Lucite pieces that have simple lines. For another real Art Deco touch, how about an Art Deco inspired mirror—one that takes its inspiration from the architecture of the period? Hang the mirror against a spicy paprika-red suedecloth wall, just for punch.

If you like the sound of all this, go up to your attic and dig out that old cocktail cabinet. Turn that old 1930s radio into a bar. Slipcover your sofa in an outsized print. Put up an Art Deco mirror. Then put on some old big-band tunes and get in the Art Deco mood!

A large-scale floral print in sand and emerald, plus the punch of an architecturally inspired mirror against a paprika-red wall, brings back a Thirties mood with a touch of Art Deco. Chrome, Lucite, and glass pieces remind us we're still up to date.

Greeff's "Lotus Flowers and Herons"

THE ETHNIC LOOK

The "ethnic look" is any style that has the flavor of another culture. We've already talked about a few of the most popular ethnic looks—Moorish, American Indian, Egyptian—but of course it would be impossible to cover all of them.

Suffice it to say the look is very big right now, not only in home decor but in apparel. Shop windows are filled with peasant blouses, colorful embroidered shawls, ankle-laced canvas espadrilles, and wide swirling peasant skirts in vivid floral prints.

As you can tell, I like the new look, but I'm not suggesting you turn your living room into a pasha's tent or that you throw out your sofa in favor of sitting on Japanese floor mats.

Give your living room a touch of the ethnic look by skirting a round end table in an African-inspired print of tangerine, wine, emerald green, black, and white. Or hang a colorfully patterned American Indian or Moroccan rug on a wall above a solid-color sofa. Or stack three or four giant batik-covered pillows on the floor and put a brass tray table of North African origin in front of the sofa.

THE PRETTY LOOK

Another super look that has never gone out of fashion in home decorating is the pretty look.

The essence of a pretty room to me is floral wallpaper with matching fabric used with soft-line furniture. Pretty rooms mean pretty things sitting about or hanging on the walls—skirted table, chaise longues, handsome handpainted or upholstered folding screens, cachepots filled with potted plants, tea sets, bookcases or painted breakfronts filled with handsome appointments such as collections of interesting china plates, jardinieres, bird figurines, etc.

Many people love the look of a room with a white painted dado and a floral wallpaper above. I am one of those people, and I like dadoes not only painted white but other pretty colors too— soft tones of pink, yellow, blue, mint green, or beige. A room in a friend's home that I can call a "pretty room" features a white dado with a multicolored floral wallpaper of pinks, blues, reds, and yellows. The cotton curtains are in a matching pattern and are edged with red braid

and tied very high in the prettiest fashion. The rounded soft-look sofa is covered in the same floral, and club chairs are slipcovered in white linen. At the focal-point fireplace end of this pretty living room is a chaise longue with flouncy skirt, also covered with the floral pattern. Once chaises were relegated to the bedroom—why I don't know. I like the look of the chaise in the living room. To me a chaise is prettier than a club chair with ottoman or a contour chair.

To complete this pretty room, blue china plates and jardinieres are displayed in wall bookshelves painted the vivid red in the floral pattern of wallpaper and fabric. In this charming corner, a pair of cane-back French chairs of antique-white finish are pulled up to a skirted table, perfect for afternoon tea. The fireplace mantel is also accessorized with valued plates. Horizontally laid blue-and-white striped carpeting give dramatic width to the room.

THE CASUAL LOOK

From Madison Avenue to Madison, Wisconsin, and beyond, casual is becoming a twenty-four-hour-a-day life-style. I remember when New York's Madison Avenue was the land of the gray flannel suit. Today it's the land of the jogging suit. And all those joggers and tennis players, squash players, and backpackers are not coming home to Hepplewhite and Louis XVI drawing rooms, you can be sure. They're coming home to casual, comfortable rooms.

If you want to go from a formal decorating style to something more casual, here are a few starting points:

Replace fussy drapery treatments with shades; mini-slat blinds; washable, rod-hung draperies. Or do away with window treatments altogether, assuming they're not needed for light control or privacy.

Take down that damask or flocked wallpaper and repaper walls with butcher paper, or paint with textured sand or stucco paint.

Look for a pair of wood-framed beach chairs or deck chairs with colorful striped or solid-color sling seats. They're comfy, inexpensive, and very, very casual.

Take up your wall-to-wall carpeting if there's wood underneath and adorn that casual wood floor with wool or straw scatter rugs. If you must

"Roundalay" wallpaper by Brunschwig & Fils

*Here is a charming corner of a pretty living room. Wallpaper above the white
dado is a multicolored floral pattern of pinks, blues, reds, and yellows. Matching
fabric is used for curtains and for chaise longue with flouncy skirt.*

carpet, choose one of today's nubby Berber-look
wall-to-walls.

Slipcover your moiré, satin, damask, or silk
upholstery with casual, washable canvas, cotton
piqué, or chintz.

Store your ornate Louis lamps in the attic and
purchase replacements of rope, wicker, brass, or
beaten copper—or go the track-lighting route.
Lighting in the casual room should be unobtru-
sive.

Above all, make sure everything you buy is
easy-care: unpolished, distressed woods; washable upholstery fabrics; wipe-down mica laminates, and washable curtains are excellent choices.

Another approach to the casual, rustic look involves a bit more work. Start by sanding all the
dark stain off the floor, and bleach it to the
lightest wood tone you can get. Scrape paint
off wood doorframes and doors at the same time.
Keep scraping! The paint on window mullions
has to go too! Everything has to look bleached
and natural-dried-grass in feeling.

Walls can be stark white, accented with some
groupings of primitives and a macramé panel.
You might use a bleached wooden mallard duck
on a wall bracket as part of the wall grouping.
For your bleached flooring, choose a beige grass
or sisal rug, maybe an Irish Tintawn carpet. At

Contemporary spring-green walls and a classically styled love seat and side chairs blend beautifully with stripped pine Queen Anne furniture and a display of sculpture.

windows natural rattan roller blinds will go along with some white linen overdraperies.

Furnishings for this setting might include a heavy woven wicker sofa and club chairs covered in batik upholstery in a combination of russet with magenta, chocolate brown, and purple. Add a white linen skirted table and a wicker lamp with a wicker shade. At a natural scraped, bleached, and unstained Parsons-style card table, use some old David Copperfield wooden swivel-base office chairs with straight, flat spindle backs —you know the kind, really sturdy and very reminiscent of the early days. The chairs should be scraped, too, and bleached to the lightest shade.

Accessories could include candlesticks you can make from old balustrade uprights to place on a console table-buffet, also in a natural finish. The balustrade candlesticks should be scraped, too, bleached and left very natural. Complete this natural living room by hanging some straw baskets, planted with natural greenery, from chains in a corner of the room. Place some of the straw baskets on the floor, too.

UPDATED TRADITIONAL

As I said earlier, traditional furnishings need not look old-fashioned. If you are one of the many people who started out married life with Queen Anne, Victorian, or Early American furniture and you now have a yen for something more contemporary, here are some thoughts on how to achieve a contemporary look without discarding your old furniture.

For colors, go clear and bright, or neutral. Stay far away from muddy, grayed-out shades.

Have a couple of your larger wood pieces refinished in a light pickled or bleached finish.

Instead of recarpeting in plush, try sisal matting or lay one or two colorful area rugs over bare wood floors.

At windows, choose bamboo roller-blinds or vertical blinds instead of a heavy drapery treatment.

Traditional furniture does not have to be wrapped in velvet, chintz, or brocade. Instead, try a bold Scandinavian cotton print on your Queen Anne chairs; a nubby white cotton on your colonial sofa, or a batik on your Victorian side chair.

You might want to take inspiration from this scheme I saw recently. The love seat had the kind of simple lines that blend well with any decor and it was upholstered in a fresh fern print of white on a clear green background that matched the wall color. Side chairs were covered in nubby white cotton. Underfoot was a rug of geometirc design in soft pinks, reds, and greens on a creamy background. The Tyndale desk, occasional tables, and lamps were of graceful Queen Anne design, but had an up-to-the-minute stripped pine finish that matched the finish of an authentic antique grandfather clock. Instead of a heavy, traditional drapery treatment, the uncurtained windows were filled with a garden of lush green plants and a collection of animal horns and primitive sculpture.

THE ECLECTIC LOOK

Webster's defines "eclectic" as something "composed of elements drawn from various sources." I define eclectic as "great." Believe me, you can mix and match elements from each of the periods and styles I've just described and come up with the ultimate in terrific living rooms.

I know people who have successfully mixed tuxedo-style upholstered pieces, Early American ladder-back chairs, and Mexican and African artifacts and rugs. I've seen exciting, original rooms that combine antiques with up-to-the-minute molded-plastic furniture. I've visited rooms where rich velvet lives happily with inexpensive Indian cotton prints.

I recently saw an eclectic living room that started out as a straightforward Early American room. With a change here and an addition there, the owners had gone eclectic—without throwing away any of their Early American pieces.

They started by painting walls white, using one of the new stucco-look paints. Their floor was covered wall-to-wall with natural sisal matting. The living room's Early American maple-frame sofa was upholstered with an antique patchwork quilt of poppy red, emerald green, and white. One of their original round end tables was transformed with the addition of a skirt of pretty flower-sprigged cotton in the red-green-and-white combination. An emerald-green Chinese jar lamp sat atop the table. The other end table was a new, inexpensive, poppy-red molded-plastic Parsons table, also topped with an emerald-green lamp. Club chairs in this eclectic room were covered in sporty emerald-green suedecloth, and an Early American end table, which originally sat near the sofa, now rested comfortably between the chairs. The room's green-red-and-white color scheme held the decor together, while the eclectic mix of plastic table, antique-quilt upholstery, Early American furniture, and suedecloth for chairs lent individuality and excitement.

Today's mix is handled in a subtle way, and it is controlled and harmonious in its look. Today we are playing straight lines with curved and rounded forms, and it's not unusual to see a very straight modern sofa used with a Queen Anne coffee table and with molded contour lounge chairs. Nor is it unusual to find an Oriental rug used under a steel-and-glass coffee table, or a geometric floor pattern—be it in vinyl or carpet—used with the most traditional English furniture.

One living room I recently saw was furnished just this way. Walls were oak-paneled, and in the center of the ceiling a modern glass-and-steel multiglobe fixture was hung. (What the traditionalist would have used as lighting would have been a crystal chandelier or a brass Williamsburg piece—you know the kind, with the clear hurricane globes or pleated shades.) Modern art was

hung on the oak-paneled walls where once traditional pastoral oils had hung. On the floor,
instead of the former Persian rugs, was a black,
chocolate-brown, yellow, and emerald-green
geometric rug with a bright yellow border. A
modern sofa, big and cushy, was covered in
toast suede; and pulled up to the tortoise-
finish coffee table were traditional walnut-framed
Queen Anne chairs covered in a yellow-and-
emerald-green gros point fabric. The mix of
traditional with modern was carried through
with Chinese vase lamps on steel-and-glass end
tables. To further enhance the mix, a traditional
walnut English breakfront was filled with modern sculpture and accessories.

Whichever style you choose for your living room,
it should reflect *you*—your personality, your life-
style, your imagination. So don't be afraid to
express yourself—you'll find it a vastly reward-
ing and liberating experience.

3

The Master Bedroom

The Romantic Bedroom

We've all heard the joking expression "the honey-moon is over" used to describe the end of a beautiful experience. I would like to offer these words of advice to brides and grooms: Don't let your honeymoon end at the threshold of your new home; keep it alive in the bedroom.

I firmly believe that whether you're starting out on a shoestring or on a comfortable budget, decorating plans can and should include a touch of honeymoon romance. Thinking back to my own newlywed days, I can recall many romantic touches my wife and I included in our decorating scheme. Here are a few I can remember:

• Candlelight—unsurpassed for setting a romantic mood.

• Fresh flowers—a must for romance. If you saw the film *The Great Gatsby*, you may recall that when Gatsby wanted to set a romantic stage for wooing Daisy, he filled their meeting place—a shabby cottage—with masses of roses. But I'm not advocating masses of flowers—one fresh bloom on a bedside table will make a room romantic.

• A spray of your favorite cologne on bedroom light bulbs to gently—and romantically—perfume the air.

• Soft lighting. Try filling a bedroom corner

with baskets of tall plants, lit from below with floor-mounted spotlights. If you turn off the rest of the lamps, turn on some soft music, and light the candles, you'll see how these few touches of decorating romance can prolong that honeymoon for—well, who knows for how long!

Romance is getting a boost in decorating now. Upholstery is soft and very puffy; ruffles are in; the color palette is warm and subdued. Several shops in New York are featuring products bedecked with valentine motifs—heart-shaped pillows, heart-emblazoned crockery, heart-shaped picture frames, and heart-print fabrics.

One of my associates is in a romantic decorating mood and is doing the bedroom of a newly-wed couple in the romantic vein. He's starting off with walls covered in shimmery, dusty-rose moiré. (A warm color for bedroom walls is definitely romantic—and very flattering to the lady of the house.) The same moiré will be used for tieback draperies hung over silky white sheers. Underfoot, fluffy white rugs will be used to warm and soften the look of a wood floor. The focal point of the room is an antique walnut bed covered with an antique-white, channel-quilted satin comforter and mounds of ruffled white and antique-white pillows, edged with antique lace and old eyelet. For lounging, there's a button-tufted chaise longue covered in a print of softest

"Bed of Roses" pattern traces the beauty of the rose from its birth to maturity; from the tender young bud to the magnificent full bloom. Available in sheets, towels, and comforters—in pink and yellow.

St. Mary's "Bed of Roses" by Fieldcrest Mills, Inc.

blue, paled-down rose, quiet apricot, and cream. The same fabric is used to skirt a bedside table —the other bedside table is wood. Both hold polished brass bedside lamps with ivory silk shades lined in shell pink to cast a warm, flattering glow.

A single print, be it floral or geometric, can look stunning in bedrooms, and much more romantic than a room full of coordinating prints and solids. I like pretty florals for bedrooms— even for bedrooms shared by man and wife—and I often lavish one print everywhere. My own bedroom, decorated by my wife Suzanne and me, has a yellow, apricot, blue, and pink floral stripe as its theme. We used the print fabric on a skirted bedside table, for Austrian shades at windows, on a love seat, and on a bergère and matching stool.

If you prefer the look of solid colors, you can use the same decorating principle by choosing a single color and varying the fabric textures. If you take this route, though, please stick to subtle colors. I wouldn't like to see an entire bedroom full of red or purple furniture and fabrics.

Try the one-color look in a formal bedroom decorated in one of my favorite colors, sky blue: Choose a sky-blue ribbed cotton for the spread, and a sky-blue-and-ivory polka-dot jacquard or sky-blue vinyl suede for chairs. Draperies can be sky-blue linen. Paint walls creamy ivory and paint trim sky blue. Lay a Chinese-style rug of sky blue and ivory. Add warm walnut or mahogany night tables, accessories of polished brass, and you have a winning scheme without the worry of whether your colors blend!

Ruffles are romantic, too. If you love the look of pine and maple furniture, ruffled chintz bedspreads are for you. Choose a soft floral in misty mauve, petal pink, apricot, and sky blue, with green foliage, on a white ground.

If you can't afford a new spread, you might make a ruffled flounce or ruffled pillows for your bed. You can make these pillows out of pretty lace handkerchiefs: Sew four together into a square, back it with a solid color, and trim with ruffles of lace or eyelet. Or use floral-print scarves or fabric remnants in pretty florals, pastel plaids, or gingham checks. For variety, make pillows and ruffles of contrasting fabrics: for example, pink-and-green plaid with a pink-and-green floral ruffle; or stripes with a color-matched gingham ruffle.

Just one word of caution: Ruffles are soft-looking, and the furniture they go on should be soft-looking, too. Ruffles do not belong on foam-slab Scandinavian platform beds.

If you decide on the ruffled look, go ruffles at windows, too. I will never tire of white ruffled priscilla curtains. I love them in country bedrooms, even when those "country bedrooms" are in the city. For the sake of practicality, choose the drip-dry variety.

BEAUTIFUL BEDS

These days, beds are so good-looking it's almost a shame to turn out the lights and sleep on them. Here are just a few of the exciting looks I've seen recently: a headboard, box spring, and mattress all upholstered in quilted poppy-red glazed cotton, and topped with a quilted paisley print spread of crisp black and white . . . a chrome four-poster, with a soft chocolate-brown vinyl-suede quilted spread, against chocolate-brown vinyl-suede walls with red lacquered ceil-

Simmons Maxipedix mattress

With its built-in cabinets to hold clothing below, stereo speakers above, this small bedroom now does double duty as a music room. A king-size mattress is a comfortable place to perch while listening to anything from symphonies to rock.

ing and trim . . . a simple padded plywood head-board upholstered in a multicolor floral with matching pillow shams and blanket cover.

That gives you some idea of the range of looks that is available. And there's more. People are putting their beds right on the floor and cover-ing them with fake-fur throws and sumptuous pillows. People are building plywood platforms, carpeting them to match their floor, and popping a mattress on top of the platform.

And did you know that you can make a plat-form bed even if you don't know a hammer from a screwdriver? It's done with stacking crates or modules—the type you normally stack one on top of the other to make bookcases. To make a platform bed, simply lay the units side by side on the floor and top with a foam mattress.

Traditionalists and modernists alike love brass beds, which first gained popularity back in the 1850s.

If you have an antique brass bed in the attic, or are interested in purchasing one, you should know that antique brass beds come in twin, full, or three-quarter sizes—never in king or queen. You should also know that antique brass beds don't accommodate standard bedding. For these reasons, new brass beds, designed for today's living, are generally a more practical choice. You'll find styles ranging from authentic antique reproductions to super-streamlined contemporary. Whichever style you choose, here are the features to look for:

• Finish—A finely applied lacquer finish will keep your bed gleaming for years without ardu-ous polishing.
• Frame—The brass bed you choose should have a specially designed frame that holds the bed firmly together. To test, first sit on the bed, then try moving the footboard. There should be no jiggling or rattling whatsoever.
• Parts—Finials, those decorative ornaments that sit atop the head and footboards, should screw on or be riveted into place.

What about brass-plated beds? That's a ques-tion I am asked from time to time. My answer? I have never believed in "lookalikes," and that holds true for brass beds. Brass-plated or ano-dized beds, which are made of aluminum, nickel, and plastic parts coated with thin layers of brass, don't hold up as well as the real thing. They are known to peel, fade, and change color. So if you can't afford solid brass (which is the industry's term for beds made of 100 percent brass tubing), you're better off with a bed of wood or one with no headboard or footboard at all.

What could be more romantic than a canopy bed? I love the look of a curtained bed. The cur-tains can be made of sheer fabric or of a pretty print or solid-color fabric—it's really up to you; canopy beds today are mostly for effect and ro-mance, whereas in the early days they had to be draped in heavy fabrics to keep out drafts in those unheated bedchambers.

The mahogany canopy bed will never be out of vogue—there is nothing like the look of pol-ished wood. But the canopy bed is also available in brass, and even up-to-the-minute chromium. Why not purchase a brass four-poster bed, and curtain it in a filmy, romantic fabric? Complete the look with a romantic color scheme: for walls, perhaps pale, pale pink with white woodwork; cyclamen-pink carpeting to bring the garden look inside; and a bedspread in a blossom print that ties everything together with its color scheme of pinks, cyclamens, apple green, and lavender blue on a white background. Use warm wood furnishings. What about a Louis XV desk trimmed with ormolu? And for relaxing, a comfortable chaise, upholstered in the bedspread print, would be my choice.

If your budget won't allow for the purchase of a new bed, you can make a canopy frame for your old bed with pipe—ordinary industrial pipe. A friend of mine created a canopy bed just that way. He fitted the pipe into screw plates attached to the floor and ceiling at the four corners of his double bed. All four pipes were covered in white fabric, and the plates were spray-painted white. A valance of white swags, lined in a yel-low-and-green stripe, was installed on the ceiling around the perimeter of the bed. Side curtains were white, faced and lined in the colorful stripe.

There are many ways to have a draped or canopy bed.

Even simpler—and least expensive of all—is the draped look created by hanging two brass towel rings on the headboard wall and looping a length of soft fabric between them. Hang rings

In a romantic bedroom setting, a queen-size bed is truly fit for a queen when framed in brass and curtained in sheer, sheer fabric.

about three feet apart, one slightly higher than the other. The effect—a soft swag-and-jabot look—is a lot richer than you would think for the small investment you made in creating it.

At the moment I am in the midst of creating a much more ambitious canopy look for a client of mine, a pretty lady who loves the pretty look for the bedroom.

Her walls will be covered in yards of shirred white cotton, and the head of the bed will be draped in the white fabric, too. To create the canopy look, a curved rod will be installed above the head of the bed and white tieback draperies will be hung from the rod and tied back to the headboard wall, enclosing the pillow area. The drapery lining, headboard wall, and bedskirt are to be a soft cotton chintz print of celadon green, petal pink, sky blue, and white. Bedspread is white. The chintz print will be used at windows, too, on laminated window shades. And since I believe that even the prettiest bedroom should serve many purposes, there will be a chintz-covered chaise longue for relaxing and reading in the bedroom.

Second cousin to the canopy bed is the tent bed. I believe in raising tents indoors as well as out, particularly in the bedroom. Some people tent the entire room, but if that's a bit much for you, perhaps you would like sleeping in a tented bed. A natural-look bedroom I saw recently featured such a bed. It was lavishly draped in simple off-white cheesecloth—an elegant version of the very practical mosquito netting of the tropics. The tropical-island effect was heightened by a sand-and-white seashell-print cotton used for ruffled pillow shams and Roman window shades. The bedspread and an upholstered chaise longue were both off-white, which contrasted dramatically with deep olive-green walls. An unusual seashell pedestal table and two rattan chairs formed a cozy breakfast nook between the win-

dows. And pulling the great natural look together was a sand-beige carpet.

The Seasonal Bedroom

Summer fruit season—the time of melons, berries, peaches, and plums—is the time I like to invent new color schemes, all inspired by the lush colors of fresh fruits. Let's see if one of these schemes will whet your decorating appetite.

The background is a blue-and-white wallcovering—the color and pattern of a lovely old Royal

The natural look of a tropical-island bedroom is pulled together by an elegant "mosquito net" tent for the bed and a sand-beige carpet.

"Gateway" carpet from

Copenhagen fruit bowl. The ceiling is the blue of a summer sky. Trim is fresh white. The bed and sinkably-soft chaise are dressed in a luscious peach color, accented with plump honeydew, lemon, and sky-blue cushions. A skirted bedside table in the blue-and-white print is topped with a solid-color peach linen minicloth. And underfoot there's a cloud-soft plush carpet of softest peach.

Wherever there are fruit colors, I like to place a bowl of real, fresh fruit. In this lovely bedroom, I picture a tiny breakfast table in front of a white-curtained window. The table can be skirted in the blue-and-white print and centered with a cobalt-blue bowl, brimming with ripe peaches. Team the table with a pair of rich wood Queen Anne–style chairs and you've got a super spot for a light midnight or morning snack.

Another way to begin might be with striéd walls of watermelon pink. (To strié, walls are painted one shade, then repainted either a darker or lighter shade. When the second coat is still wet, the wall is "combed" to give a dimensional, ribbed look.) With those strié walls, try trim painted fresh coconut white. Ceiling can be pale sky blue. Stain the wood floor rich walnut.

Another summery scheme is the garden-party look, sure to chase away the winter chills.

We'll start with walls of airy sky blue, overlaid with white trellis—or, if you prefer, shop for a trellis-design wallcovering of white on sky blue. Paint your trim fresh white and the ceiling sunny buttercup yellow. Underfoot, we'll lay a carpet of shaggy grass green.

The bed—the center of attention—we will dress like a bed of flowers, in a ruffled chintz comforter-and-pillow ensemble of pinks, reds, yellows, and blues on a grass-green background.

At windows, let's keep it simple with white louvered shutters and a hanging garden of flowering plants.

If there's room for a small sitting area, why not a chaise longue or love seat slipcovered in white cotton and lavished with pillows covered in the bedspread print? That's a garden-party bedroom, to be sure!

The natural look and summertime are natural partners. Everyone and everything goes natural in the warm summer months. There is an abundance of farm-fresh fruits and vegetables for our tables, and there are natural easy-to-wear fashions —straw hats and cottons—for the summer scene. Stores are full of great summer naturals for the home, too—for your own home and to give as gifts to your weekend hostesses at the shore or in the country.

You can dress your bed for summer in cool, natural, 100-percent cotton sheets—they're back, you know. And you might top that bed with a powder-blue-and-white striped cotton bedspread from India. Wouldn't that be a cool natural look against walls painted pure sparkling white?

Underfoot, lay a natural crocheted sisal mat in a pretty openwork pattern, and shop the stores for summertime accent pieces of wicker and bamboo. There are many attractive and inexpensive pull-up chairs, bedside tables, shelf units, and baskets. My favorites are the bamboo nesting tables from China; they look so pretty next to a bed or tucked between a pair of bedroom chairs.

Autumn colors—oranges, golds, and shades of green—are America's favorites. Yet they're also America's most abused colors.

So many people tell me that their fall-tone rooms are drab, drab, drab! Nine times out of ten it's because too much of one color has been used. After all, have you ever seen an autumn scene that's all maple-leaf red, or all coppertone, or all brown? Of course not. Fall colors in decorating, as in nature, are meant to be mixed— light with dark, vivid with dull.

To see what I mean, try this fall-tone bedroom scheme. I guarantee no one will be able to say it's drab! Paper walls in a cork-textured wallcovering of nut brown. Stain wood floors berry brown. In the center of the floor, lay a rya area rug of pumpkin, camel, chocolate, maple-leaf red, and cinnamon. Choose a bedspread of wide-wale camel corduroy, and toss pillows on that camel spread of pumpkin, maple-leaf red, harvest gold, and grass green. Club chairs can be upholstered in a geometric cotton print of camel, harvest gold, black, and pumpkin. At windows, hang maple-leaf-red draperies over dark-stained bamboo roller-blinds.

On nippy autumn nights, wouldn't it be nice

to snuggle down in a bedroom decorated around these rich fall hues? Start by painting walls a restful chocolate brown. Carpet in a russet shag. For the bedspread, how about a striking quilted geometric in chocolate, cinnamon, and autumn-leaf yellow. Give those brown walls a lift with a bold graphic copied from the bedspread pattern, and add an all-important touch of bright white with a headboard and accessory pieces in white and harvest gold. Believe me, that white furniture looks smashing against chocolate-brown walls.

The Period Bedroom

WILLIAMSBURG

Visit Williamsburg, Virginia, with its historic houses and restorations of eighteenth-century buildings, for some true decorating inspiration. To me, Williamsburg represents beauty. It is a living book of American decorating and taste and that no one will really ever want to put down. Williamsburg is simple, elegant, and tasteful.

A warm fall-tone bedroom is the best defense against nippy autumn nights. Restful chocolate-brown walls are the backdrop for a zingy yellow and cinnamon graphic, white and harvest-gold headboard and night tables.

"Dialogue Collection" from Stanley Furni

What decorating inspiration I find in the governor's palace. In the bedchamber, once occupied by the governor himself, you'll see the big four-poster Chippendale bed with side curtains and a pagodalike valance. The governor's bedroom has a polished wood floor, and there are great pieces of furniture, including a high-back wing chair covered in gold damask. The window curtains, bed canopy and side curtains, as well as the upholstery on a desk chair, are all of gold damask, too. The Williamsburg era in decorating often worked around one fabric pattern, and that was used on everything.

Williamsburg is the country look. It is miniature spice chests (why not hang one on a wall above a bedside table?) and flocked wallpaper in rich golds and subtle green. It is embroidery and quilted coverlets. It is leather-topped stools with brass nailhead details. It is Queen Anne tea tables and big bold geometric plaids. And it's pale green painted walls with subtle gold painted trim. Williamsburg is total inspiration.

If you have a yen for the Williamsburg-inspired bedroom, why not start by painting your walls pale green? Wood trim, window mullions, and doors can be mustardlike gold. At windows hang draperies and chinoiserie valances of gold-on-pale-green damask. Use the same fabric for the spread on a mahogany four-poster bed. A wing chair and a high Williamsburg chest of drawers with a pediment top would be welcomed. Polish dark-stained wood floors, and do not carpet wall-to-wall. If you insist on doing so, go celadon green, champagne beige, or gold.

VICTORIAN

A touch of Victorian in the bedroom can be an interesting note, and many young homemakers today are finding that the large, overly carved and ornamented Victorian-style chests—bedroom highboys are also good buys. "Victorian furniture is big, I know, but, believe me, the drawer space is ample and commodious," a recent bride told me.

Well, I'm all for the look, particularly when the Victorian pieces are stripped of the mahogany finish and left in the natural wood with simply a coat of clear sealer. Victorian furniture does not look so big when the dark stain has been removed.

For my yellow country bedroom I found a Victorian armoire of ample size, complete with ornate carving and ornamentation as well as mirrored doorfronts. My wife and I lacquered the large wardrobe white, then lined it in a yellow-and-white checkered fabric.

There are many handsome Victorian tables with marble tops about today, and when painted, refinished, or left in the walnut or mahogany finish, they could be handsomely used as night tables. Or consider a single Victorian table with a marble top as a tea-service or breakfast-service table in a cover of the bedroom.

Here's a Victorian decorating idea for the bedroom from a London friend. Create a headboard for a double bed from a richly carved and upholstered Victorian sofa frame with sides that can embrace the bed. Remove the sofa seat and front legs and upholster the back and sides in rich velvet, brocade, or some other fabric of your choice. Slide the boxspring and mattress directly into the sofa frame. Bedspread and bedskirt can be made of the fabric used for headboard upholstery.

THE FRENCH LOOK

How best to achieve a French look in a bedroom is a question I have often been asked. My answer usually begins with a point that's least expected. I feel that a French room requires, first of all, wall moldings.

Thus, if you wish to create a French look in the bedroom and are decorating on a budget, start off with wall moldings. Plan where you would like to apply them and then order from the nearest lumber yard or supply house, choosing perhaps a stock molding that is 1 or 1½ inches wide. Before applying moldings to walls, you might paint them a clear, clean French blue and the wall surfaces a sparkling white. (It's easier and neater to paint first.) After mounting the moldings, the wall panels inside them might be covered in blue-on-white damask or toile wallpaper. If your budget doesn't permit covering the panels with paper, you might consider leaving the panels white and painting the ceiling French blue.

For the French-bedroom look in this case, I would recommend white furniture trimmed in the palest blue, with yellow moiré tieback draperies trimmed with white, yellow, and French-blue fringe. Headboard and bedskirt can be yellow moiré, and bedspread a frosty white. Crystal bedside lamps; a gold-frame mirror hanging over a bedroom chest; and white, lemon-yellow, or French-blue carpeting would complete the picture.

And when thinking of French furniture, don't overlook the bombé chest. Despite what you may have heard, bombé chests are not from India. These chests, which bulge in a graceful curve at the middle, are definitely of French origin. There are all sizes of bombé chests, and they are available in stain finishes, painted finishes, and just about any other finish you can imagine.

Recently I decorated a bedroom with French bombé-style furniture. There were bombé night-table chests at each side of a king-size bed, and there was a long bombé-style chest, above which hung a large gold-leaf French mirror. The bombé pieces were painted sunny yellow, trimmed in bright white, and hardware was antique white. The chests were delightful in that large bedroom, which had lemon-ice carpeting and white silk draperies under a swag-and-jabot valance of delicate yellow flowers on a white background. The bed was covered in quilted fabric matching the valance.

If you find an old bombé chest in a thrift shop, and have a place to use it, why not consider painting it yourself in a color or colors to suit your fancy, your decorating scheme, and your Francophilia?

The French Provincial look is another Gallic touch that many people love for the bedroom. But, alas, it is often misunderstood.

The word "provincial," you know, refers to the provinces—the countryside—so the French Provincial style, which developed during the reign of Louis XVI, should have a country look. Yet people who wouldn't dream of mixing American country furniture with the formality of gilt, silks, and damasks insist on decorating their "French Provincial" rooms in luxurious trappings.

Here is my view of a French Provincial bedroom—a country room with a French accent.

The walls are painted crisp, fresh white. There's a fruitwood armoire for storage and a flower-patterned rug of pinks, blues, and cream underfoot. The bed is a simple style in brass with white porcelain detailing and is topped with a puffy quilt covered in a charming provincial paisley print of dusty pinks, blue, cream, and sunny yellow. Lace- and eyelet-edged pillows and an eyelet bedskirt are used with the quilt. At windows, I picture natural wood shutters framed with tieback curtains of the paisley print. And I would flank the bed with tables—one skirted with the paisley; the other a small wooden French-style chest. Painted china lamps with white shades would complete the country-fresh scheme.

And for a perfect formal or provincial French bedroom, remember those little details that make a room something special. I'm talking about the doorknobs, the switchplates, the hardware for curtains. Stunning furniture and beautiful wallpaper don't make a room by themselves; you need the right details to give a room style.

When a woman dresses, she chooses accessories that match her outfit's color and style; she doesn't (we hope) wear an evening bag with blue jeans, or a straw hat with gold lamé. When dressing a bedroom, the same rules apply—the wrong detail can ruin a room; the right detail can make it.

Picture a charming French Provincial bedroom with the great French furniture that's so well loved. On the walls is a French striped wallpaper of pink and blue, and the bed is topped with a matching fabric. But, alas, there are white venetian blinds at the windows, a chromium switchplate, and chromium doorknobs, too!

Now picture that charming French bedroom with white, full-length, embroidered tambour curtains. Then add painted china doorknobs and a switchplate in a pink-and-blue design on a white background. And why not carry out the scheme in the adjoining bathroom? Carpet in Wedgwood blue. Paper walls in a pink-and-blue floral on a white background. And don't overlook the details—painted china of pink, blue, and white for soap dish, drinking cup, and for tub and washstand handles, too.

THE ORIENTAL LOOK

The lure of the Orient to Western travelers will always remain strong, and so will the look of the Orient—the look of China, Japan, and Korea; of lacquerwork, shoji screens, and tatami mats; of ginger jars and rattan.

The Oriental look is simple and serene. Couldn't we all use a little serenity in our bedrooms? Orientals have known for centuries that a room doesn't have to be crowded with furniture and knickknacks to be beautiful. In Japan a room may contain nothing more than a few tables and some floor cushions. And those rooms are beautiful indeed!

Westerners have discovered another fascinating aspect of the Oriental look: Because of its simplicity, Oriental furniture blends beautifully with the Western look of things. For centuries in Europe and in the United States, Chinese-style ginger-jar lamps have graced night tables and illuminated bedrooms filled with European-style furniture. And they've always looked right at home.

Many people love the serene Oriental look for their bedrooms, such as the one pictured. A simple Korean-style four-poster bed is the focal point of a terra-cotta-tiled room with soft gold walls. Drapery and bedspread fabric of soft russet and blue is in harmony with the room's restful mood.

The serene mood of the Orient is captured in a gold-painted bedroom furnished with pieces from a Korean collection.

Korean Collection furniture by Baker

ADAPTING A STYLE

I recently overheard a lady remark: "Those decorators have their heads in the clouds!" She had just been thumbing through one of the deluxe decorating magazines.

But she missed the point. True, the rooms seen in decorating magazines are from another world; they are not meant for everyone. But they are meant to be inspirational; they can be adapted to suit a simpler, more down-to-earth life-style.

Of course the rooms of an Italian palazzo, or an Edwardian estate, or an Oriental mansion will be sumptuous, but you can recreate and adapt many of the ideas shown in those rooms at just a fraction of the original cost.

If you see a bedroom in an Italian palazzo with walls covered in biscuit-beige suede, what's to stop you from painting your walls biscuit beige and covering your bed in biscuit-beige velveteen or corduroy? Those simpler materials are probably more in keeping with the kind of casual life-style Americans like anyway.

If you see the bedroom of an English duchess in a color scheme of pale water blue and gold, what's to prevent you from using the color scheme? As for the rest—the swags, the gilded carving, the heavy damasks—you wouldn't want that in an American home anyway.

If you fall in love with an elegant photo of a bedroom that features a gilded Japanese screen, an apricot satin spread, and a white fur rug, adapt the ideas. Make a screen yourself, using Japanese mural wallpaper. Paste it to a three- or four-panel plywood screen, and presto! As for the bedspread, and rug, cover your bed in a heavy apricot cotton twill instead of satin, and carpet in champagne-and-white hi-lo shag. Replace the heavy white satin draperies you saw in the picture with simple white dead-hung panels over white sheers. And instead of the off-white damask the decorator used on the walls, paint your walls soft ivory with white trim and cap with an airy sky-blue ceiling.

Leafing through the pages of travel magazines or the resort pages of newspapers is the way I feed my travel fantasies and my decorating fantasies, too!

Reading about a Caribbean sailing trip aboard an old-fashioned sailing vessel conjures up visions of a *belle epoque* sugar plantation with the master bedroom decorated in rich navy blue and sparkling white. The room of my dreams would have navy-blue upholstery with white trim, blue-and-white wall covering, and lots of teak and mahogany.

Another day—and with another magazine in hand—my travel fantasies take me to the exotic and timeless casbahs of the Middle East. Go there yourself—decoratively, that is—with brass lamps; rich purples, blues, and reds; pillows galore; and handsome pierced woodwork. Let simple white stucco bedroom walls be the backdrop for all that Oriental richness. Carpet in a low-pile plush of rich, dark purple and top with a scattering of bright Oriental rugs. Cover the bed with a rich purple throw and, if you choose, add a small colorful Persian-print throw. Toss on armloads of pillows in hot pink, rich golden-rod yellow, midnight blue, and amethyst. In place of a headboard, I would like a natural pierced-wood screen. At windows, hang stained wood louvered shutters.

The Contemporary Bedroom

When I do a contemporary bedroom I'm often asked, "Where does your inspiration come from?" I can answer it in one word: Everywhere! Sources of inspiration *are* everywhere and they are free for the taking. You don't have to be a decorator to have and use inspiration.

I stepped into a lovely bedroom recently and asked the young lady who decorated it what had inspired the scheme of navy blue and white. She told me the room had been sparked by a chic lady's suit of 1940 vintage that she'd seen in the window of a thrift shop.

The suit was navy blue, so the young lady painted the bedroom walls rich navy. The suit had been accessorized with a crisp white lace collar and cuffs, so there was lace in the room too—white lace curtains at the windows. Doors and trim were also painted frosty white. Thrift shop and hand-me-down furniture had been refinished by the young lady herself for night tables and a comfortable chair was covered in white cotton. The gold jewelry shown with the suit was translated into brass— there were brass lamps sparkling on the night tables and brass-toned frames for the pictures on the walls.

This "amateur" decorator had created a simple and lovely room—all inspired by a cast-off lady's suit!

Perhaps you have a favorite outfit that could become the inspiration for your next decorating endeavor. Maybe it's a pantsuit of apple green that you like to wear with a green, red, pink, and white print shirt. Wouldn't that be a winning scheme for a bedroom: white walls, apple-green quilted spread, and pink, red, green, and white draperies and bedskirt?

Nature—her colors, textures, and shapes—often inspires schemes in my mind. The beige and white of a seashell with the blue of a summer sky; or the rich green of a pine forest with the earthy brown of the forest floor and the delicate pinks and violets of spring forest flowers.

Whatever inspires you, it can be translated into a new and exciting look for your contemporary bedroom. And one of the best ways to achieve an exciting contemporary look is by using the element of surprise.

The next time you see a bedroom done by a decorator—in a home, department store, or magazine—look closely and I bet you'll find an element of surprise somewhere. Very often this element of surprise involves using objects, fabrics, or colors in unexpected, surprising ways—like putting a top on an old barrel and using it as a night table, filling a shiny copper cooking pot with flowers for that night table's accent, upholstering a contemporary molded acrylic chair with a scrap of antique patchwork.

The best part of most decorating surprises is that they spring from inspiration and daring, not from an overstuffed wallet. For example, you can create color surprise in your bedroom by reversing the usual look of light walls with a dark spread. Instead, paint your walls surprising coral red, paint trim and ceiling creamy ivory, and choose a creamy ivory quilted spread. Carpet can be thick champagne-beige shag, and for window drama choose a print of roses with green leaves, coral red on a cream background in the largest scale you can find. Hang those surprising draperies from poles painted ivory.

For another example, consider the placement of the bed. Does it always have to be on the wall facing the door to the bedroom? The architectural layout of most bedrooms dictates this placement because the room usually has one long wall for the bed and two windows on a side wall, and rarely do bedroom layouts vary. But today creative people are trying to get away from the architect-forced placement of the headboard and night tables on the long facing wall. And in so doing, those who have large bedrooms have decided that they would like the bed—surprise!—in the *center* of the room.

You gasp, but consider. This arrangement leaves open space for seating groupings such as sofa or chairs, or a table grouping for morning coffee or for letter writing. With the bed in the center of the room, you can turn the master bedroom into a sleeping/sitting room.

If your bedroom is large and has a view, place the bed in the center of the room facing the windows. Behind the headboard you can have open filigree panels installed from ceiling to floor. On the wall previously used for bed placement, a small sofa grouping would be an all-day delight. The sofa should be flanked by a small slipper chair and ottoman. And in front of the windows, why not place a breakfast table and a pair of chairs?

The bed-in-the-center-of-the-room arrangement also is great for one-room apartments. You can even use a king-size bed in the limited space of a studio apartment by placing the bed front and center, framed ceiling to floor in painted wood. You might say it creates a room within a room.

One middle-of-the-room bed placement that I saw in a studio apartment used 2 x 4 uprights, painted a snappy apple green, to frame a king-size bed that was upholstered in vivid red-green-blue-and-white geometric-patterned no-iron sheets. Two headboards, joined at right angles, framed two sides of the bed and were upholstered with the geometric-design sheets, which had been treated against stains. Into the space created by the uprights, laminated window shades were installed. Actually, the shades were made with bright red-green-blue-and-white floral-patterned no-iron sheets. Accent pillows were covered in coordinating towels. Walls, curtains, and campaign chest in the studio apartment were all white. In the corner behind the headboards of the centered king-size bed was space for an intimate dining area, which was accented with various green plants.

After a period of strict prohibitions against

For the one-room-apartment dweller with a king-size bed, my advice is place the bed in the middle of the room, framed ceiling to floor with painted 2 x 4 uprights. Decorate the bed and headboard with brightly colored no-iron sheets.

mixing patterns, the pattern-on-pattern look also evokes surprise, even though the look goes way back in history. The Orientals and the Arabs have always known how to mix patterns. And what about our great-grandmothers who mixed patterns daringly in their patchwork-quilt designs?

The look is now going strong. I often mix patterns in my decorating work, and have used anywhere from two to five—and sometimes more—patterns in a single bedroom. There's no limit to where that pattern can go, either. Walls can be patterned; floors can be patterned; ceilings can

be patterned; even wood furniture can be patterned, through the use of stencils or fabric.

The most important rule when mixing patterns is that the patterns must have some relationship to one another—be it in color, scale, or mood.

If you want to try your hand at mixing patterns, here's a bedroom scheme for you: Walls are papered in a cool variegated stripe of leaf green and pure white. The floral bedspread and floor-length draperies feature the same green for foliage to complement blossoms of peach, coral, lemon yellow, and cornflower blue, all on a white background. For carpeting, I picture a tiny all-over geometric in the same green and white as the wallcovering. Bedside tables are white. And for lamps, I envision a small-scale floral in the bedspread colors, with pleated white lampshades.

For more on the use of pattern-on-pattern, see Chapter 2.

FURNITURE FLEXIBILITY

There was a time when bedroom suites were relegated to the bedroom; living-room suites stuck together in the parlor, and dining-room furniture never dared show its face anywhere but in the dining room. Today, that's all changed. You can use a small, low chest of drawers as a living-room end table, or you can keep a casual sofa in the bedroom for intimate relaxing. Many people even tuck a small refrigerator into the bedroom to hold cold drinks and snacks.

Furniture flexibility makes every room in your home a multipurpose room. You can turn your bedroom into a home office by substituting a convertible sofa for a bed, using a living-room end table for a night table, and placing a double-decker cocktail table at the foot of the bed. The cocktail table will hold blankets and linens below and a pretty bowl of flowers above, and a Queen Anne desk will provide a quiet place to write letters and keep the household accounts. I've always believed that desks can live happily in any room of the house.

A graceful table desk placed near a bedroom window can be outfitted with a small standing mirror and can then be used as a dressing table. Or put a cloth over that desk and it becomes a romantic dining nook for weekend breakfasts or candlelit dinners.

And what about an easy chair for the bedroom? So many people use the bedroom as a TV room, yet never think of watching from a comfy

BarcaLounger recliner

Peters-Revington Queen Anne desk

Two cocktail tables and a Queen Anne desk are right at home in a pretty bedroom done up in gingham and flowers. With the desk closed, a velvety recliner tucked in the corner becomes a comfy spot for watching TV.

chair. A recliner in the bedroom will fill the bill perfectly. Covered in nutmeg velvet it combines beautifully with apple-green-and-white gingham walls and floral spread and draperies in sharp citrus tones.

NOSTALGIA IN THE BEDROOM

If there's something you feel sentimental or nostalgic about, your bedroom—your private domain—is the perfect place to express it.

I once spent a morning on the green goddess of the sea, *Coronia*, a Cunard steamship. Believe me, I was not getting ready for a cruise to the Caribbean; I was visiting the ship to look at all the furnishings that were being sold. The *Coronia*, unfortunately, was being scrapped. And, alas, another era was over. But for the many people at the sale who purchased chairs, tables, and other *Coronia* memorabilia, the era of the great trans-Atlantic steamships can go on.

For one of my bedroom decorating projects, I purchased a pair of *Coronia* night tables with bowed fronts. The tables are small—only 13 inches wide—but they'll fit perfectly into the space for which they are intended. Besides, where can you buy a pair of night tables for $40? The tables also have drawers from top to bottom—small drawers, yes, but wide enough and deep enough to hold all the things one keeps at the bedside. I lacquered the night tables white and replaced the old drawer hardware with some Lucite pulls.

There were other great buys on the *Coronia*, such as deck chairs for $25. The deck chairs on the *Coronia* were used over and over again by many, many people, so you can be sure that their construction is sound. When painted and recushioned, they were comfortable, relaxing bedroom accessories. The adventurous and creative might paint an old sturdy wood deck chair with bright red lacquer and outfit it with a cushion covered in a red-pink-and-white geometric print. Use the fabric for toss pillows on a pink bedspread and create an unusual bedroom with plenty of punch.

THE LIGHT AND AIRY LOOK

It seems everyone these days wants a light and airy look. And I'm all for it, particularly since today's small bedrooms with their low ceilings can so easily be dark and dreary.

If you like the light and airy look as I do, start with light, airy colors and add light, airy furniture—wicker, acrylics, rattan—or furniture painted in sparkling clear tones.

A bedroom I designed recently featured the light and airy look. Walls were painted dazzling sunny yellow, and carpeting was the same happy shade. Moldings and ceiling were frosty white. Because the room was small and dark, I furnished it with white wicker and brightened existing wood pieces. Two small dark-wood dressers took on a lighter-than-air look when laminated with a geometric-print fabric of lemon yellow and white. The old brass dresser knobs were replaced with contemporary pulls of clear Lucite.

And how do you make a large bed look light and airy? I did it by upholstering the box spring, mattress, and headboard in the same cotton print used on the dressers and dropped a cheery, white-grounded patchwork quilt over the whole thing.

A dusty, gray city view was concealed behind light, airy white louvered shutters, framed with yellow-and-white-floral drapery panels.

THE CHIC CONTEMPORARY LOOK

I've heard the word "chic" bandied about for years. A lady will say, "I really want a chic bedroom," or, "Aren't those love seats chic?" "Chic" in decorating means understated, up-to-date. A bedroom designed with white walls, white draperies, a white spread, comfy white modern chairs, and glass-topped end tables on white Lucite bases can be chic.

Chic, however, is not to be confused with chichi. A "chichi" room is an overdone room that has too much of everything.

If you want to create a chic contemporary bedroom, here's a way to do it with one color. (One-color rooms have always fallen into the chic category, you know.) Color your room pale yellow—pale yellow walls, pale yellow shag carpeting—and paint woodwork white. At windows hang sheer white undercurtains, ceiling to floor. For overdraperies, go pale yellow satin, hung on clear Lucite poles with clear Lucite rings. For your bedspread choose yellow satin, and welt the top of the spread. The bedskirt should be shirred and ruffled, please; ruffled shirring is very chic. Your headboard, or, better yet, a bamboo-style four-poster, without the canopy, should be painted white.

Skirted tables make chic end tables. In your yellow bedroom, skirt bedside tables in white and use clear glass tops to protect the fabric. (Chic isn't always too practical.) For lamps,

Yellow walls and carpeting, white wicker, and cotton "upholstery" for dressers and bed turn a dark city bedroom light and airy.

Simmons box spring, mattress, and headboard

white Lucite or lemon yellow would be right up to the minute. If your bedroom has a fireplace, paint the molding white—no elaborate mantel, please. And above the fireplace, hang a large Venetian mirror—very chic, even though they've been around for years.

The Bedroom Retreat

Don't you find that you really need a place to refresh yourself and take a breather from the exciting and sometimes frantic world outside? I know I do. For this reason I believe that get-away rooms, as I call those relaxing havens, are important at any time of year.

For many people, this type of room is the bedroom, a place where soft, soothing colors and comfy furniture hold sway. Even better is a getaway bedroom that's opposite in mood from your everyday routine—like a country-style bedroom in the city, complete with beamed ceiling and patchwork; or an Arabian Night's tented bedroom in a farmhouse; or a tropical-paradise bedroom in snow country.

Flowers and blue skies are always part of my getaway plans. I recently completed such a bedroom in a hotel—the room is to be used by busy executives after long days of meetings and conferences. Three walls are papered in a multi-colored floral on a white background, and the fourth wall—the wall behind the bed—is covered with a matching fabric, shirred into soft folds. Above wide white crown moldings floats a sky-blue ceiling which is reflected underfoot by cloud-soft sky-blue carpeting. Furniture is painted white, and upholstery on comfortable chairs is cool sea-foam green. The beds, simply dressed in pastel-embroidered white sheets and snowy white quilts, are skirted in hyacinth pink.

Privacy, of course, is essential to the get-away room. We all have those days when we want to shut out the world and enjoy utter privacy, but unfortunately many of us are victims of the "to-getherness" trend that hit builders several years ago, resulting in homes with no doors and very few walls to separate one room from another.

If you like privacy, but aren't getting enough of it, why not think in terms of making privacy a part of your bedroom decorating scheme? One

trend I'm behind 100 percent is the bedroom/bathroom combination. That's right—many people are including bathtubs in their bedroom plans. (What fun in a vacation home, too, and what a thoughtful addition to a guest room, where privacy is of paramount importance.)

In a country home I visited recently, the sunken tub in the master bedroom was placed right next to a window (insulated, of course) with a serene woodland view. The bedroom, painted a soft off-white, also featured a platform bed and a mix of modern conveniences and family heirlooms, such as a panel of old stained glass suspended in front of the window. The modern conveniences were represented by the solid comfort of a foam-slab mattress, dressed up with a fitted beige spread, and by a soil-hiding tone-on-tone nylon carpet in two sunny shades—spring green and a soft, happy yellow.

The floating look is a good choice for the bedroom retreat because it says up, up, and away! Furniture with the floating look has no visible means of support; sits on a recessed base or on a support of clear glass or acrylic. The result is a serene look that's perfect for the bedroom retreat.

The floating look is a wood-, metal-, or glass-topped table with a clear acrylic cube for a base.

The floating look is a cushy, leather-covered sofa on a recessed brass base.

The floating look is a sling chair suspended in a plate-glass frame.

The floating look, as you may have gathered, is not just up-to-date but even futuristic.

That doesn't mean, however, that the floating look is all hard edges. Far from it. To prove it, here's a bedroom that combines all the futuristic drama of the floating look with the soft prettiness of a sand-beige nylon carpet, gently shirred draperies, and a welter of ruffly pillows.

The center of attention is a do-it-yourself floating platform bed that seems to be resting on nothing more substantial than a pool of light. The effect is achieved by supporting the plywood mattress board on a recessed plywood box that is illuminated around its upper edge with strip lights. When the lights go on, the bed seems to float up, up, and away!

The head of the bed is slipped into a lacquered modular wall system that beautifully stores any-

*Modern conveniences and family heirlooms live happily together in a bedroom/
bath carpeted in tone-on-tone plush of soil-hiding nylon.*

thing and everything in its drawers and on its shelves. The bed is painted a soft terra-cotta, and windows and bed are dressed in sea-inspired patterns and colors from a new linen collection. Pretty draperies of rust-and-sand rickrack-print sheets are combined practically with a Stoplite window shade.

While the floating bed is undoubtedly the most exciting, there are lots of other new looks for the bed.

The most popular of these new looks is the casual, easy-care open-bed fashion. The open bed consists of a comforter tossed over matching sheets and pillowcases—at least they usually match; there's no law that say they must.

A reversible comforter of two solid colors can coexist happily with any print and also offers a seasonal—or even weekly—change of decorative moods. If you prefer a print comforter, buy some sheets that coordinate as well as some that match: If your comforter is a pink-and-white floral with green foliage, mix it with sheets striped in pink and white, or green and white, or with checks of pink or green; if your comforter

The futuristic look of a floating platform bed, lit from beneath, is combined with the soft prettiness of a beige plush nylon carpet, ruffly pillows, and softly shirred draperies in a bedroom decorated in soft earth tones.

is a tailored geometric of navy and white, use matching sheets, solid navy sheets edged with white, or white linens monogrammed in navy.

If you prefer a more formal look, think of a fitted bedcover with matching upholstered box spring on a sleek platform.

In the room pictured, inspired by the exotic East, all eyes will focus on the bamboo-trimmed platform bed, neatly topped with a shirred, fitted bedcover and matching pillow shams. The colors—tones of salmon on hand-printed batik— are picked up in the smoky-salmon carpet.

Walls, papered in a print that simulates the

look and texture of sisal squares, are echoed by handwoven macramé and basket accessories, and by the bamboo of the bed and its matching bench.

Blue is a good color for the bedroom retreat. It is, after all, one of nature's most relaxing colors. (Have you ever stared up into a clear blue sky?)

I predict that all the blues—from navy to ice —will be making decorating news. I myself like blue so much I once decorated an office of mine in blues—royal blue for the carpeting, a blue-

—bring the look indoors in your bedroom retreat. Vegetarian designs for wallcoverings, fabrics, and accessories abound on today's market, so you'll have plenty to choose from.

One of the prettiest cotton prints around these days sports bunches of two-tone green asparagus tied up with flying pink ribbons, all on a white background. I would like to see a fabric like that used in a bedroom for the bedspread and for an upholstered headboard. Paint the room white, and carpet in garden-fresh emerald green. Skirt the bed in pale pink cotton moiré. Use the pink moiré for tie-back draperies, too, under a shirred valance of the asparagus print. Next to the bed, place a table skirted in green, the color of those first garden shoots. And on that fresh-looking green table, place a white ceramic cabbage lamp with white shade. I know the cabbage isn't considered one of nature's more glamorous creations, but, when you stop to think about it, those lowly cabbages look a lot like full-blown roses!

While most people seem to prefer bright, airy rooms, some people find dark rooms more restful. If you're one of those who are forever drawing the curtains or pulling down the shades, why not consider black? If you associate black with depression or unpleasantness, you're missing out on a good decorating bet. Black for furniture, black for floors, black for walls—black can be used in many ways in the home, and believe me, if done right, a touch or more of black will be anything but depressing.

For a cozy bedroom, you might choose matching wallcovering and fabric in a medium-scale print of pink and green on a black background. Use the fabric for tieback draperies and for the bedspread. Skirt the bed in shell-pink polished cotton, and paint woodwork and ceiling shell pink, too. Leave your wood floor bare except for a hooked rug in the pink-black-and-green color scheme of your fabric and wallcovering.

For plaster walls that are badly pitted, black is a happy color choice that will camouflage the wall's imperfections. Team black walls with natural wicker or rattan furniture. Paint ceiling and woodwork white. Cushion wicker chairs in a cotton bandanna print of red, white, blue, and black. Spread the bed with the same bandanna print. For flooring, my choice would be wall-to-wall natural sisal matting. Accessorize your black walls with framed bandannas and with natural straw baskets in interesting shapes.

If you prefer your black in small doses, remember even diehard pastel fans find that a touch of black—a lacquered night table or black patent upholstery on a bedroom chair—enhances and dramatizes a pastel decor. The impact of just one or two black touches provides the contrast that keeps all those pale tones from looking washed out.

The Celebrity Bedroom

Polly Bergen, television personality and beauty expert, loves white. And no wonder: White is a great brightener for dark rooms, and the white treatment can make small rooms look larger. White is restful, too, so it's ideal for bedrooms.

Polly's Malibu, California, home has lots of windows to let in stunning ocean views. She didn't want her decor to compete with those dramatic vistas, so she went white all the way—white floors, white walls, white furniture. The only touch of color is on the bed, which Polly accessorizes with colorful sheets, pillowcases, and coordinating coverlets.

Perhaps you like the idea of a white bedroom, but are afraid it's impractical. Well, believe me, today's miracle products can make a white room as practical as any. Try this scheme and you'll see what I mean.

Paint walls and trim white, using washable paint. Paint floor white, too, with scrubbable polyurethane paint, and over that floor lay a fluffy white area rug of machine-washable fake fur. For a bedspread, how about treated white canvas? And make sure the bed you choose has a frame of warm, honey-tone wood. Night tables

A bedroom that invites relaxation starts with a soothing one-color scheme of ice blue for walls, floor, and furnishings. There's relaxation, too, in a mattress with built-in bedboard, concealed under a simple quilted spread.

can be cubes of that rich wood, and for night-table lamps, gleaming brass would be my choice. Upholster a club chair in that white canvas. And for your second chair, how about an old-fashioned bentwood-and-cane rocker? At windows, hang natural bamboo roller-blinds, and make sure that you place some live green plants at that window, too. If you want some more color, put up a few wall posters and paintings, and accessorize your bed with toss pillows of raspberry pink, chome yellow, emerald green, and tangerine.

Van Johnson is a pewter addict—and a ship addict, too. That's what the star of some 100 motion pictures told me just the other day. Van was raised in Rhode Island and he loves Americana and New England decoration—colonial furniture, polished hardwood floors, harvest tables, bright happy New England countryside colors.

When planning a bedroom scheme for himself, the all-American movie star chooses white walls, a navy-blue carpet, a pine colonial poster bed—a masculine look in the fashion of Paul Revere. And you can be certain you'll find pewter accessories around, maybe a pewter lamp or a pair of pewter candlesticks on the chest of drawers.

For bedroom wall decoration, Van chooses the things he likes, including some of his own paintings. Did you know there are many original Johnsons around—paintings of New England flowers, vegetables, red barns in the snow, lighthouses, the rockbound coast of Maine? Van paints the things he really loves.

Arlene Dahl decorates to enhance her looks. That's what I learned when I dropped in on her in her river-view apartment.

Arlene, a well-known entertainer, is also a beauty consultant and she firmly believes that a room's colors should flatter its occupant. She herself loves bright, happy colors and warm wood tones—colors that act as a backdrop for her famous looks. "If the color of a room isn't sympathetic, I'm unhappy," she told me.

Unhappy colors for Arlene are the grayed-down colors. "Those colors to me are like a rainy day."

For her bedroom, Arlene chose a warm mauvey

pink—over her husband's initial objections. "I brought him around by explaining that feminine colors enhance a man's masculinity, just as a man-tailored suit can make a feminine woman look even more feminine."

Bedroom colors to stay away from, says Arlene, are gold and green. "Gold makes the skin look sallow. Green is okay only for redheads with nearly colorless skin."

Arlene's other musts, besides sympathetic colors, are room fragrance and good lighting. She likes rooms to have their own scents, like people who wear a signature perfume. In her husband's Persian-look dressing room Arlene burns exotic incense, and in the bedroom she uses a combination of potpourri plus her own perfume. She puts the perfume on the bulbs of the bedside lamps; when the light goes on, fragrance fills the room.

When it comes to lighting, Arlene Dahl is a perfectionist. "You can't look your best if you apply makeup in bad light." Arlene's dressing room has natural light—"The best for putting on makeup." The next best thing is incandescent light, she says. "No fluorescent light, please."

Bedroom Details and Decorating Problems

DECORATING WITH RIBBON

Don't reserve ribbons for tying up your little girl's hair. Ribbons are for home decorating too. The French make beautiful embroidered ribbon —some with rich gold or silver geometric designs; others with delicate pastel floral designs; still others with traditional peasant designs in brilliant colors. The ribbons are available in widths up to two inches.

Use wide embroidered ribbon to tie back draperies in a period bedroom. I like pink-and-powder-blue floral ribbon with white silk draperies or with lemon-yellow velvet draperies. Or how about rich black-gold-and-white ribbon, to hold back draperies of emerald green? Or red-emerald-green-and-white ribbon teamed with sky-blue draperies? The combinations are numberless!

Ribbons are also being seen a lot these days as trim for boudoir pillows, and some ambitious handicrafters are making entire pillowtops of ribbons that they weave together. Simply choose two, three, or even four different ribbons and weave them as you'd weave a basket. Back your ribbon pillows with a contrasting fabric, and trim with a deep white eyelet border. Whether they're made with gingham ribbons, embroidered ribbons, or solid-color ribbons, I love those pretty pillows for bedrooms.

And when thinking of ribbons, don't overlook the beautiful ribbon-design fabrics and wallcoverings on the market. One of my favorite bedrooms is done in a ribbon-print fabric and matching wallpaper. The ribbons of buttercup yellow are combined with nosegays in pink, blues, greens, and apricot, all on a white background. The ribbon design is used for bed canopy, draperies, and bedskirt. The bedspread is pure white, as are the sheer, filmy undercurtains. Bedside tables are skirted in white trimmed with buttercup-yellow ribbons. The room's two slipper chairs are upholstered in a small-scale tapestry fabric of buttercup yellow and white. And underfoot is a soft, soft yellow plush carpet.

BORDERS

North of the border or south of the border, wherever I roam, I still love the look of borders on bedroom draperies, rugs, carpets, curtains, window shades, walls, floors—you name it. A border can be the finishing touch that makes the difference between an attractive bedroom and a super one!

Picture this, for instance: a bedroom with moss-green draperies, moss-green carpet, white walls, moss-green spreads. It's pleasant, but not exciting. Now picture those draperies and valances edged in a wide embroidered ribbon of petal pink, forget-me-not blue, buttercup, moss green, and white. And picture those spreads bordered in that wide ribbon, too.

I'd go on to lay an area rug—perhaps in a floral design in the same pretty springtime colors as the ribbon, and leaving just a border of moss-green carpeting to set it off. And how about using that ribbon all around the top of the wall, where it meets the ceiling? That's another kind of border I enjoy.

THE UPHOLSTERED LOOK

Padded or unpadded, the upholstered look is everywhere these days. No longer confined to sofas, chairs, and ottomans, upholstery is also being seen on walls, tables, chests of drawers, and even curtain poles.

A bedroom I saw recently was softly pulled together with upholstery on dressers, occasional tables, and chairs. Curtain poles were also upholstered. The print used was a delicate hydrangea-blue floral with green foliage on a white background. The fabric was applied with wallpaper paste to two inexpensive dressers, and was also used for floor-length draperies, hung on white rings from a wood pole wrapped in the fabric. Walls were painted hydrangea blue with white trim and ceiling. Carpet was fern-green shag. The bedspread, of the same print, was complemented by a lacy white eyelet bedskirt and a scattering of eyelet-edged baby pillows. A penny-bright brass headboard and two brass sconces added twinkling warmth to the soft, soft upholstered room.

Even softer is the look of stretched or padded fabric walls for the bedroom. I love the look in the city and in the country, but if you decide to go with fabric walls, do it right. Whatever you do, don't staple fabric directly to the plaster and then try to cover the seams with glue. Start by first stapling narrow wood slats or lath strips around the perimeter of the wall to be covered: under crown molding, above baseboards, and around doors and windows. Then stretch ¼-inch cotton flannel from top slats to bottom slats. After stretching and tacking the flannel to the slats, you can begin applying the fabric. Stretch fabric from slat to slat, matching the seams. Cover tacks with a handsome gimp, braid, or with self-welting made from the same fabric.

Remember, stretched fabric walls do not have the look of walls covered with paper-backed fabric. Stretched fabric walls are far more elegant and soft. And one thing is certain—stretched fabric on the walls will hide cracked or badly plastered wall surfaces.

If you are planning new bedroom decor, consider walls covered in a pale-blue-and-white damask print with draperies and valances in the same fabric. Tie valances with a buttery yellow, and carpet the floor with yellow shag. For bedspread and headboard, use the damask print, and skirt the bed in a lemon-and-white stripe. Night-table lamps can be white opaline with soft white silk shades to shed a good light on those soft upholstered walls. (And by the way, you can hang pictures on fabric-covered walls with ordinary picture hooks.)

SKIRTS

As you may have gathered by now, I love the soft look of skirts for bedrooms—for bedside tables, for beds, and for chairs. Skirt a bed in a pastel floral cotton of apricot, raspberry, and lime green on a sky-blue background, and use the same floral fabric on a skirted night table. For the bedspread, use apricot glazed chintz—quilted, please—and if you have room, a dainty slipper chair, upholstered in the quilted apricot cotton and skirted, of course, would be a pretty touch. Walls can be sky blue, trimmed in white. Carpet in grass green. For draperies, white sheers would be my choice.

CHINTZ AND BAMBOO

I'm a dyed-in-the-wool window-shopper and often find myself gazing into pretty shop windows on my walks to and from the office. This year I find window-shopping more enjoyable than ever, and the reason can be found in a single word—chintz. Beautiful glazed chintz in rich colors and patterns is in for women's fashions and for bedroom furnishings, too.

Chintz, as you may know, originated in India way back when and was brought to England as early as the thirteenth century where it was an overnight success. That explains why chintz is so often associated with English decorating. But why stop there? Chintz needn't be reserved for those whose taste is English; these days, chintz is being designed to complement any bedroom decor—period or contemporary.

While window-shopping last week I saw a lovely lady's umbrella made of chintz with a tortoise bamboo handle. I liked it so much I decided to design a bedroom scheme combining those elements.

For walls, I pictured a tiny geometric print of soft spring green and white, with white ceiling and trim. Carpet would be pastel-pink plush. For headboard, bedside tables, and occasional chair and ottoman, I visualized tortoise bamboo with

chair seat pad in a pretty pink-white-and-green floral chintz. Bedspread and draperies would be of the same print. On a bedside table skirted in pale pink and trimmed in spring green, I would place a gleaming brass lamp shaded in spring green.

PATTERNED LINENS

As everyone must know by now, the plain white sheet is a thing of the past. Sheets have gone wild with color and pattern. And not just sheets: There are blankets, comforters—even curtains—to match.

Patterned linens are a boon for the busy housewife who doesn't have time for the bedspread routine every morning. With linen sets, just pull the comforter or blanket over the matching sheets and the bed is made! Furthermore, when you want to change the look of your bed, you can simply substitute a different set of sheets. Try an apricot-and-white striped sheet with an apricot-blue-and-cream floral comforter, or substitute solid blue sheets with that comforter. And to give your bed a finished look, you can buy or make a dust ruffle to match your sheets.

If you are a dyed-in-the-wool bedspread fan, do what a neighbor of mine did. The walls of her bedroom are painted a soft peach. The floor is covered in pale straw-colored sisal matting, and there is a fluffy white wool rug next to the low platform bed. Sheets on the bed are a chocolate brown with a cream-and-peach geometric print. The bed is covered with an off-white fringed bedspread of nubby Indian cotton. All that shows of the linens are the pillowcases. They add a touch of warm color to the bed and look super against that off-white spread.

When a change of mood is desired, my neighbor switches over to pillowcases and sheets in a museum reproduction of a peach-blue-and-green floral on a cream background. Off comes the Indian spread to reveal a comforter covered in peach polished cotton.

FABRIC BARGAINS

These days, everyone is a bargain hunter. And one of my favorite hunting grounds for budget-minded decorating inspiration is the remnant table in the fabric department of any department or variety store.

Fabric remnants, as our ancestors knew, can be turned into unique and colorful patchworks for bedspreads, curtains, pillows, whatever. Remnants made into skirts can transform a ho-hum night table into an exciting asset. And fabrics laminated onto window shades or applied to screens can also give a custom look to rooms.

My favorite fabric bargains are those that are versatile. I'm talking about gingham, mattress ticking, bandannas, and those super Indian bedspreads in colorful paisley prints. Indian bedspreads offer a bonanza of color and pattern for little money. And for only the brave, entire rooms —walls, ceilings, upholstery—can be decorated with Indian paisley bedspreads.

Picture the walls and ceiling of a bedroom covered in a print of red, orange, black, brown, and beige on gold, with wood trim painted Tabasco red! Window shades can be natural bamboo, and floors can be covered in sisal matting of pale beige.

If the country look is more to your liking, look into bandannas of red and navy blue. They can be sewn together into many attractive accessories. Sew them back to back for happy toss-pillow covers—great on a denim-covered bed. Or sew several bandannas together to cover a tabletop that's skirted to the floor in solid blue or red. The bandanna overcloth will add eye appeal and will protect the underskirt, too.

WOODEN POLES

Do you think wooden poles are only for the closet? I don't. And I don't think wooden poles should be relegated to the drapery-and-curtain department either, even though I have always advocated hanging curtains the "painted-pole" way. I love the look of bedroom windows decorated with draperies in a geometric print of ginger brown, white, and yellow, hanging on ginger-brown wooden poles and rings.

The bedroom pictured blends the traditional and the contemporary through the use of poles to create a contemporary version of our old traditional favorite, the canopy bed. To further update that fabulous canopy look, the bed has space-age controls that allow you to raise or lower the bed's head and foot for old-fashioned

comfort. A pole-leg dressing table matches the canopy, and for contrast with that contemporary pole furniture there are a couple of ornate accent pieces in bamboo and carved wood. The floral bedspread colors of pink, lavender, and green are repeated in a boldly patterned supergraphic that forms a dramatic backdrop for the bed.

PROBLEM RADIATORS

Concealing the ugly bedroom radiator is a challenge that almost everyone faces at some time or other.

If your ugly radiator is the type that bulges out from under a window and gets in the way of draperies, try boxing the radiator attractively and using bamboo shades, shutters, or sill-length curtains at windows. Make sure that the box you build has some kind of openwork in front, such as lattice or metal cane, so that the heat can escape.

If your under-the-window radiator is the flat type, sheer curtains can be used in front of it, with tieback or loose drapery panels on either side. For the radiator window with no view, I like the idea of a screen in front of the window area to conceal both radiator and window. Again, some type of openwork material, such as lattice, wicker, louvers, or pierced wood should be used. I would especially like an openwork wicker screen painted white against apple-green walls. For the bedspread, choose a print of floral sprigs in green, hydrangea, daffodil, lavender, and grass green.

LOW CEILINGS

Oh, those beautiful high-ceilinged rooms of yesteryear—most of us can only dream about them. In the meantime, what to do about the claustrophobically low ceilings we have?

One answer to low ceilings is low furniture, and that includes furniture that sits right on the floor. In a low-ceilinged bedroom, keep your bed close to the ground by removing the legs. Just think, you may never have to clean under the bed again! Draw attention to your arrangement by covering the box spring and mattress in matching sheets. And for a contemporary look in your

Beautyrest's Space-age Adjusto-Rest

Traditional and modern meet in a bedroom that combines an old idea—the canopy bed—with space-age innovation: controls that raise and lower the bed's head and foot to the desired height.

low-slung bedroom, use a quilt to match your sheets.

For night tables, choose low models in natural light wood. And atop those bedside tables try a bit of high-style fakery with white-shaded wicker-look ceramic lamps. Keep storage units low, too. On the white painted window wall you might build in a shelf-and-cabinet arrangement to windowsill height to hold knickknacks like a happy menagerie of white ceramic animal accessories. Complete the contemporary look with white bead curtains against white walls; other walls could be painted deep eggplant.

THE TINY BEDROOM

There are two ways to approach the really under-size bedroom. One is to capitalize on its small-ness by making it seem appealingly snug and cozy, rather than merely confining. The other is to expand it visually—make it seem larger than it actually is. In the first chapter we talked about some ways to do this in entryways, and some of those suggestions can be used equally well here.

First of all, paint walls and ceiling a light color, and paint trim around doors the same color to avoid breaking up wall expanses.

Second, choose a space-expanding wall treatment, like mirror or trelliswork. Mirror is the more expensive, of course, but it will visually double the size of your room.

Third, keep furnishings at a minimum, and keep them low and small-scale.

The bedroom shown illustrates all three of these points.

Decorating for Singles

We've talked, in this chapter, primarily about bedrooms for the couple, but the single life is the way of life for millions of Americans. As a decorator I've decorated for both singles and families, and take it from me, singles have very different decorating needs.

A low-ceilinged room reaches new heights when a gingham-covered bed is placed directly on the floor. Illumination on natural wood night tables is provided by wicker-look ceramic lamps.

Tyndale's wicker-look ceramic lamps

A bedroom for the single man or woman should be easy to care for. Here, flame-red walls are a backdrop for modular furniture, including a platform bed. Bed and other furniture go right to the floor so dust can't collect underneath. And the bed looks super dressed in nothing but a toss-on comforter, so bedmaking is a snap.

Singles generally live in smaller quarters, have busy careers and social lives, and have little time to maintain their abodes. Singles are on the move every minute of the day, but often, when they're home, they love to entertain and do it beautifully, yet simply.

The single person is often young, but may also be a senior citizen. But whatever his or her age, the theme song of every single is "Give Me the Simple Life"—they don't want to be bothered with complicated bedmaking, or with vacuuming under the bed either. For them, the platform bed —maybe in perky pecan veneers and oak solids —is a perfect solution. It looks super dressed in a simple box-quilted comforter, which makes bedmaking a snap.

Shown here, against flame-red walls, the bed is part of a modular furniture group that includes chests and glass-fronted bookcase and storage units. I'm all for modular furniture for singles. It can be moved easily and repositioned easily in new quarters. And it can be beautifully augmented with additional pieces if the single decides to become double!

A mirrored wall plus happy springtime yellows and blues and small-scale furniture create a spacious feeling in a small bed/sitting room.

4

Rooms for Kids to Grow in, from Nursery to College

A child's room should be a happy, colorful, and safe place to be. It should also be practical—easy to clean; resistant to damage; suitable for the favorite activities of his/her age level; and with ample space for storage, both open and closed. For walls, washable paint or vinyl is best. For floors, easy-to-clean vinyl, at least until the preschool years are past. For furnishings, choose sturdy, safe, easy-to-clean pieces. Look for rounded, smooth edges on furniture, plastic-coated fabrics, dent-proof metal tubing, nontoxic paints (especially on secondhand cribs and playpens). Plastic laminate is an excellent choice—it can even be used as a surface for fingerpainting!

My son Nicky's room is a good example. The walls are covered with a cloud-design vinyl—white clouds on a blue sky. The floor is blue vinyl, banded in canary yellow. Nicky's desk is laminated in white, so dirt, crayon marks, paint, and spills wipe up with a damp sponge, and his bright red bed is painted with nontoxic paint.

The Nursery

In planning the nursery, think ahead. Choose furniture with classic styling that your child won't outgrow, and use fabrics, prints, and wallcoverings the child will grow into. Pass up the nursery-rhyme motifs and little boats and doll prints; instead, go for bright plaids, gingham checks, big floral prints, stripes—all in happy colors, of course. Instead of furniture decals depicting Wee Willie Winkie and Bo Beep, paint nursery furniture in bright colors and stencil on big graphic stripes or chevrons in contrasting hues. (A navy-blue chest with kelly-green and red chevrons would be super.) Or you could forgo nursery furniture altogether (except for the crib, of course) and create a storage wall with stacking shelves and cupboards. Such a unit would be useful from crib to college.

Here are two nursery schemes to think about:

Walls—a pencil-thin stripe of grass green and white
  Ceiling—sky blue
  Trim—grass-green tweed
  Furniture—washable white laminated crib and wall unit
  Window treatment—white louvered shutters.

Or try a scheme with Early American flair:

Walls—covered in a patchwork print of red and white
  Trim—white
  Carpet—cherry red
  Furniture—maple crib and wall unit
  Window treatment—white balloon shades.

As you can see, I'm a great believer in wall units for baby's room. The reason? Wall units made up of drawer, shelf, and cupboard modules can be rearranged and added to as baby grows. In fact, I know a "baby" who is now a fully grown eighteen-year-old college student, and his nursery wall unit—with a desk and more shelves added—is still in use.

I recommend that you not use real antiques in a child's room, since most pieces are too frail to withstand the rough-and-tumble that your tiny baby, in just a few short years, will be indulging in. If you're an antiques collector, by all means include antique children's furniture in your collection, but place them elsewhere. I like to collect antique children's chairs, but would never put one in the nursery; instead, they are kept in the living room, on the porch, or in the family room where the children use them rarely.

You might use some semiantiques, however, brought down from the attic and given a fresh look with some paint. For a girl's room, paint an old carved desk a pretty lemon yellow. Use the same sunny hue on an old wicker trunk that can be used to store toys. Paper walls in a romantic floral print of pink, yellow, orange, and green on a hyacinth-blue background. And how about a really elegant window treatment to make that little girl feel, oh, so grown up? Raspberry pink tieback draperies, lined in raspberry-and-white plaid, would be my choice. Hang the tiebacks over window shades laminated with the plaid fabric, and trim the shades with pink gimp. When the crib goes, use the plaid for a tailored bedskirt under a soft pink quilted spread.

Auctions are a good source of furnishings and other items for the nursery, and going to country auctions is a favorite weekend activity of the Varney family. The country newspapers are full of advertisements for auctions where you can still find many decorative items for a song. Here's a sampling of items you can look for:

• Damaged patchwork quilts to be cut down for crib-size comfort.
• Old crockery jugs to top with pleated parchment shades for dandy nursery lamps.
• Old round wooden boxes; when sanded and

stained they're great for holding flowers or plants (with glass liners, of course) or for storing nursery accouterments.
• Old wooden medicine cabinets to hold lotions, oils, and baby powder. You sometimes find these cabinets covered with layers of paint, but they're well worth the trouble it takes to strip them down.
• Antique rocking chairs, great for rocking the new baby, and one of the few antiques I favor for the nursery. Choose a sturdy one, strip it down, and add a soft foam-filled seat pad covered in sunny yellow-and-white gingham cotton. Paper nursery walls in a patchwork wallcovering in pastel shades—pink, powder blue, daffodil yellow, peach, and lime green.
• An old crib. Strip it down and leave the wood in its natural state, oiled for protection. Cover nursery floors with cushioned vinyl in a white brick pattern. Hang natural wood shutters at windows, and over those shutters how about yellow-and-white gingham checked curtains?

Special Rooms for Growing Boys and Girls

Although pink is no longer *de rigueur* for girls' rooms, it's still a wonderful color to use. It's a very flattering color, it seems to work with every other color, and—what's more important—it seems to delight most little girls. There are many shades of pink, ranging from pale cosmos to rich hyacinth, and of course there are all those hot Siamese pinks and rich shocking pinks.

I have planned many bedrooms with pink walls, coordinating the pink tone with printed drapery and bedspread fabric of a royal blue, azure blue, pink, and leaf green, along with a royal-blue carpet.

One mother I know delighted her young daughter with a pink-and-white room featuring wallpaper that I designed—a parade of pink elephants holding red and yellow flower arrangements in their trunks. The wallpaper comes with coordinating fabric, and the creative homemaker laminated the elephant fabric onto the window shades for a charming touch. She also made pink-and-white gingham curtains, tied back in cascades of bouffant poufs and finished with pink and white streamers. The bedspread was of the pink-and-white gingham also.

Furniture for the pink-elephant bedroom was

Conso's pink gimp t

An elegant window treatment of tieback draperies over coordinating laminated window shades gives a little girl's bedroom a grown-up feeling.

white wicker. A child-size table was skirted in pink-and-white gingham with elephant appliqués to match the cushions on a small wicker chair.

Of course her daughter will outgrow the elephants, but those frothy gingham checks are timeless.

Did you know that the monkey motif in decorating goes all the way back to eighteenth-century France where it was called *singerie?*

In those rococo days, the monkey motif was popular on wallcoverings and was often combined with another favorite—*chinoiserie* (the

This pink-and-white room, with a parade of pink elephants holding red and yellow flower arrangements in their trunks, would enchant any little girl. The parade starts at windows with elephant-fabric laminated window shades and marches right on to the matching wallcovering. Pink-and-white gingham curtains are tied back in cascades of bouffant poufs and finished with pink-and-white streamers. A child-size table has a pink-and-white gingham skirt with sewn-on elephant appliqués.

The red carpet treatment is always royal in a dining room.

For the dining room beautiful, murals on walls always add character. In this room, vibrant green draperies, trimmed in persimmon, hang at the windows. Persimmon is the color of fabric in dining chair seats.

For a dinner party in my own dining room, we rented gold ballroom chairs with red velvet seats. Folding dining tables were skirted with acid-green moiré.

Chinese look). In those *singerie* designs, the little creatures, dressed in brightly colored costumes, juggled, played musical instruments, and frolicked amidst scrolls, flowers, ferns, and palms.

Plan a pretty room for a little girl around an up-to-date monkey-design wallpaper. One I like is a bold leaf-and-flower design in several shades of sharp green, tangerine, and hot pink; through the colorful foliage, charming brown-and-white monkey faces peer. Paint trim and woodwork white, and for furniture that's practical and pretty, too, how about white laminate? Bedspread can be a quilted style in hot-pink polished cotton, and I would skirt the bed in lime green. Carpet can be lime green too. Chair pads and floor-length curtains, hung from white rings and poles, can be a monkey-print fabric to match the wallpaper.

Here's a way to put a little swing into your young lady's life. It's not only charming and colorful, it's fun!

Suspend a swaying hammock-style bed from the ceiling with stout nylon marine rope. Cover the mattress with a fitted spread of easy-to-wash pink-and-white striped seersucker, and pick curtains that are washable and light in look also. (White trimmed with pink borders?) Complete the light and colorful look with a soft apple-green nylon carpet.

When I was a small boy growing up, spring wasn't spring without a brand-new overcoat of natty navy blue. Although I'm a good many years older today, I still associate navy blue with the spring season. Indeed, dark though it may be, navy blue blends beautifully with all the spring colors—anemone red, daffodil yellow, tulip pink, grass green. And it takes red and white beautifully; think of the flag!

In a little boy's room, what could be more appropriate than nautical navy blue? I would paper walls in a washable rope-print vinyl wallcovering of navy on white. And with those walls I picture navy-blue fitted bedspreads trimmed with white rope trim. Carpet can be bright anemone-red shag, and at windows my choice would be tomato-red café curtains trimmed in navy and hung from shiny brass poles.

No one enjoys the beach as much as kids, and I know many children who would love a beach scheme for their rooms. One artistic mother I know went so far as to paint a beach mural on her young son's walls. The sand, dotted with colorful umbrellas, was rendered in sand paint on the bottom half of the wall. The blue sea, frosted with whitecaps and tiny sailboats, covered the top half. Puffy white clouds on a sky-blue ground brought the ceiling to life. Carpet was sand-beige shag. For bedspreads, of course lipstick-red terry cloth was the choice, lined and quilted for durability. A director's chair enameled emerald green had a canvas seat and back wide stripes of emerald and white. And for lounging there was a pale bleached-wood beach recliner with a sling of the green-and-white striped fabric.

Polka dots are making the decorating scene in wallpaper as well as in fabrics, and their festive, bouncy look makes them perfect for children's rooms. Why not style a little boy's room with red-white-and-blue polka-dot vinyl wallcovering? Flooring could be slick red vinyl or, if you prefer carpet, fire-engine-red shag. Soft and cuddly polyester would be my choice for durability and practicality; it's easy to care for and always bounces right back, even after the wildest round-up of little cowboys.

For furniture you can use some of the great new children's designs that have the modular look, sophisticated enough to be used right through the teen years.

For fun, try mixing polka dots with florals, stripes, plaids, checks—you name it! Dots, like stripes, mix well with most other prints.

Canvas is appearing all over the map, and it's an excellent choice for children's rooms. Not only is it attractive, it's durable—and washable—which means it can take the patter of little footsteps, even when those footsteps march across the sofa, the chairs, and the beds!

Use canvas on walls, or for upholstery, quilted or unquilted. Those with artistic flair might try stenciling on canvas—I like the idea of a table skirt with stenciled border.

In a boy's room, use rough, tough canvas for fitted bed and bolster covers on a studio couch.

"Cloud Land" carpet of Allied Chemical Nylon

This bedroom for a young girl swings with color and fancy. Hammock-style bed is suspended from ceiling with stout nylon marine rope. Color scheme is pink and green with white accents: Bedspread is pink-and-white striped searsucker; carpet is apple-green nylon; wallcovering, featuring dominant pink-green colors, is handprinted floral stripe.

My color choice would be royal blue, welted in white. Paint walls periwinkle with white trim and royal-blue doors. At windows, striped canvas Roman shades in navy, kelly green, and white would be a nice change from the usual curtain treatment. Carpet in kelly-green shag and pile the bed with canvas-covered pillows of kelly green, white, and periwinkle blue. If there's room for a lounge chair, my choice would be a beach chair with sling of the striped canvas used at windows.

Blue denim, that all-American favorite fabric, actually originated in the French city of Nimes, so the fabric was dubbed "deNimes"—that's "from Nimes" in French.

Durable denim, in shades ranging from deep slate blue to faded pale blue, looks great in almost any room where you want a casual look; and for a boy's bedroom, of course, it's a natural. You could decorate around a blue denim spread. On the ceiling and the wall above a wood dado, use a multicolored, patchwork-look washable wallcovering. Roughhouse flooring can be fire-engine-red vinyl. Complete your denim room with fire-engine-red, sunny yellow, and royal-blue accessories.

But blue denim isn't only for boys, as anyone can see by looking at today's fashions. For a feminine look, team red-and-white dotted swiss with blue denim. Bedspread can be quilted blue denim (it's wonderfully washable), and use red-and-white dotted swiss for ruffled crisscross curtains, ruffled bedskirt, and ruffled edges on denim toss pillows. Cover floor in powder-blue vinyl or shag carpet. And if you're handy with a crochet hook, how about making a granny square afghan of the new denim-look yarns? Use faded-blue and deep-blue denim yarns along with pink, red, and sky blue to create a newfangled throw to place at the foot of that blue denim bed. Strip the finish off an old rocking chair and outfit the seat with a blue denim cushion piped in red. A brass headboard would be my suggestion for the bed. And as a storage unit or hope chest, why not give an old trunk a paint job to match your blue denim decor? Clean the old hardware with lots of elbow grease and steel wool.

No one wants to make a decorating mistake. And who can blame them? These days every mistake, no matter how small, is costly. So of course everyone wants dos and don'ts—surefire decorating rules that never fail. But, alas, decorating is not like picking a box of "never-fail" cake mix off the supermarket shelf.

There is one trick, however, that almost never fails. It's the all-in-one-print scheme, using either matching fabric and wallcovering or matching fabric for upholstery, walls—everything.

The only pitfall to avoid in the all-in-one scheme for a child's room is a print that's too loud or jumpy to live with. Test this out beforehand by obtaining a large sample of the fabric you want to use. Take it home to the room you're redoing and live with the sample for a few days or, better yet, a few weeks. If you still like it after the test period has elapsed, start decorating the all-in-one way.

One safe bet for boys is a small-scale, all-over plaid in clear colors. Another look I favor is the check, but it can get monotonous unless you break it up with stabs of bright solid color or even with touches of a complementary print. Florals and abstracts work well with checks. Or try checks of a different color.

For a girl's room the flower-garden look is one of my favorites, particularly in crisp red and white. Who can resist fresh, snowy white punctuated with sparks of scarlet? If you decide to use it, choose a red-and-white posy-print wallcovering and matching cotton polyester fabric, ruffled on the bed, on the bed canopy, and at windows. In the room shown, the important additions that keep the one-pattern look from going stale are the white-painted dresser and nightstand and the happy strawberry-red rocker.

The second bedroom in today's apartments is often not much larger than a walk-in closet. "My son's bedroom is only eight by eleven," one woman complained. "How can I decorate such a small room?"

One of my favorite ways of making space in a small room is to decorate in the corners. The corner way of decorating leaves the center of the room free.

In this boy's tiny bedroom, for instance, you could decorate the corner way with a side convertible chair or ottoman instead of a space-wasting bed. Place the chair on the diagonal in the corner and leave it closed until bedtime. Place a corner wall system that includes a desk, bookshelves, and drawer space in the opposite corner, leaving the center of the room free for play space. As the child grows and a bigger bed is needed, you could consider a built-in corner banquette topped with a thick foam mattress.

Some of the suggestions for small entryways (in Chapter 1) and undersized master bedrooms (Chapter 3) could also be adapted for use in a

A girl's room furnished with cast-offs becomes a posy-filled dream room when redone in a single print. Walls are covered in a red-and-white floral. Bed and windows are ruffled in matching cotton polyester.

child's room. Please don't try a mirrored wall here, however. It would be too hazardous.

Do-It-Yourself Ideas for Children's Rooms

Anything you make or do yourself to brighten your child's room or make it more comfortable is a special way of saying "I love you." Here are some suggestions:

▶ *Tie a little girl's room up in bows.* Turn a plain, solid-color bedspread into a super surprise by sewing on a pretty party "bow" of contrasting strips of fabric. Crisscross the strips to make the bed look like a gift all wrapped and ready to be opened, then tie the loose ends into a bow over the pillow end of the spread and tack down the bow's center to keep it from untying.

Try a powder-blue spread tied up with a pastel plaid, or a yellow-and-white gingham spread tied up with a yellow-green-and-white sprigged calico.

"Tie up" a little girl's wall with a floor-to-ceiling bow you paint or tape onto the wall. And while you're being artistic with paint or tape, letter your bow with the child's name.

▶ *Decorate with the letters of the alphabet!* You could start by painting walls sunshine yellow, then stenciling your child's initial, giant-size, in fire-engine red above the head of the bed. In a little girl's room, you might adorn the initial with handpainted flowers of pink, sky-blue, and sunshine-yellow flowers with green leaves. Cover the bed with a pretty floral calico spread in pinks, yellow, red, and blues. And add a fire-engine-red shag carpet, too.

While you're at it, wouldn't your little boy or girl love to see his or her name on the door? Paint the door to your child's room a happy color and use white press-on letters, purchased in an art supply store, to spell out the child's name. The letters come in various styles and sizes up to three inches high. They can be used as well to mark the contents of colorful toy-storage boxes.

▶ *Refurbish an old stepladder.* In the hands of the do-it-yourselfer, the old wooden kitchen stepladder can become a fun decorative accessory piece for the a child's room.

The first step is to create shelves by nailing a piece of wood of proper dimension, front to back, on the two narrow steps and top surface. You can then lacquer your ladder and shelves bright red or another color to complement your color scheme.

For a little boy's room, I could see a ladder with its frame painted bright royal blue and the shelves wrapped in red-and-white ticking. For a little girl's room, a ladder lacquered petal pink or covered in a pink-and-white garden-flowers vinyl wallcovering would be fun and delightful.

▶ *Staple it.* Lots of do-it-yourselfers have discovered the staple gun for home-decorating tasks. You can buy one for under $10, and a box of staples for a dollar or less. It's a fast, fun way to accomplish a great many decorating tasks.

Try striping the headboard wall in a boy's room with the help of the staple gun. All you have to do is cut ceiling-do-floor lengths of fabric into 3-inch widths, then staple the fabric stripes to the way at the top and bottom, leaving three inches between each stripe. Finish by gluing a border of 2-inch-wide grosgrain ribbon to the top and bottom of the wall to cover up the staples.

You can staple a colorful lining to the inside backs of storage units, too. Rmove shelves when lining, if possible, so you can cover the back in one piece. If shelves are not removable, cut fabric to fit back spaces and staple into place, trimming away any excess fabric with a razor blade. To cover staples, apply a narrow piece of matching fabric with paste. Or you can paste attractive gimp over the staples. Gimp, which is a flat trimming or edging, usually of cord, is available in the notions departments of local stores.

Another easy project is stapling a low-maintenance fabric onto slip-seat pull-up chairs for a child's room. Each seat probably requires about a half-yard of fabric; and be certain to purchase a fabric that has a bit of give as you will have to pull the fabric over the seat. Staples should be applied to underside.

Lots of people are also discovering that shag carpeting can be easily stapled into place. If you plan on carpeting your child's room, why not try the staple method of installation? Choose shag carpeting that does not have a heavy backing, order a piece slightly larger than the area to be covered, and lay carpet from one wall to the opposite. Cut off the excess after stapling is completed.

▶ *Try carpet tiles.* These 12-inch carpet squares with latex foam backing are "in" with do-it-yourself homemakers on budgets. They're easy to install, and I particularly like them for children's rooms because you can easily replace a worn or badly soiled spot by installing a new square. Carpet tiles also are washable and, because they're rubber-backed, skidproof.

One should begin installing the tiles from the center of the room, working to the walls. (Find the center by stretching two lengths of string from corners to opposite corners to form an X, then center the first tile under the point where they intersect.) It's easy to cut carpet tiles with either a carpet knife or scissors.

I recently used carpet tiles in a children's room to create a decorative geometric pattern with three different colors—orange, gold, and green—and it was truly a fall inspiration. Walls were painted gold, white-lacquered louvered shutters with brass pulls were installed at windows, and furniture was white plastic laminate. Bedspreads were of orange corduroy, accented with pillows of gold and green corduroy.

► *Frame it.* Art belongs in children's rooms as well as any other place in the house, even if you can't afford the kind of artwork and framing you splurged on for the living room.

Colorful, inexpensive posters are a great solution. They pack a lot of punch, and their small cost means they can be replaced as the child grows and changes. I like to see posters used headboard-fashion in a child's room. You can frame them yourself by mounting on plywood and nailing lath strips around, enameled or left natural. Or you can have them framed by a professional the new, inexpensive way: The framer first mounts the poster on a stiff backing, then applies decorative tape around the edge to provide a narrow "frame." Finally, the backed poster is laminated with a clear plastic film.

An even better source of artwork for your child's walls is your child's own work. Children's art is colorful, abstract, primitive, and fascinating. If you've been giving it short shrift by sticking it on the wall with Scotch tape, make it more important by framing it, and watch your child's eyes light up! One easy way to do it is with plywood, cut larger than the picture by about 3 inches on all sides. Wrap the plywood with solid-color or print fabric that goes well with your color scheme and ties in with the picture's colors, then center the picture on it and glue down. Trim the edge where paper meets fabric with contrasting ribbon, braid, or bias tape and you're done—unless you want to frame the whole

with lath strips painted to match the interior trim.

► *Whip up some pillows.* Think of all the wonderful decorating tricks you can do with simple pillows you make yourself: colorful pillows to brighten a drab room; ruffled pillows to soften a too-tailored room; pillows to add soft comfort to hard chairs; and pillows, on a grand scale, to substitute for furniture or to supplement conventional furniture.

To decorate an older child's room with pillow furniture, build a low plywood platform along one wall for seating, and top with a row of fat colorful pillows in a corduroy print of poppy red, sunny yellow, and white on a forest-green ground. Carpet the room and the platform in poppy-red shag. Walls can be sunny yellow. Use the corduroy print for a tailored bedspread and top the bed with lots of colorful pillows in red, yellow, and green. For extra seating, pile three or four giant floor pillows, covered in red, in a corner.

If you want to make your own pillows, here are a few important tips that will help you get a professional look:

1. Always cut fabrics with the grain so that your rectangles and squares have neat straight edges.

2. Cut your fabric at least ½ inch narrower all around than you want your finished pillow to be. This will give you a nice plump look when your pillow is stuffed.

3. Always make pillow covers with zippers so that covers are easy to remove and clean.

► *Try prepasted wallpapers.* If you tried papering a room a few years ago and swore never to do it again, give it one more chance—with prepasted wallpapers. There's no more trimming the edges, no more pails of glue to mix and mess with; these papers are pretrimmed, scrubbable, and strippable, and they come in a host of designs.

Prepasted paper can be installed easily on a painted wall or one that was wallpapered previously (not with vinyl, however). If the wall has been painted with enamel, be certain to sandpaper the slick finish before attempting to hang the new paper.

When installing prepasted wallpapers (which are available in widths of 27 inches or 21½ inches), the do-it-yourselfer needs the following: scissors, a sponge, a razor blade, a putty knife or a straightedge ruler, and a water box (available at any hardware store for about $1.50) filled with lukewarm water. In cutting strips, allow a little extra for overlapping at ceiling and baseboard. Roll a strip from bottom to top, glue-side out, and dip it in the water box for about thirty seconds—or until the water stops bubbling. Then lift it by its top edge and apply from the top down. You'll find that prepasted wallpaper goes up in a jiffy, strip after strip. Smooth out any wrinkles or bubbles with a wet sponge, working from the middle out, then trim the excess at ceiling and baseboards with your razor blade, using the putty knife as a straightedge.

In a colonial bedroom I am designing for a young girl, I'm using a prepasted wallpaper with bright, happy flowers in pinks, oranges, and greens on a white background White crisscross organdy curtains was my selection for windows, and I also chose white organdy for the bedskirt, used with a pink quilted spread. The colonial furniture, a set from the attic, was lacquered white and the brass hardware polished up. White-painted rocking chairs, used as lounge chairs, were decorated with orange-white-and-pink plaid cushions tied on with orange grosgrain ribbon. The prepasted wallpaper was also used to cover an old trunk at the foot of the bed, as well as a wastebasket in the adjoining bathroom. And bathroom walls and ceiling were covered with the same floral paper.

▶ *Build a wall of cubes.* For a young child's room where storage is needed for books, toys, and everything else, you can make a complete wall of cubes, stacked one on top of the other. The cubes can be painted in alternate colors of red, white, and blue lacquer, or, if you prefer, all cubes can be painted one bright color—perhaps paprika orange or fire-engine red—to complement his decor.

Easy-Maintenance Suggestions

I met a young mother of four recently who told me, "I'm so tired of cleaning up after my kids!"

You probably are too. But do you know that you can liberate yourself from many tiresome cleanup chores simply by decorating the children's rooms with easy care in mind?

The young mother of four finally did just that. First, she provided storage facilities that the children can easily use themselves—large bins for stashing toys; and hooks, instead of hangers, for hanging clothing. Next she has purchased furniture that sits directly on the floor so there's no need to clean underneath—or crawl underneath looking for lost shoes and toys. (The bed's platform, by the way, houses extra storage space in the form of roomy roll-out drawers.) Bed-making can be done by the children themselves because instead of cumbersome bedspreads this smart mother chose colorful blankets and fitted sheets that match the room's emerald-green and fire-engine-red decor. A colorful red-and-green tartan carpet of tough nylon is flat and dense, providing an easy-to-clean surface that's also great to play on. The pattern, by the way, hides spots and soil.

All furniture in the boys' room is painted with washable emerald-green and white paint, and the tailored campaign styling is a look they won't outgrow for years to come.

Here are some ideas that may help to make *your* life easier.

▶ *Use chests for storage.* Did you know that for many hundreds of years the chest was the most important piece of furniture a family could have? Back in the early days of our country, chests held all of a family's possessions. When the family moved, so did the chest and the worldly goods within.

Today, chests and their kissin' cousins, trunks, are still excellent choices for clearing children's rooms of clutter. Even young children who can't reach high shelves can learn to keep their own rooms neat by returning toys to low chests.

A wicker chest, painted a happy color, is a pretty way to solve storage woes in a girl's bedroom. Picture that brass-trimmed wicker chest painted a cheery lemon yellow. Walls can be lemon yellow, too. And for bedspread and draperies, how about a wicker print in grass green, lemon yellow, and white? And don't forget a grass-green shag carpet underfoot!

A boy's room I visited recently had two small, squarish, knotty pine chests on either side of the bed. Those chests neatly held toys, games—you name it. Wall-mounted lamps on either side of the bed provided light for bedtime stories while keeping the tops of the chests free for easy open-

Easy care and good looks come together in an emerald-green, red, and white boy's room carpeted in colorful green-and-red tartan-pattern nylon.

ing. The bedspread on the pine-framed bed was a flag-blue-and-white Early American woven pattern in a flower design with borders woven in a locomotive design. Walls were covered in a scrubbable vinyl stripe of patriotic red, white, and blue, and on the floor there was a cheery fire-engine-red carpet.

► *Try sleeping bags.* Sleeping bags filled with down are now part of the decorating scene in the children's or teenagers' rooms. Many a mother, weary of trying to keep the children's beds made, has resorted to topping the beds with sleeping bags instead of quilts or blankets. The sleeping bag, which I hope is filled with down, can be kept rolled up at the foot of the bed or can be pulled up to cover the bed in place of a spread—sleeping-bag covers are very colorful and decorative these days, you know.

A busy working mom of my acquaintance has chosen the best of both worlds for her son's room. His bunk beds are made up with channel-quilted down comforters, but to sleep overnight guests there are a few down sleeping bags rolled up in the closet. The sleeping bags, however, aren't

strictly for company; when her son goes camping or sleeps over at a friend's, he takes one along. The room has lots of other fun features, too. My favorites are the snappy blue-and-green tartan carpet—the pattern hides soil—and the super-graphic blinds of royal blue, emerald green, and sunny yellow.

► *Create a small playroom.* Even a very small room in your home that's not being used to any real purpose can be turned into a playroom for the children. And being the father of young sons, I have learned the need of such a room in a home with children; otherwise you can be certain that toys will be all over the house.

Begin by building seating units around the perimeter of the entire room, directly against all walls except the doorway so you have ample space left in the center of the room for toy boxes, carts, wagons, etc., as well as for a game table. The units can be created by building a platform of plywood, maybe 9 inches or so off the floor, around the room. The depth should be some 36 inches. To really maximize your space, you can hinge the seats of the built-ins, and use the platforms for storage. Paint the platform a gay color, perhaps red enamel, and top with foam mattresses and wedge-shaped foam bolsters. Cover the bolsters and mattresses with a sturdy, colorful fabric, such as green corduroy, which can be easily zipped off and thrown into the washing machine.

For flooring, choose a durable vinyl—I would like a black-and-white checkerboard design; laid on the diagonal, the squares will make your small playroom look larger.

For wallcovering, choose a vinyl of a happy color. With green corduroy bolsters and mat-tresses on a red-lacquered platform base, what about red walls? Hang children's art and family creations on the walls for the very personal touch.

And for toy storage, if you haven't provided it under the seating, what about using heavy cardboard file boxes, 14 to 16 inches high, which have been painted happy colors? Paint each toy box a different color—perhaps red for one young-ster and yellow for another. The painted file boxes, put together, can make a colorful table, too.

Redecorating the Teen-ager's Room

A lot has changed in the teen-ager's room since I was a high-school boy. In those days, a corduroy bedspread, a maple bedroom "suite," and a wall covered with pennants was all a boy needed. For girls, the look was all pink frills and ruffles.

Today's teen-agers are different, and so are their bedrooms. Many young teens these days want an all-purpose room where they can sleep, do homework, entertain friends, even hold small parties. Such a room might be furnished with a sleep sofa or studio couch and a wall storage unit for books, clothing, and sports equipment.

Other teens, particularly those with small rooms, might like the novelty of a loft bed with desk and storage space built in below. By getting the bed off the floor, you leave most of the floor area free for hobbies and crafts or for trying out the latest dance steps!

And I know many a teen-age girl or boy who would love the cozy privacy of a sleeping alcove complete with shelf space and telephone. In the room pictured, the alcove was created by building a plywood arch around the bed. To highlight the architectural effect, two wallcoverings were used —a yellow-and-white stripe on the arch and a feminine print in pink, coral, orange, tomato, and bright greens for other wall areas. Track lighting was concealed behind the arch to light the alcove. A hand-me-down dresser and old ice-cream parlor chairs were given new life with white paint. The dresser front has also been brightened with "de-cals" cut from leftover wallpaper. A cheerful bed-spread, dust ruffle, and table skirt are all made from five-and-dime coral and white polka-dotted cotton. The look is grown-up and lighthearted at the same time.

Trundle beds are another good idea for teen rooms. And did you know that they actually came

Bunk beds are ideal for one overnight guest in a boy's room, but how do you sleep more than one visitor? In a puffy, down-filled sleeping bag! It tucks into the closet ready to be brought out for company or for camping trips.

over on the *Mayflower*? The "truckle beds" of our ancestors were for the children of the family. To save space in cramped quarters, the trundle bed was slipped under the larger bed when it was not in use.

Looking around today, I see that the concept of the trundle bed has never really left us. Convertible sofas of all kinds, high-risers, and convertible ottomans are all descendants of the humble trundle bed. One of the latest and greatest variations is a full-size foam "mattress" that folds lengthwise to form a sofa with back. A strap-and-snap arrangement keeps the "sofa" from popping open. I'd like to see one of these cozy sofas in a teen-ager's room in poppy orange. Put a lamp and roomy table nearby and you have an attractive reading area.

The new illuminated furniture is a great look for teen rooms. Today wall units are glowing with soft illumination; cube tables are shining brightly; even antique furniture is being wired for light, light, light!

In a young man's bedroom, all the decorative excitement was provided by illuminated furniture. The room was painted a rich bottle green, with bedspread and shag carpet of the same shade. The wall unit was lacquered bottle green and illuminated. Magic flowed from that green-lacquered wall unit, which glowed softly from within, and from an illuminated bedside table of acrylic. Shoji screens at the windows with green-lacquered frames were also illuminated, by small bulbs placed on the sill between the windows and the screens.

You can achieve the look yourself without too much difficulty. Light shelves from the side by installing bulbs along the inner edge of the unit's front, or install bulbs under each shelf to light the shelf below. In either case, bulbs should, of course, be hidden by a cover or strip of wood. Hiding the workings of your lighting is part of the magic.

Put a little humor into your teen-ager's room—it will make the atmosphere more friendly.

For a young man with a sense of humor, we styled a bedroom with golden yellow walls, white trim, carpeting of brown-and-gold tweed, and a bedspread of a plaid in brown, golden yellow, and white. Humorous posters ware hung on the walls, and a sturdy work table/desk of chrome and pecan vinyl veneer was accessorized with a fish tank. Since height-conscious teen-age boys like to keep daily tabs on their progress, we included a giant-size measuring stick, hung on the wall next to the desk.

You'll find wallpapers and fabrics with a humorous touch all over the market. A word of caution about humorous wallcoverings, though: Just as the same old joke ceases to amuse, wallpaper humor can grow stale after a while. A wallcovering that pleases at the same time that it amuses will not go out of style.

Paper furnishings and accessories are fun, too—and very much in the news. Paper furniture, paper lamps, and paper decorative accessories got their start hundreds of years ago in the Orient, and today the East still supplies us with many decorative paper objects.

I like those Japanese white paper lamps in rounds or ovals. And did you know that Japanese paper lamps come in cube shapes too, for stacking?

Furniture makers these days are turning out snap-together furniture of paper—corrugated cardboard to be more precise. The cardboard furniture comes in bright hues—red is my favorite—and it would be perfect for a teen-ager's room. Decorate a young man's room using a couple of boxy red cardboard chairs as a focal point. Other furniture can be dark wood. For the bedspread, choose tough emerald-green sailcloth piped in red. Use the sailcloth for café curtains too, hung from red poles with red rings. For carpeting, a red-and-green tartan world be a good choice. Cover the walls in rich brown cork, and paint the ceiling sky blue. Accessorize the dark cork walls with Oriental paper kites; they come in many designs—dragons, fish, mask heads—and are great wall accessories for decorators on low budgets. Paper accessories of another kind could take

An ordinary teen's room becomes something special when the bed is tucked into a "privacy alcove" where books, prized possessions, and a telephone are all close at hand. Two complementary wallcoverings underline the architectural effect and set a lighthearted mood.

Heywood-Wakefield's trundle bed

JS/Permaneer's sturdy work table/d‹

Humorous posters and a giant graphic ruler hung on walls lend a light and friendly touch to this teen-age boy's room. The work table/desk provides ample area for study or work projects, and matching sliding-door record cabinet and wall units offer roomy storage space. Walls are golden yellow, carpeting is brown-and-gold tweed, and the bedspread is a brown-gold-and-white plaid.

their place in a girl's pretty, old-fashioned bedroom. I'm talking about old, lacy valentines purchased in antique shops. Matted in pastel colors and framed in handsome dark wood or gilt frames, they'd be the perfect touch in a Victorian- or Edwardian-style room.

You and your teen-ager can have fun decorating his or her room together with dyes. You can dye a white cotton table skirt your teen-ager's favorite color. They are available in powder and liquid form—in fact, there are eighteen liquid colors and thirty-five powder colors as of this writing, and of course you can mix your own colors by following the color recipes.

Lots of teens tie-dye their own wearing apparel, and I know people who have tie-dyed their living-room slipcovers, too. In this method of dying, you create interesting designs by tying portions of the fabric so that it will not absorb the dye. Visualize this teen-age girl's room: Walls are painted frosty white, and the floor is covered with a tangy tangerine shag. The white bedspread has been tie-dyed with tangerine and yellow irregular sunbursts. White cotton curtains are hung on yellow poles, and a table is skirted in tangerine. The room is exciting yet simple, and you could translate it into your teen-ager's favorite colors.

Off to College:
Decorating the Dormitory Room

Now I'm writing to all those bound for college—those who will be living in dormitories for the next few years.

Oh, those dreary dormitory rooms! I remember them from my own college days at Oberlin—and I remember how some students transformed them, with more imagination than cash.

One of the first things you'll need to make your room more inviting is a comfortable chair of some kind. You probably won't want to go out and buy a new one, nor should you; part of the fun of dormitory decorating is doing it on a budget. So ask relatives if they have a chair they no longer want, or scout the junk stores near the college for a suitable one.

For those living in unfurnished dormitory facilities, the junk store offers endless possibilities. One recent college graduate I know decorated her entire room the junk-store way. She and her roommate bought chairs, lamps, pictures, even two old patchwork quilts to brighten their room. The quilts served as bedspreads.

And speaking of bedspreads—those used in college dorms take a beating, believe me, and should always be chosen for strength and washability as well as for good looks. Flimsy Indian cottons won't hold up, particularly if the bed doubles as a sofa. Good choices are corduroy, denim, sailcloth, or heavy cotton-polyester blends. Since the bed will certainly be used for sitting and lounging when friends drop by, I like a pair of bolsters covered to match the spread.

And don't overlook decorative accessories when feathering your college nest. There's no reason why a dorm room must be as bare and spartan as a prison cell. Look for attractive lamps for desks. Look for colorful desk accessories. Look for old picture frames to hold personal photographs or colorful prints. (I prefer the look of framed pictures to unframed ones.)

For the floor, a shaggy rug of washable fake fur or a colorful carpet remnant is a warming, homey touch.

5

The Dining Room

There are three types of dining rooms—the full room reserved for dining; the "dining room" referred to as a "dining area" because it's really part of the living room; and the breakfast room. The second type, the living/dining combination, is the one most frequently found in today's new homes and apartments, so it might be best to begin our discussion there.

The Living/Dining Room

The living/dining room combination is a decorating challenge. What you want to avoid is the cramped, cluttered look that results from squeezing too much furniture into a relatively small area.

Avoid a crowd scene in your living/dining room by choosing furniture that can serve more than one purpose—convertible sofas that double as beds in a one-room studio apartment; upholstered dining chairs that double as comfy occasional chairs; a dining table or console table that doubles as a desk and work area for hobbies.

Make your room seem even more spacious by selecting airy-looking furniture—furniture with long legs, for instance, and see-through furniture of glass or acrylic.

You can heighten the spacious look with a monochromatic color scheme for carpet, walls, upholstery, and accessories. A scheme of greens with touches of white would be a happy choice. I recently saw a charming living/dining room combination that featured a cool, summery patchwork-design fabric in mint, lime green, and white on sofa upholstery, console and bunching tables, and also on walls. High-back dining chairs and club chair were upholstered in lettuce green, and dining chairs were paired with a see-through glass-and-chrome trestle table. The color underfoot was cool lime, a mix of sherbet and mint, in shag carpet with bands of low loop pile running throughout to create a suggestion of tracery.

Let's visit a typical furniture "supermarket"—a store where the customer buys disassembled, crated furniture and puts it together at home—and fill our carts with the colorful wares we find for the living/dining room.

A monochromatic color scheme of greens and white unifies this living/dining room combination. A cool, summery patchwork-design fabric in mint, lime green, and white is used on bunching tables, console, sofa, and walls. Carpet in shades of mint and lime green sets the tone for the room.

Simple, molded-foam modular furniture is a staple of many furniture supermarkets. Let's pop a few units, covered in chocolate-brown canvas, into our shopping cart and move on to the chair department for a pair of brown-lacquered tubular-steel chairs with brown canvas seat and back pads. On to the rug department where we find a handsome 9 x 12 white sisal rug.

Now we need a dining table—and most furniture supermarkets have a wide selection. Choose a round, a rectangular Parsons, a lacquered, or a plastic-laminated model. For our living/dining room, my choice would be a Chinese-red laminated Parsons table and a group of dining chairs made of natural cane and tubular steel.

All our imaginary living room needs now is the background—how about walls painted warm peach melon?

Accessories—also found in many supermarket shops—can include brass floor lamps, colorful posters, large storage baskets, and colorful molded-plastic occasional tables.

Molded-plastic furniture, by the way, is a good choice for a young couple on a limited budget and for families with young children. (You know how hard kids can be on fine wood furniture.) And don't think for a minute that contemporary molded-plastic pieces belong only in contemporary surroundings. Whether your decor is Early American, traditional, or modern, believe me, the simple lines of molded plastic will blend.

For a cozy dining area under the stairs, how about a color scheme of rich coffee-bean brown and gold? Place a glass-topped molded-plastic table and molded-plush chairs on an Oriental-style rug in golds, brown, ivory, and leaf green. Walls can be covered with another of my favorites —tortoise vinyl.

The living/dining room is also an ideal place to display a handsome cupboard. The armoire, the hutch, and the wardrobe belong in the cupboard family, and in my opinion every home should have at least one of these good-looking and functional pieces.

The owner of a country home I visited recently had a lovely old pine corner cupboard that was oh, so handy when table-setting time came around. There were the glasses, dishes, placemats, napkins, and silver all close at hand, and all attractively displayed, too, on open shelves lined in the same blue-and-white floral fabric that was used for café curtains.

A cupboard with open shelves can be a fine focal point for your living dining room when used to display colorful china, or glassware. I also like a hutch of dark polished wood or of homey pine in colonial-style decors. The hutch has always said colonial to me. An Early American living/dining room I saw recently featured a hutch on one wall. The hutch's open shelves held a collection of pewter, china, and glassware. The rest of the room was comfortably furnished with sofas covered in a warm persimmon and a club chair done in handsome burnished gold. For color contrast, walls were papered in a narrow blue-and-white striped wallcovering. The carpet was a pretty pale gold that complemented the rich wood of the hutch and the polished dining table.

Banquettes are a good choice for seating in a dining area that's part of the living room. An L-shaped banquette built into a corner of the dining area can comfortably seat four people around a circular or square table and folding chairs can be set up for extra seating when guests come. Moreover, banquettes with hinged seats can provide valuable extra storage space.

The easiest way to create a banquette is with plywood. Simply build an oblong box of the desired length and place against the wall. The sides of the box can be carpeted to match the floor carpet, or can be padded and covered in fabric. For comfort, the depth of the box should not exceed 20 inches and there should be a backrest at least 5 inches deep. For back support, I

The contemporary lines of molded-plastic table and chairs in espresso brown plus the traditionally patterned Oriental rug in rich gold tones add up to cozy dining.

Karpen's Herculean-covered sofa and cha

*A comfortable colonial living/dining room features sofas and chairs in persimmon
and gold and a spacious hutch filled with prized antiques.*

would suggest a firm foam-rubber bolster. And
to soften the look, toss cushions galore.

Whatever the size of your dining area and whatever you choose for furnishing it, make sure it
has personality.

Give your dining area personality with a focal
point—an antique chandelier or Tiffany lamp, a
beautifully lit painting or a wall of colorful plates.

Give your dining area personality with color.

Since the area is small, don't be afraid to wash
it with a coat of brilliant color. In a gold-and-
green living room, I can picture a rich gold or
persimmon dining area.

Give your dining area personality with an
exciting wallcovering, one you might not dare use
on the large expenses of the living-room wall. In
the room pictured, a tiny, intimate dining area
with a big personality focuses on a red-and-gold
geometric wallcovering. The sparkling gold and
rich red give the area a festive look that is

carried over to red-lacquered Chippendale-style chairs matched with an airy bamboo-and-glass table for four.

Where do you store tableware and such in a small dining area? Here the problem is solved beautifully with stacks of Chinese wicker suitcases. One holds the silver chest, another the place mats, and two more are filled with tablecloths. Above the "storage" area, a red-lacquered shelf neatly solves the serving problem.

In a small dining area like this one, beware of the overpowering window treatment. Here the solution is a plywood frame that neatly splits a too-wide window into two manageable rectangles. The window is simply treated with narrow-slat blinds and the frame is covered with wallcovering.

Red woodwork, a red-stencil-bordered ceiling,

plus wicker baskets of plants, add to the dining drama.

You'll notice that in this dining area a table for four was used. It's a very popular size for small city dining areas. Another good choice is a 48-inch round table with a see-through top and see-through chairs that will appear to take no space at all.

Otto Preminger, the movie producer and director, likes the look of see-through furniture in small spaces and large spaces, too, for the airy feeling. In fact he told me once that he was furnishing a house completely in the see-through look!

If you are budget conscious, a skirted round table is an ideal answer for a dining area where

"Sansui" Mylar wallcovering by Sieglinde

A tiny, intimate dining area with a big personality focused on a red-and-gold geometric wallcovering. The sparkling gold and rich red give the area a festive look that is carried over to red-lacquered Chippendale-style chairs together with an airy bamboo-and-glass table for four.

the look you've decided on is one of casual charm. You can use a stock metal restaurant table and skirt it to the floor. Restaurant tables come in all sizes, but my favorite is the 60-inch round with padded top. You can make floor-length table skirts for all seasons of the year. For summertime, what about gay polka dots, a daisy print, or a gingham check? For the fall, you can use felt or a gay country print.

In the charming dining area of her vacation house, a friend of mine used a round table skirted to the floor in a dainty white floral print on a blue background. Dining-seat covers and napkins, too, were of the same print. The blue-and-white-skirted table was decorated with a vase of yellow and white daisies and sat on a blue-and-green sculptured carpet. Above the table a large white Japanese lantern was hung. Walls of the dining area were covered with a supergraphic wallpaper with a white background and bold beige design, which cleverly concealed handy storage cabinets. Windows, with light curtains of modacrylic, were filled with white pots containing colorful blooming plants.

For the casual way of dining, here is a dining table in the round, skirted to the floor in a dainty blue-and-white fabric. Chair seats are covered in the same print. Blue-and-green patterned carpet is of sculptured polyester.

"Arista" carpet by Collins & Aikm

You can dress up casual dining tables in no time at all with low vases of floating flowers, a cornucopia filled with vegetables, or a basket-of-fruit centerpiece. And what wonders for a casual dining area when the color scheme comes directly from the fruit bowl. Paint dining-room walls the color of honeydew melon, and hang flower-print draperies in shades of honeydew, cantaloupe, and purple grape. Chair upholstery can be a practical cantaloupe-colored fabric. For the area rug, I would suggest deep grape.

The Separate Dining Room

If you're lucky enough to have a whole room for dining, no matter how small, make it unique, and those wonderful, family-time holidays might be just the moment to effect the transformation.

Where can you come up with a reasonably priced, sturdy table to replace your old, down-at-the-heels model?

Some of the cleverest hostesses I know solve that problem by using big, round restaurant tables. You can find them in eateries that are going out of business or in restaurant supply stores. (Call ahead to make sure they'll sell to a retail customer.) Buy the kind that has leaves that drop down to convert the table into a square.

The restaurant table is unsightly, to be sure, but you make it beautiful with a long, flowing skirt made of the permanent-press fabric of your choice. You might keep a dark, solid-color skirt on at all times and change the look with wash-able, short square overcloths. (Here's where the square cloths from your old table will come in handy.) The skirted-table look is soft and pretty, and, depending on the fabric you use, can work with any decor.

In a natural-look room, toss a beige-and-chocolate bamboo-print cloth over a long brown skirt. Try a real patchwork crib quilt or a square of patchwork-print fabric over a solid-color skirt in an Early American room.

If a quick overhaul is needed in the dining room, the most dramatic way to a new look is to change the background—that is, the walls and floor. For a warm traditional look to go with your antiques, choose a prepasted floral wallcovering of Williamsburg blue and white. Change the look at windows with a fabric that matches your wallcovering. Stitch fabric into simple floor-length panels that tie back by day, hang free at night for coziness and privacy.

Don't fret about a color scheme—simply look for the colors in your favorite china pattern. One handsome dining room I saw used simple blue-and-white willowware as the china service. Walls were richly lacquered deep blue, and trim and ceiling were bone-china white. Draperies were a soft blue shade from the willowware and trimmed with light blue and deep blue willowware-colored braid. On a pale blue area rug with sculptured border stood a white-lacquered dining table and white Chinese fretwork chairs with seats covered in deep-blue velvet. A crystal chandelier with candle bulbs covered with white pleated shades was hung above the dining table. The entire look of the dining room was superb, especially when the white-lacquered table was set with rich blue place mats, crystal glasses, and, of course, with the room's entire inspiration—the blue willow-ware.

One of my favorite china patterns is all flowers and leaves on a white background, so delicate and soft in color. For a dining room decorated around this pattern, there are lots of color choices for walls—pale yellow, soft blue, delicate pink, and, of course, white. If this is your china pattern, why not paint walls white and the molding and door trim metallic gold? Paint ceiling pale pink. Hang polished-cotton draperies of a floral design—maybe pink and soft blue morning glories en-twined with green leaves on a white background. Lay a morning-glory-blue carpet under a ma-hogany dining table and framed chairs. The chairs can be covered in pale yellow, pale pink, or vine green.

Even if your china pattern is white and gold, you can create a room to flatter it. Cover the walls above a white dado with a gold-flocked damask design on a white background. At windows hang gold silk or taffeta curtains under gold valances; draperies can be hung over white Austrian shades. Choose an off-white area rug with sculp-tured border. Cover the seats of fruitwood-framed dining chairs with a gold-and-white cut-velvet stripe. In the center of your dining table, set with the gold-and-white service, place a low, hand-some arrangement of white and pink tea roses. A large colorful gold-framed painting, maybe a still life or a landscape, would be an eye attraction over a large fruitwood service buffet.

For those of you whose china patterns are less than inspiring, here are some other suggestions for choosing a color scheme or a special look for your dining room.

GO WITH GREEN

The green light is permanently flashing on Decorating Street, U.S.A. Never have I seen so many people selecting green for upholstery, carpeting, furnishing—just about everything that goes into the home.

The "Go" light is on green-grained furniture, which can be most attractive in brilliantly colored rooms. Many of these grained furnishings are trimmed in a contrasting color—some in red, others in yellow, and still others with white or russet trim.

Why not try green-grained wood furniture in your dining room if you're looking for a new touch? Cover walls with an olive-green-and-white checked wallcovering (the pattern should resemble a café tablecloth) over a dado painted bright white. I would recommend fire-engine-red carpeting; and louvered shutters, also of fire-engine red, would be a welcoming note at your windows. Seats of the green-grained wood dining chairs can be covered in a fabric matching the wallpaper. Lots of greenery in natural straw baskets or clay pots would complete the setting.

If you are a green thinker, you can come up with a host of different shades of green that are so great on today's decorating scene—apple green, emerald green, kelly green, chartreuse, sea green, pea green, avocado, and many more.

After a concert my wife Suzanne and I often enjoy a late-night snack at a New York City landmark—the Russian Tea Room. And for all those people who have been searching for a great look for the dining room or dining area, let it be known that I found it there.

The exciting mood at the Russian Tea Room begins with walls of a rich fir-tree green (somewhere between hunter and emerald.) The color is as relaxing as can be. For contrast, tables are covered with pretty pink cloths, over poppy-red cloths!

To keep things from looking too dark, there's lots of sparkle everywhere. The RTR is the only place I know of where Christmas decorations are left up all year round—how festive can you get—

so there's a bit of tinsel here and a string of red Christmas balls there. And there's more sparkle in a narrow strip of mirror that runs around the room, right above the top of the wall-mounted banquettes. The mirror is there so that patrons who face the wall can still engage in the RTR's favorite sport—people watching. For an added touch of magic, those dark green walls are hung top to bottom with paintings of every description —seascapes, landscapes, portraits—you name it.

If you would like to create a bit of that Russian Tea Room excitement in your own home, start with the most important ingredient: those dark green walls.

Carpet in the same rich hue. Instead of the solid pink used at the Russian Tea Room, choose a floral fabric for draperies and chair upholstery: a design of pretty pinks, burgundy, and hunter green on a white ground.

For contrast with all the dark green, I would like chairs lacquered pale shell pink around a table of glass and sparkling brass. Overhead, hang a sparkling chandelier of crystal and brass.

When setting that table, my choice would be poppy-red place mats, pink-and-white flowered china, and glittering cut crystal with a centerpiece of red and pink carnations.

A BOUQUET OF GERANIUMS

Summer is scarlet and pink geraniums with their ruffled leaves spilling out of window boxes, lining porches, and peeping from city windows and terraces. And did you know that those geraniums are a terrific source of decorating inspiration?

Geranium-print fabrics are all over the market right now and would be a welcome addition to any room of the house. Picture a bouquet print of red geraniums tied with sky-blue ribbons on a white ground used to upholster the seats of white-lacquered dining chairs. The walls of that dining room can be pale geranium pink. To contrast with those pale walls, I would stain the wood floor ebony. At windows I would hang floor-length draperies of the geranium print. And of course those windowsills would hold many pots of pink and red geraniums.

My table choice would be a geranium-red Parsons-type table set with place mats of the geranium print.

A BASKET OF SHELLS

As I've said before, I find shells a great source of inspiration, for dining rooms and for every room in the house. I love their interesting shapes, and obviously other designers agree with me. I have never seen so many super shell looks in decorating. Fabric designers are coming up with shell-design fabrics in natural colors and brighter hues.

Shell colors are naturally harmonious, so with a shell-inspired color scheme you can't go wrong. Take the handsome conch shell, for instance, with its dappled beige-and-white exterior and glowing pink interior. Wouldn't that beige-white-and-pink scheme translate beautifully into a dining room? I would paint walls soft shell pink with white trim. At windows, hang shell-print cotton draperies of beige, pink, and white, and line those draperies in soft conch-shell pink. Use the shell fabric for upholstery on a set of fully upholstered high-backed dining chairs and finish with pink braid. I picture those chairs grouped around an oval table lacquered shell beige. Cover the floor with a chevron-patterned rug of beige and white. On one wall I would hang a shell-framed mirror. And when setting the table I would center it with a basket of shells and a group of shell candle holders. Set each place with pink linen place mats and matching napkins rolled into shell napkin rings.

THE SPATTERED LOOK

The word "spatter" is usually associated with unwanted spots on the kitchen wall. But there's another kind of spatter that is far from unwanted in the decorating world—I'm referring to spatter painting and spatter-look fabrics and wallcoverings.

I have personally spatter-painted many flowers and walls in my day, and you don't have to be a Rembrandt to do it. Simply paint your floor or wall the background color of your choice, choose one or two colors to spatter, dip your brush, and shake. That's all spatter painting is, you know—shaking the paint off the brush so that it forms interesting drips and spots of color. Even a child can do it.

The spatter look, as you can imagine, is a great soil hider, but it's more than practical and fun to do—it's pretty, too. In fact, so good-looking that wallcovering and fabric manufacturers have made the spatter look their own.

How about a dining-room scheme with spatter-print wallpaper of spring green, hyacinth blue, lemon yellow, and white? In the room I picture tiebacks of matching fabric trimmed in spring green, and they frame spring-green window shades and café curtains of green-blue-and-white checked cotton. Antique pine ladder-backs with seat pads of the check are pulled up to an antique table of mellow wood. The green of the spatter-print walls is picked up in a chandelier fitted with old-fashioned green glass shades and in a pine hutch filled with green butterfly china.

TOILE

Toile—or more accurately *toile de Jouy*—is that, oh, so pretty scenic fabric depicting French aristocrats and peasants at work and play. Despite its French name it was developed by a German, Christophe Phillippe Oberkampf, in the eighteenth century. The aristocrats of the day were crazy for print fabrics from the Far East, so Oberkampf set up shop in Jouy, a town near Versailles, to try his hand at reproducing the popular Eastern prints. But soon he turned his talents to the more familiar scenes of French life he saw around him—and those motifs are still loved today.

Oberkampf's fabrics came in only four colors—red, green, blue, or eggplant—all on a cream background. Today the choice of colors is wider and there are pure white backgrounds available in addition to the traditional cream.

I like red-and-cream toile wallpaper in a formal dining room above a wood-paneled dado. It's a super look with tieback draperies of a matching toile fabric. On a polished wood floor, under a mahogany or walnut dining room table and chairs, lay an Aubusson-type area rug in reds, pinks, and greens on a creamy background. Cover the seats of dining chairs in red cotton moiré. Leave your dining table uncovered so that warm polished wood shows, and make sure you include a centerpiece of red and white blooms and green ferns in a silver bowl.

Toile is a favorite with traditionalists, but that doesn't mean it can't work with contemporary furnishings. For example, you could do the same dining room in a less formal vein and still use the toile for walls and draperies. I would choose a

Spatter-print wallpaper is the perfect foil for rustic country pine furniture. Curtains are of the spatter print also and frame spring-geen window shades and checked café curtains.

white Parsons table. For chairs, I would use the high-back French country type. Lacquer the exposed arms and legs a bright Chinese red and upholster the seats and backs in red-and-white toile. Paint the paneled dado white and carpet in emerald green!

ARGYLE

Argyles are socking it to today's decorating, if you'll pardon the pun. At any rate, the argyle pattern is all over the home furnishings market.

The family of Argyle was originally a branch of the Scottish clan of Campbells from whose tartan the argyle design was adapted—the design being a geometric knitting pattern of varicolored diamonds in solid and outline shapes on a single background color. Many of us have been wearing the pattern for years—especially as socks. Now we are living with it in our homes. I guess if houndstooth can cross the bridge between clothes and home furnishings, why not argyle? I feel that argyle designs will soon be giving houndstooth a real race for the money—for the money in the wallcovering, carpet, and fabric fields, that is.

I have seen a host of great argyle-patterned carpets in royal blues with burgundy reds or with deep forest greens. Why not consider an argyle-patterned carpet for a contemporary dining room—maybe one that features mulberry, beige, and melon diamond geometrics on a pearly gray background. Paint walls a very pale pearl gray and all woodwork a shiny champagne-beige lacquer. At your windows hang beige open-weave casement curtains on a melon-colored pole. Spray the frames of bentwood chairs the same melon color as the curtain pole and cover chair seats in champagne-beige Naugahyde or rich mulberry suede. For the modern look, the dining table can be glass with a stainless-steel or chrome base. For the walls, lots of modern paintings, or you could hang a horizontal piece of argyle rug—maybe 6 feet long by 42 inches high. Place the piece of argyle rug on a canvas stretcher and frame with chrome stripping.

STRIPES

Stripes are great in dining rooms. There are carnival stripes in yellow, pink, white, and green. There are patriotic stripes of red, white, and blue. There are horizontal stripes and vertical stripes. There are ticking stripes in gray and white, blue and white, pink and white. And ticking stripes are no longer relegated to the box spring and mattress.

Stripes now climb the walls and stretch across floors. You've seen those striped rya-type area rugs, haven't you? Striped rugs can make a small, chubby room look longer and sleeker. And a striped carpet across the width of a narrow room can make that room look wider. Widen a narrow dining room by laying a vinyl flooring of stripes. I do it all the time by forming colorful stripes of 12-inch vinyl squares. Lay a stripe of red, then one of white, then one of blue. Cover walls above a white dado with red felt, and accessorize your dining room with a gallery of prints, paintings, and *objets d'art*.

If you are a traditionalist with mahogany dining-room furniture and you have an Oriental rug on the floor, there's no reason why you can't use a striped fabric for chair upholstery, draperies, and valances. Select a stripe that takes its colors right from the Oriental rug—perhaps a stripe of champagne beige, autumn orange, pale blue, and burgundy.

And going from the formal to the informal in dining, why not create a year-round summer delight by setting off a dining room/game room combination with a colorfully striped tent effect in cheerful poppy red, daffodil yellow, and snowdrop white? It successfully brings together indoor and outdoor living by framing both a garden view and a summery-looking white plastic table with tempered glass top and commodore chairs. White brick walls and white wall-to-wall carpeting enhance the outdoorsy, summer-garden feeling without competing with the view of the great outdoors.

PATTERNED SHEETS

Decorating a dining room with sheets is no longer news, but what continues to be news is the ever-growing selection of sheets to choose from. The homemaker who wants to decorate with sheets doesn't have to settle for pale, washed-out florals or polite little candy stripes. Today we have batiks, Navajo designs, and rich florals on dark or light backgrounds. We have Persian motifs, bold geometrics, even scenics. And did you know that for the first time ever a limited number of sheet patterns are now available in yard-goods form?

In other words, if you've been thinking about decorating with sheets, there's no time like the present. And sheet manufacturers are lending a hand, not only by offering a super selection of prints, but by offering instructions for making all sorts of things.

For instance, look in on the decorating service at your local department store. I stopped by recently at a display featuring a home economist on videotape who was demonstrating how to make lampshades, draperies, folding screens, harem pillows, tablecloths, dust ruffles, and more.

The demonstration inspired me to dream up a country dining room. I would use the sheets, shirred, on walls and would strip the woodwork and leave it natural. Ceiling and doors would be white. I pictured a natural wood floor, topped with a floral needlepoint rug in shades of yellow, pink, green, and blue on a cream ground. A table and chairs of rustic bleached pine with seat pads of apple green would be my choice, and I'd line a pine hutch with the sheet fabric to display pretty china. The table would be set with quilted placemats, grass-green pottery, and a centerpiece of pink and white geraniums with green leaves in a straw basket.

FOIL

Foil wallpapers are big decorating favorites. Nearly every client of mine today wants a touch of foil somewhere in the home.

Foil wallcoverings have that metallic look and you can find many different colors on the market. There are foils in silver, gold, blue, pink, and pale green. There are tortoiselike foils in a number of colors: mottled blue-and-silver combinations are very often seen, as are brown-beige-and-gold tortoise foil. There are foils on which designs are screened. There are white damasklike designs screened on all the background colors.

In a dining room I recently decorated I used a white damask pattern screened on a blue-and-silver tortoise foil. The pattern was used on all the walls, with white-lacquered woodwork and a royal-blue ceiling. Drapery in the room was white with a pale sky-blue swag valance. The valance and blue ceiling set the tone for a handsome crystal chandelier. Carpeting was a deep royal-blue velvet, and on it stood a white-lacquered Parsons dining table with modern chromium chairs whose backs and seats were upholstered in a rich banana-colored nylon. There were many colorful modern paintings on the walls, brought to full life with chromium picture lights. China used on the table was lemon and royal blue with a silver rim. The setting was truly a pleasant mix of traditional and contemporary styling.

When you are decorating the dining room, consider foil for the dramatic effect of today. The papers have a shimmery quality and are very exciting when proper lighting is used. Please don't tackle this paperhanging job yourself, however. Foils usually require a liner and are difficult to handle unless you're an expert.

BRASS

Remember when the word "brassy" was used to describe something brazen and crass? Of course, it still is. But in the world of furniture today, brass isn't crass, it's beautiful. And we're seeing a lot more of it, along with bronze and copper. These are what I call the warm metals, and they are definitely edging out the shinier, cooler look of chrome.

The brass I like best? I like it all. I love the bright gleam of polished brass andirons beside a stone or brick dining-room fireplace, and the glow of chunky polished-brass lamps illuminating a long buffet. When the look is natural, I like the softer, more subdued look of brushed or antiqued brass.

Want a super combination for dining chairs or occasional tables? Look for dark-stained rattan banded with antiqued brass or bronze. Combine it with a blue-and-white Oriental willowware wallcovering, off-white slipcovers, and snappy lacquer-red and black accessories and you've got a winning scheme.

The brass-and-glass table shown has a matching étagère and also a matching console table on casters that can be teamed with the dining table for large groups. The table's mellow brass frame is set off by a cheery scheme of cornflower blue for walls and dining chairs, blue-and-gold Bargello upholstery for side chairs, and accessories of bright peach.

THE TROPICAL LOOK

Take me to the tropics, and I don't mean because of the fuel oil shortage. I would love to be sitting under a mango tree someplace in a world of lush vegetation during the cold winter months. If you can't get yourself to an island this winter, you can certainly bring a bit of the tropics right into your small dining room with decorating touches.

Begin by selecting wallpaper with scattered island flowers on a white background. Add an area rug in tropical lime green and a compact table with a bamboo motif in antique yellow and a laminated pecan top. Seat pads of matching chairs can be covered in a green-and-yellow bamboo latticework print. For window treatment, no heavy curtains, please! Plain wood-slat blinds

A red-yellow-and-white carnival-striped tent effect brings together the great outdoors and the definitely great indoors in this combination dining room/game room. White brick walls, white carpeting, and white plastic glass-topped table and commodore chairs set just the right outdoor mood.

A bit of the tropics is reflected in this charming dining room accented with green plants and floral wallpaper with scattered colorful flowers on a white background. Junior dining group is made of hardwood in an antique yellow finish with a distinctive bamboo motif; tabletop is laminated pecan finish. Chair seats are soft green-and-yellow bamboo print, and carpeting is lively lime green.

Liberty Chair Co. dining group

will do the job effectively and airily, provided you hang some baskets of greenery from the ceiling in front of your window.

THE BUILT-IN LOOK

As you know, I rarely advocate built-ins for today's life-style because these days people are always on the move and built-ins are hard to take along.

As an alternative to real built-ins, I use free-standing look-alikes. I suggested an L-shaped banquette in our earlier discussion of living/dining areas, and I like its built-in look in dining rooms, too. The whole thing can be constructed of plywood platforms and loose pillows that are easy to take apart. I also love the built-in look of a corner cupboard, filled with pretty china and glassware. To make the built-in illusion work even better, I would line the corner cupboard with wallpaper to match the dining-room walls.

As an example, picture a dining room papered in a flowery batik of spicy mustard, magenta, royal blue, jungle green, and white. In the corner, I see a bamboo-trimmed corner cupboard, lined with the batik paper. And with those batik walls, wouldn't a natural wood floor and scorched bamboo roller-blinds be just the right touch? My choice for a table would be a circular natural

The mellow look of brushed brass on glass tables and étagère sparkle up a small blue-and-yellow dining room.

rattan model with a glass top, tucked into a corner banquette setup. And I would upholster those banquettes in a batik fabric to match the wallcovering.

If you have the space in your dining room, a wall of bookcases with a built-in look can be very effective. Built-in bookcases always remind me of a leathery English library, and what could be cozier? But if you've priced carpenters lately, you know that a whole wall of real built-in bookcases could break the Bank of England. The alternative? Free-standing look-alikes using stacking bookcases now on the market. They come in a range of wood finishes for a warm, mellow look.

THE GRAND-SCALE LOOK FOR A SMALL-SCALE ROOM

Do you think that the grand scale of things must be relegated to grand palaces and villas? Not so! I am a lover of the grand scale in decorating —plump furniture styles; large-scale floral prints; sumptuous, grandly scaled drapery treatments— and I believe that it can work even in a small house or apartment.

One of the most attractive dining rooms I've ever seen was the small but grand creation of a young bachelor. Walls were lacquered a rich chocolate brown, and the high ceiling was chocolate, too. On one of those dark walls the owner had hung a huge, colorful poster that extended from the floor to within a foot or two of the ceiling. Moldings, doors, and louvered shutters were all white. In the center of the room sat a simple Parsons-style table and, instead of skimpy, spindly chairs, fully upholstered Parsons-style chairs in a paisley print of chocolate, tomato red, and off-white. The total effect was really smashing.

If you're still in doubt, let me assure you that I've seen it work many, many times, as long as certain rules were followed.

First, large-scale furniture should not be confused with large furniture. I believe in the grand scale, but I don't believe in the impossible—such as trying to fit an 8-foot sofa into a 7-foot space. Grand-scale furniture can be a look, rather than an actual size. A 4-foot sofa, providing it is plumply upholstered and skirted right down to the floor, can be as grand as an 8-foot sofa.

Second, grandness should not be confused with price. An inexpensive 3-foot glass-topped coffee table will be much more grand-looking than a tiny one made of priceless woods inlaid with gold. And at windows, which do you think is grander-looking—two thin panels of precious raw silk, or yards and yards of less expensive cotton chintz? The silk has snob appeal, but the chintz is grander, believe me!

Grand-scale prints can also be used in small rooms. My only rule for doing so is to choose prints in bright, clear colors and pretty pastels.

THE PERIOD LOOK

The period look is achieved by mixing elements from your favorite period with other elements that brighten and update it to suit today's lifestyle. Here are some ideas you can try.

Queen Anne

I never tire of the beauty of Queen Anne furniture. The furniture designs of Queen Anne's reign (1702–14) were graceful and curvaceous. Chair backs were high and legs were cabriole (that's a leg that bulges at the top and curls out at the bottom). The scallop shell was a popular carved motif of the period.

With all that grace and charm going for it, is it any wonder that Queen Anne furniture is still loved today?

Queen Anne chairs in particular are all over the market. You can buy them in warm wood tones, in lacquered versions, and even unfinished. I love Queen Anne chairs in dining rooms. Not only are they pretty to look at, but their high contoured backs and softly upholstered seats make them as comfortable as can be.

And like all decorating classics, Queen Anne chairs are versatile. You can place Queen Anne chairs around any kind of table—from a contemporary glass-and-steel rectangle to a polished antique oval or round—and the look will always be right. Or you can mix Queen Anne with other chair styles. Try two fully upholstered Parsons chairs at either end of the table with a grouping of Queen Anne chairs along the sides. For a more traditional look, place wing chairs at the ends of the table.

For another kind of mix-and-match look, I favor the idea of using painted Queen Anne chairs around a wood table. In the room shown, the

An all-print treatment for a dining room featuring wallcovering and a matching fabric is accented with painted Queen Anne–style chairs and the warm wood of an oak table and mahogany lowboy.

James Seeman Studios "Nottingham" wallcovering

Draperies of Bloomcraft cotton

chairs are painted a soft lime green to match a lime green, gold, and eggshell wallcovering. In a room like this where a great deal of a single print is used, a solid-color accent is a good idea; it helps break up the all-print look. Warm wood accents are another good foil in an all-print setting. The woods in this room are polished oak for the round pedestal table and glowing mahogany for a Queen Anne lowboy.

At windows, there's more of the print, this time in a cotton, tied back softly over an arched valance covered in the print fabric.

Princess Anne

If you've always dreamed of having a dining room fit for royalty, why not plan a dining room like the one in the country home of England's Princess Anne and her husband, Captain Mark Phillips?

You'll need to begin with host and hostess chairs along with six side chairs—all in rich, gleaming mahogany. I have always liked the regal look of high-backed host and hostess chairs, and sitting in such chairs when you entertain—or even when it's dinner-for-two time—will certainly make you feel like royalty, believe me.

The dining chairs selected by the princess and her husband are reproductions made by the prestigious London firm of Algernon Aspry. The chairs have open backs, carved in an elegant three-petaled tulip pattern. You can bet they look fit for a princess when placed around a circular mahogany pedestal table.

For upholstery on the seats of those chairs, Princess Anne chose a striped fabric of cocoa, chocolate brown, and creamy beige. But you don't have to be a princess to know that the stripe is one of decorating's common denominators.

Here's a royal decorating scheme that you can

adopt for your dining room, using a stripe similar to Princess Anne's on your chair seats. Start with a mahogany dado, stained dark. Above the chair rail, hang a beige-and-cream damask wall-covering. At the windows, use beige silk for draperies and a shaped valance, and trim those window hangings with burgundy, beige, or brown fringe. Under the dining table, lay a burgundy-red carpet. To complete that English look, accessorize the walls with landscape paintings in gilded frames. And to crown the whole setting, how about a crystal chandelier outfitted with cream-colored silk shades?

Ming Dynasty

In the time of the Ming dynasty (1368–1644) artists were encouraged to do their own thing—and many beautiful things those artists did! It was during the Ming dynasty that the blue-and-white porcelains were developed, and the porcelains of the previous times, which were very plain, fell into obscurity.

Oh, those beautiful flowers in all shades of blue! How handsome they look on those creamy white backgrounds. The blue-and-white Ming porcelains were most often covered with a thin bluish glaze. And if you are a Ming lover, then you know that Ming porcelain patterns were also made with white flowers on a blue background.

One of my friends is decorating her new dining room with a Ming dynasty look based on these colors. Walls are being painted a pale blue, and woodwork and door trim will be done in white semigloss enamel. The ceiling will be painted flat white. Underfoot, a blue-and-white area rug will be laid on a polished walnut floor. The rug is Tibetan, and the blues in the flower pattern certainly are handsome against the creamy background. Draperies and window-seat covering will be made up in a fabric of royal blue and white in a Chinese script-and-flower design. The same fabric will be used for chair seat upholstery. A large breakfront will be placed against the blue dining-room walls and painted to match the wall color. The breakfront's interior will be royal blue, and an assortment of blue-and-white Ming plates, cups, and saucers will be displayed on the shelves. How very Ming the dining room will look when the walnut dining table is set with the blue-and-white china. For visual punch, I will recommend a centerpiece of red poppies in a clear glass bowl.

Jacobean

In our earlier discussion about living-room styles, I mentioned that Jacobean pieces are having a revival. The reason, I believe, is that today's homemaker wants some detail in design, including a curved look on furniture legs, to offset the straight, Parsons-style look of the Sixties.

I like Jacobean furnishings, and I like the modern, too—and I frankly believe that you can mix the two periods. For example, in a dining room with white walls and a walnut parquet floor, why not place a glass-and-steel dining table in the center of the room on a burgundy-blue-and-beige Oriental rug? Chairs can be high-backed Jacobean pieces of solid oak. The straight chairs can have seat pads of a burgundy-champagne-and-blue cut-velvet stripe. At windows, beige velvet curtains can be hung with oak rings on heavy Jacobean oak poles.

The room shown is another example of the successful blending of Jacobean with modern. In this small dining room a handsome Jacobean gateleg table and cane-back chairs—sharing urbane Jacobean turnings—are placed in front of a bay window. In tune with this "country English" setting is a cabinet with glass-enclosed shelves at top for china and hideaway storage below. To unify the bay window arrangement, dado-length print curtains are set off by shades in the rich red of the print.

When thinking of colors for Jacobean settings, think of burgundy, beige, olive, rich deep blue, and mustard gold.

Sheraton

Oh, Mr. Sheraton, your name will go on forever! I'm speaking, of course, of Thomas Sheraton, who way back in 1793 wrote *The Cabinetmaker's and the Upholsterer's Drawing Book*.

There were many folk around who claimed that Tom Sheraton took all of his designs directly from other cabinetmakers of the time—from the French as well as the English—and indeed experts often find it difficult to distinguish the Sheraton designs from those of Hepplewhite or Shearer. Be that as it may, I am a Sheraton fan,

itage's Jacobean gateleg table

Breneman's Ribcord shades

Jacobean furnishings are having a revival. In this dining room a Jacobean gateleg table with cane-back chairs, also with Jacobean turnings, make a handsome setting in front of a bay window. Dado-length curtains are set off by shades in the rich red of the curtain print.

and I love many of the characteristics of the Sheraton contrivances. Old Tom loved secret compartments in his tables, and you can be certain that when he designed a piece it had a hidden drawer or two.

Sheraton is best known for creating unusual pieces for unusual purposes and he used a lot of satinwood as inlay on his furniture, generally with mahogany. (Imagine a beautiful dining table of mahogany with a satinwood inlay top.) He also liked to decorate his furniture with delicate painted designs, especially urns and wreaths. Delicate openwork lyre designs characterize his

chair backs, a pickup from the period of Louis XVI, and another French influence in his styling was reeded and fluted legs on tables.

So if you want a graceful-looking design when decorating your dining room, think about Sheraton. Paint walls a delicate pale yellow with white trim. Use a Sheraton sideboard, one with convex corners, and above it hang a handsome mirror or perhaps an ancestral portrait. Around a long rectangular mahogany table use lyre-back Sheraton chairs; seats can be covered in an apricot-and-lemon-yellow stripe. The stained wood floor can be decorated with an Oriental rug, and at windows I'd like apricot velvet draperies and valances, lined in yellow. Don't you think an apricot-and-lemon color scheme goes well with the delicate Sheraton line? I do.

LIGHTING

I once heard a story about an architect who designed a house that was magnificent in every detail but one: He'd forgotten the electrical outlets! So let's remember that if a professional can forget it, anyone can, and talk more about lighting for the dining room.

No matter what look you've decided on, it won't come to life without proper lighting. Lighting can flatten or highlight the colors and textures of drapery and upholstery fabrics. Lighting can put your beautiful paintings in the dark or make them focal points. Lighting can flatter your guests or make them look pale and sickly.

I recently had a dramatic demonstration of what I call "The Power of Positive Lighting." A plain-Jane dining room with the usual chandelier-over-the-table was transformed through the use of dramatic lighting—all of it mounted on a track. A painting on the white wall just sat there until a spotlight hit it. An African sculpture on the buffet came to life when it got the spotlight treatment. Plain, off-white draperies became a dramatic dining backdrop when downlights, concealed in the valance, were switched on. The tables itself, though set with inexpensive white china and a plastic flower arrangement, looked spectacular when a downlight concealed in the chandelier was turned on. Suddenly, the table was alive with shadows cast by the flower arrangement.

If my description sounds theatrical, perhaps it's because the dramatic power of lighting has been relegated to the theater for too long and ignored in the home. I say it's time to shed some light on that outdated notion!

The Breakfast Nook

The sunny breakfast nook—lucky are the folks who have one. But even if your home didn't come

with a breakfast nook, you can create one. And it doesn't necessarily have to be in the kitchen!

An attractive table and chair set in front of a sunny living-room or bedroom window makes for a nice breakfast nook. And if you don't have sun, you can create a bright atmosphere with gro-lights and lots of greenery. Tall green palms make a refreshing backdrop, even in a dark corner.

Some friends of mine created a breakfast nook in their large bedroom by setting a small round skirted table and chairs in front of their sunny window. The room is painted lemon yellow with white trim and a sky-blue ceiling. Carpeting is sky blue. The white bedspread is a hand-crocheted heirloom, and the bedskirt is a floral chintz of lavender, sky blue, and pinks with green foliage on a pale lemon-yellow ground. The breakfast table is skirted in chintz and the top is protected with clear glass. Dainty white wire café chairs have seat pads upholstered in chintz, also. Draperies are lemon-yellow cotton moiré, and the city view is blocked by sheer white Austrian shades that still let in the morning sun. I don't have to tell you that breakfasting in that room is a delight!

If you're one of those lucky folks whose breakfast nook is in the kitchen, why not decorate it with a country flair using wallcovering? Use rustic wood-grain vinyl on the walls and a blue-and-yellow pattern on the ceiling. Choose a sapphire-blue trestle table and benches, and cover the bench pads in a yellow-and-white cotton geometric. Use the same fabric on a laminated window shade, too.

The picnic look is another good choice for a breakfast nook. In fact, I love picnics and the picnic look so much I've dreamed up a picnic look for an indoor breakfast nook that can be enjoyed all year round.

The look starts with walls of fresh white above a dado painted grassy green. Overhead, paint a sky-blue ceiling and, if you choose, brush or sponge on a skyful of puffy white clouds.

Checks—checkered tablecloths and napkins—are a must at all picnics; I can't imagine a picnic without them. And those checks are a must in

A sunny breakfast nook takes its country flair from rustic wallcoverings used on walls and ceiling.

my picnic room, too. I picture a checkered floor of yellow and white vinyl tiles. At windows, I would hang fresh-as-a-breeze café curtains made from pretty yellow-and-white checkered dish towels, and I'd make sure those windows were filled with green plants galore.

Furniture, of course, would be a redwood picnic table with two redwood benches, or a table and chairs of peeled pine logs. And I would top chairs or benches with seat pads covered in sturdy washable grass-green sailcloth. When you set that table with a checkered cloth and bandanna napkins, I guarantee you'll think you're picnicking in a grassy country meadow.

As you know, finishing touches are of great importance to me, so I would decorate one wall of this country nook with a wicker picnic hamper filled with green plants!

Throughout this book you've probably noticed my emphasis on plants. In fact, I like to keep a photograph on my desk of a garden in bloom. That's to remind me that no matter how much it snows, blows, and sleets outside, spring is just around the corner; and that means we'll soon be enjoying our gardens—or, in the case of city dwellers, our window boxes.

I have often turned to gardens for inspiration during the winter, and you can, too, with a year-round garden look for your breakfast area. In a country breakfast nook I decorated recently, I used a trellis wallcovering of white on a sky-blue background. Windowframes were painted white and given shutters of white trellis. Furniture was white wicker, with chair pads covered in a garden floral of pale orange, pink, sky blue, and lemon yellow with green foliage on a white background. Underfoot there was a grass-green carpet, of course, and, hovering overhead, a sky-blue ceiling.

Carpeting, incidentally, can be a good choice for your kitchen breakfast nook. The carpet industry is into all kinds of patterned floor coverings and they're both durable and easily washable.

A couple I know in Vermont chose a tile-patterned nylon carpet in golds and browns for their kitchen breakfast area. The walls were covered with paneling in buckskin tones with the adze marks of hand-hewn timber. The breakfast area with its eclectic mix of furnishings and accessories is a popular gathering spot for the family. The contemporary bamboo table and chairs, lighted with an old brass lamp overhead, serves for games as well as dining.

nd's Chesapeake print nylon carpet

Shenandoah paneling

Pattern and texture predominate in this breakfast room, a popular family gathering spot. A tile-patterned nylon carpet in golds and browns sets the tone. Walls are covered with paneling in buckskin tones with the adze marks of hand-hewn timber. An eclectic mix of furnishings includes a contemporary bamboo table and chairs with an old brass lamp overhead.

6

The Kitchen

Make It a Happy Place

Remember Cinderella, the household drudge who was transformed into a radiant princess? We're going to play Cinderella with the plain-Jane kitchen.

Today's kitchens should have style, flair, personality. Many folks, myself included, feel that the kitchen is the heartbeat and heart of the house and they want it to have loads of charming as well as practical features.

My secret: Look for products that have both qualities. Remember, it's as easy to love a beautiful kitchen accessory as it is to love an ugly one. And if well-chosen, the beautiful ones will not only function with ease, they will also lift your spirits every time you use them!

The Cinderella kitchen pictured features a raft of beautiful—as well as useful—decorating ideas, starting with soft, comfortable carpeting whose special tight weave and tweedy pattern helps hides spots and spills.

The wall treatment doesn't carry a fancy price tag, but the look is expensive. All it takes is some crisp white tile trim and a coat or two of non-yellowing white enamel for work-area walls, and a wash of sky blue for ceiling and exhaust hoods. For punch, there's one small wall covered in a wallpaper remnant—sky-blue branches on a bittersweet ground—and a slash of bittersweet paint above the stove.

Storage galore is provided in under-the-counter cabinets and in less conventional spots, too. A neat four-shelf unit, tucked far away from the smoke and grease of the cooking area, holds the family's everyday dinnerware of colorful stackable plastic, as well as the cookbook collection. A display of pots and pans, plus onions, potatoes, and a few strings of garlic, all hang from a centrally located wrought-iron rack and add warmth and personality. Below the rack there's more storage for big bulky items in an easy-to-build plywood island. It's painted white, trimmed with melon stock molding, and topped with spillproof and scratch-resistant white plastic laminate—another example of the useful and the beautiful working together.

When it comes to selecting kitchen appliances, the Great White Way is my way. Anything else

Beauty and utility combine in a kitchen that features a comfortable, soil-hiding carpet, simple white walls, and the kind of open storage that lets the family cook put his or her personality on display.

limits your decorating options. Remember, a refrigerator, stove. or dishwasher can last for twenty years. If those appliances are sparkling white, you can decorate a different way every year if you wish, but with appliances of gold, coppertone, or green, you are forced to keep decorating around those colors.

I've heard people express the opinion that white appliances are sterile or cold. They can be, of course, if they sit in a white-painted kitchen with beige-flecked tile on the floor and white curtains at the window. But white appliances in the right setting look super. With white appliances I may paper walls in a red-green-and-yellow design of fruits and flowers; or paint walls warm apricot and hang pretty chintz curtains at windows; or go sunny yellow all the way; or decorate with natural wood and brick. With white appliances, it's easy to do any one of those schemes, and more.

A kitchen pictured here, designed by an accredited kitchen designer, is a good example. All the cabinetry is rich oak-stained wood veneer. For eye appeal, walls are patterned in clean, crisp navy-and-white houndstooth vinyl. Blue and white is a classic kitchen scheme I never tire of, and the houndstooth gives it pizzazz. Navy was also used for the beams on the kitchen's cathedral ceiling, and sun pours through white curtains trimmed with navy-and-white houndstooth fabric. For added charm, there's a blue-and-white delft-style chandelier to light the breakfast nook.

I'm sure you'll agree that the look is cozy, warm, and friendly—there's no hint of coldness, despite the bright white appliances, frosty white countertops, and white brick floors.

In the fashion world, softness and prettiness are showing up as a return to lace, ruffles, and skirts to compete with all those pantsuits we've been seeing. In home fashions, I don't believe that softness and prettiness will necessarily mean lots of frills. I think what we'll see instead is fresh, clear color; soft, cushy upholstery; lots of pillows; a generous use of fabric.

Why not a "pretty" look for the kitchen? Picture this kitchen, and you'll see what I mean: Walls are papered in a springtime floral of pink tulips, golden daffodils, and fresh white daisies with green foliage on an airy sky-blue background. For flooring, sky-blue and white vinyl tiles are laid in a pattern of wide stripes. Curtains can be white washable cafés trimmed with ball fringe and hung from delicate brass rods. If a table and chairs are called for, I would choose daffodil-yellow laminate or molded plastic for the table and white for the chairs. And how about chair pads in a floral fabric to match the springtime wallcovering?

For another pretty look, try vegetables instead of flowers. Fresh vegetables know no season in decorating. I love the many vegetable-print fabrics on the market these days—especially for kitchens and breakfast nooks.

A print of feathery dill plants on a white background would be a pretty starting point for a kitchen make-over. Use the print for curtains, dish towels, a floor-length skirt for a round breakfast table, and for seat pads on bleached-wood ladder-back chairs. Paint the walls white and the ceiling and cabinets happy apple green. Trim cabinets with a thin band of white paint and add white china knobs. If you are installing new countertops, make them butcherblock. Lay a floor of terra-cotta vinyl brick.

And how about making a collection of vegetable-decorated china plates the focal point of a kitchen? A lady I know did just that, and so can you with the variety of inexpensive plates available on the market.

This lady started with plates hand-decorated with painted and raised designs of lettuce, tomatoes, parsley, cucumbers, squash—you name it. The plates are displayed against walls of lively lemon yellow. (Trim and ceiling are pure white.) Some of the plates also have a place of honor in a pine corner cupboard. And when this lady sets her table with yellow spatterware, her centerpiece is always a vegetable-decorated bowl brim-

Rich oak-stained wood veneer cabinets and lively navy-and-white houndstooth team up for a look that's cozy, warm, and friendly with no hint of coldness, despite white appliances, frosty white countertops, and white brick floors.

ming over with fresh bell peppers, cucumbers, yellow squash, and rich purple Spanish onions.

Let's shed some light on the subject of dark dreary kitchens—there are plenty of those around! Cabinets are dark. Floors are dark. And there's never more than a glimmer of light coming through the window. Or worse there's no window at all!

If that sounds familiar, you need to brighten and brighten and brighten. Start with walls. Paint them a light, happy shade—lemon yellow, snowy white, or pale cantaloupe. Whatever shade you choose, make sure paint is oil-based. Oil-based paints are easily washed; water-based paints are not. If you like the look of wallcovering, what about a plaid in yellows, white, emerald green, and olive? Wallcoverings should all be canvas-backed vinyl; in my opinion, it adheres to walls better than its paper-backed cousin.

Many people complain about wood cabinets that make their kitchens look oppressive. If that's your problem, why not take off those dark wooden doors to create open shelves? If shelves are wood, paint them to match walls or choose a bright accent color—apple green against yellow walls, or Chinese red against melon. For newer, nonwood cabinets you might choose a bright laminate instead of paint.

Since so many kitchens these days have avocado-green appliances, here's a kitchen decor built around that popular color. Cover walls with a red bandanna-print vinyl. Woodwork can be white. Select a flooring that could stand up to a trampling by a convention of railroad workers —red brick vinyl would be my choice. For your breakfast table and chairs, how about white molded fiber-glass pieces? Mats on your easy-to-clean table can be red, and napkins can be avocado to match appliances. At your windows, what about white washable cotton curtains hung on red-lacquered poles? You might even make some tiebacks out of early-vintage red bandannas. A wrought-iron plant stand filled with ferns in natural clay pots would add an antique touch. And even if you don't care for your dark kitchen, the ferns will—they thrive in little light.

Perhaps your kitchen is not only dark but tiny as well. An efficiency kitchen. A pullman kitchen. Call it what you will, the tiny kitchen is very much a fact of modern life, sad to say. But even a tiny kitchen doesn't have to be a cramped and gloomy kitchen—not if colors are bright and storage is wisely planned. And that means that dark colors, wall clutter, dark wood cabinetry, low-hanging ceiling fixtures are out.

My office kitchen is a good example of a tiny kitchen that's a joy. Wallpaper is a medium-scale contemporary floral of pinks, red, sky blue, hot orange, lemon yellow, and lavender with green foliage on a white ground. All cabinets are painted poppy red, the stove is lemon yellow, and the refrigerator is white. For carpeting, I chose poppy red. As small as that kitchen is, no one can say it has a cramped or gloomy feeling!

Perhaps a more serene, old-world setting is what you want in your tiny kitchen. Try this: Paper walls and ceiling in an overall small-scale print of sky blue, royal blue, and navy on white—and make sure there's lots of white background, please. Paint all cabinets white and cover the floor with self-stick tiles you cut out yourself to create a small-scale black-and-white diamond pattern. For eye appeal plus practicality, use a pine or maple corner cabinet with open shelves for displaying your pretty china and glassware. (More on kitchen corners later.) Save the closed wall cabinets for workaday items that don't enhance your decor. The corner cupboard is an efficient way to use precious space, you know. And make sure you line that corner cupboard with some of your blue-and-white wallcovering.

Yellow is particularly good for bringing some sunshine into those small, dark efficiency kitchens. To bring the sun into your kitchen, try this scheme.

Cover walls in a happy, sun-dappled sunflower-print wallcovering of golden yellow, spring green, and white. Paint all trim white. For cabinets and countertops, choose butcherblock or butcherblock laminate. And underfoot, how about the durability and comfort of indoor/outdoor carpeting in olive green? If there's a window, create an

Warm wood cabinetry is set off by a sunny yellow blockwork print on the beamed ceiling of this cozy brick-walled kitchen.

illusion of a sunny day with a sun-yellow window shade trimmed in yellow-and-spring-green braid.

Kitchens with International Flavor

We've talked about the popularity of the ethnic look in today's homes, and it's a look that works well in the kitchen, too. Here are some ideas for adding international flavor to your kitchen.

ORIENTAL

If you have an interest in Oriental cooking, why not give your kitchen a Far Eastern tang? Many kitchen cabinetry firms around the country today are offering the Oriental look, and you could team those cabinets with other Oriental accents.

In one Oriental-style kitchen I recently saw the cabinets had a Ceylon-black finish were outfitted with Oriental medallion pulls of brass. Into the upper door panels over the kitchen sink area, red insert panels were installed—plastic-laminate inserts, naturally, for the practical Western homemaker. Countertops were white for contrast against the Ceylon-black cabinets, and white glazed tile was used for the splashboard surfaces. For a shoji look, modern lighting was cleverly incorporated into the white ceiling, accented with black-lacquered beams. Flooring was brilliant red vinyl tile. A red pagoda-style hood was installed over an elongated octagonal cooking island stained Ceylon-black with Oriental-design brass hardware.

If you want to bring the flavor of the Orient into your kitchen decor, but have limited funds for redecorating, why not restain your present cabinets Ceylon black, and change the hardware to Oriental brass? Recolor countertops too— mandarin red or white laminate would be my preference.

If walls need redoing, choose an Oriental-design vinyl—there are on the market many trellis-, flower-, and geometric-pattern wallcoverings with an Oriental feeling, which would do the job

superbly. And an Oriental wind chime fixture over the kitchen table would be an attractive note.

For another kind of look with Oriental flavor, take your cue from an inexpensive set of blue-and-white willowware china. Paint walls pure sparkling white as a backdrop for a collection of willowware plates, or cover walls in willow-pattern blue-and-white vinyl. Stain wood cabinets dark walnut and lay a floor of blue-and-white vinyl squares.

If there's a breakfast nook, furnish it Oriental-style with a dark-stained table of *faux* bamboo (that's wood turned to imitate the knobs of bamboo). Cover seats of four *faux* bamboo chairs with a blue-and-white willowware-print fabric, and use the same fabric for pretty, bow-tied café curtains at windows.

SPANISH

My wife and I often entertain another couple or a few friends in our Mediterranean-style kitchen, turning the countertops into buffets and setting a small but adequate table with checkered cloth and napkins and earthenware mugs and dishes.

For your own Mediterranean kitchen, you might paint walls bright white and the ceiling a Spanish torero-red lacquer. At windows you can hang white café curtains with gypsy-dancer red and black ball fringe. Kitchen cabinets can be a rich, deep espresso-brown stain, and your countertops a brilliant red plastic laminate. Hang a black wrought-iron rack from the ceiling to hold pots and pans, and, if possible, plan a space in your kitchen for a butcherblock cutting board counter; cooks seem to love working on butcherblock, and I like its look.

For the floor, consider warm red carpeting with high-density foam-rubber backing in a Spanish grille design. And for counter stools I would suggest some handsome Mediterranean-villa woven reed pieces on black wrought-iron bases. A Spanish-style kitchen always looks great

A small, dark efficiency kitchen comes to life with a vinyl sunflower-print wall-covering and a sun-yellow window shade trimmed in spring-green-and-yellow braid.

For the Westerner with an interest in the Oriental mood, here's a kitchen with cabinetry of Ceylon-black stain with Oriental medallion pulls. The floor and the pagoda-style hood over the octagonal cooking island are brilliant red.

In this kitchen with a Spanish feeling, carpeting is a Spanish grille design in a warm red tone with a high-density foam-rubber back. Walls are painted bright sparkling white and ceiling is Spanish torero red. Cabinets are rich, deep espresso-brown stain with bright red countertops. A black wrought-iron hanging rack, holding pots and pans, lends a special decorative note.

with natural reed pieces and wicker baskets sitting about. The baskets can be filled with fruits, vegetables, or green house plants.

AUSTRIAN

If the Austrian window shade is the only home decoration you associate with that country, you'll be surprised to learn that an even more popular look for the home originated there too. The look is bentwood, and it's a look that's turning everyone's head these days.

Bentwood was developed by an Austrian gentleman named Michael Thonet, who began mass-producing it in 1857. The process, a revolutionary development in its time, involved steaming the wood and then placing it in molds that shaped it into the familiar swirls we love today. Of course, there are other bentwood styles now—styles created in more recent years using Thonet's process. But the styles that Thonet originally created are still going strong. The "ice-cream-parlor" chairs that Thonet popularized, for example, are having a revival in restaurants. In fact, I used a raft of bentwood chairs in Copley's, a Boston restaurant I designed to look "old."

If you want to create that old-time look in your kitchen, why not consider using bentwood of the Thonet type? I would like to see those bentwood ice-cream-parlor chairs grouped around a circular marble-topped table, just as they might have been back in the good old days. Illuminate the scene with an inexpensive dark-green-enameled hanging fixture over the table, and at windows hang forest-green-and-white-checked café curtains from shiny brass poles. Floor can be forest-green-and-white checkerboard tiles. And for a touch of bright color, paint cabinet doors poppy red!

THE AMERICAN KITCHEN

Why include our own American kitchen in a list of international kitchens? Because the American kitchen, like our country itself, is a blend of ideas from all over the world. It may contain colonial furnishings derived from English designs; tilework derived from Italy, Spain, or Portugal; wallcoverings of French, English, or Oriental inspiration; utensils and fabrics of Scandinavian design; wicker and woks from the Orient; dishes from England, Holland, Japan, or Germany—all melded into a look, however, that is uniquely our own, a look that is functional, practical, friendly, and casual.

The American kitchen is a warm, cozy kitchen with wood cabinets, beautifully colored walls, and colorful or sparkling-white appliances to suit every need.

The American kitchen is also more than a kitchen—it may be part of an adjoining family room or living room, or it may contain a sunny breakfast nook. No matter how small, the American kitchen is never just a factory for turning out meals.

The American kitchen is well organized. This is not an impossible dream—even for the tiniest efficiency kitchen—because today we have so many ways to store kitchen necessities: pegboard, ceiling hooks, revolving shelves, and, more and more often for those who have the space, an island for working and eating as well as for storage.

This kitchen pictured is typically American in its warmth and functionalism—even the accessories, from the storage boxes on the windowsill to the display of copper and iron pots and pans above the island, are useful as well as beautiful. The carpet colors—a tweed of gold, firethorn, and walnut—complement walls and cabinets of soft, buttery yellow.

Two particularly appealing looks for the American kitchen are the colonial look and the country look. The colonial kitchen is a favorite of mine, especially one with a beamed ceiling—beams lend so much charm to any room in the home. For the colonial kitchen, new pine cabinets with pewter knobs would be effective. While George and Martha Washington might have preferred a wood-plank floor or brick flooring in their country kitchen, today's homemakers can choose easy-care carpet or practical vinyl brick. Individual "bricks" are available today that, when laid in a herringbone pattern, can make a small kitchen seem larger.

A charming kitchen dining area I saw recently featured barn-red walls and louvered shutters. The kitchen cabinets were also painted barn red and accented with gold-painted wooden pulls. Wood beams accented the cabinets and countertops which separated the dining area from the kitchen. I liked the printed nylon carpeting in a pattern complete with

The all-American kitchen is famous the world over for its blend of function and fashion, typified by a handsome work island and a tweedy carpet for soft steps and hard wear.

Federal eagles and drums in golds, red, blues, greens. And on the wall of the dining area was a modern graphic of President Washington surveying the modern homemaker's colonial-style setting.

Traditional country kitchens are having a big comeback these days, especially with the sudden popularity of the natural look. The two looks are easy partners—after all, those great country kitchens came into being in an era when everyone lived the rustic, natural way.

A kitchen I'm designing now will have maple Windsor chairs teamed with a trestle table in the same rich wood. Cabinets will be an easy-care-wood grain laminate. For wallpaper I've chosen a fresh, natural floral print of red, tangerine, buttercup yellow, and parrot green on a white background.

You can mix the country look with the contemporary look, too, and the results will be super. In a friend's kitchen I saw old-fashioned wooden farmhouse chairs with rush seats used around a spanking-new white Parsons table. Underfoot was a colorful geometric-patterned

Oriental rug in brilliant blues, oranges, reds, and earth tones. Walls were white.

That kitchen, as you can imagine, is as contemporary as can be, yet it still has the look of a country kitchen.

New Ways with Floors, Walls, Counters, Appliances, Colors

VINYL VERSUS CARPET

I am often asked the question, "What about carpet for the kitchen?" As you know by now, my answer most often is, "Go to it." I strongly believe the carpeted-kitchen age is upon us. While the kitchen remains the base for food preparation, today's kitchen is also being designed to expand pleasure; it has become the focal point for casual entertaining, for family meals, and even for some home businesses. With its newly assigned function as a room for living, not just cooking, it has become as natural to think in terms of carpeting for the kitchen as it is for other rooms in the home.

So if it's carpet you want, by all means have it, you'll find washable, soil resistant, antistatic kitchen carpeting in all colors and patterns and foam-backed for extra comfort. Buy it by the yard, or choose carpet tiles you can lay yourself to create checks, stripes, or bordered effects.

If you choose vinyl, however, you can still have that soft, cushiony feeling underfoot. I walked on air recently when I visited a home that had cushion-vinyl flooring. And when I say walked on air, I'm not being poetic; I mean it! You see, cushion vinyl is made of expanded vinyl foam, which contains tiny air bubbles. This construction is what makes cushion vinyl so soft, and warm, underfoot. Yes, warm! Those same tiny air bubbles that give cushion vinyl its softness also provide insulation that keeps cold air from coming up through the floor.

I like cushion vinyl for kitchens, where spills and heavy traffic are routine. Friends of mine who recently renovated an old farmhouse used barn-red brick-pattern cushion vinyl on the floor of their enormous country kitchen. The focal point of the square room was the old woodburning stove on which my friends do a lot of their cooking. The wall behind the old black stove was tiled in delft-blue ceramic squares; remaining walls were white. A wood breakfront to the left of the stove held dishes above, linens in drawers below. To the right of the stove, an old walnut-stained washstand and mirror provided additional storage as well as eye appeal. The wall above the washstand was hung with a charming collection of antique plates. Built-in cupboards were stained the same walnut hue. A large, square, wooden table was surrounded by six rush-seated chairs and covered with a red-and-white checked cloth. At the windows were curtains of the same checked fabric with matching tiebacks. Old wicker baskets holding kitchen utensils were displayed on countertops of the same varnished-brick cushion vinyl as the floor.

Flooring manufacturers are also coming up with great new stock designs that formerly were available only on special order for the custom look. If you're texture-conscious and interested in a new flooring design for your kitchen, consider a vinyl-asbestos tile flooring that features a geometric design, prettily surrounded by a gentle scroll, that can flatter almost any decor. It's powerful fashion in a neutral room and unpresumptuously lovely in traditional interiors. Moreover, if you're thinking of doing the job yourself, you'll be happy to learn that vinyl-asbestos tiles are easily installed, and the new 12″ x 12″ tiles feature a new type of edge that takes the headache out of pattern matching.

One of the young decorators in my office created a great texture-look kitchen in his small New York apartment. On the floor he installed Indian-orange vinyl-asbestos tiles. The walls in the kitchen, where practicality counts, were covered with an orange-white-and-beige grasscloth vinyl. A row of standard metal kitchen cabinets were painted in alternate colors of hot

A modern graphic of President Washington looks over this colonial-style kitchen/ dining area with a color scheme of barn red, gold, and green. The printed nylon carpet is complete with Federal eagles and drums in all the colors George and Martha Washington would have liked—golds, reds, blues, and greens.

Carpet in the kitchen? Why not? Spots and spills won't show on a low-pile rubber-backed carpet made of soil-hiding nylon.

Monarch's "Hexagon" carpet of Antron nylon

orange, mocha grown, and white. Countertop was canary-yellow laminated plastic. For further punch, he used old wooden ice-cream-parlor chairs, painted canary yellow, at the small kitchen counter.

Steel

The decorative value of steel was first realized by the French, way back in the nineteenth century. You can still find examples of steel day beds, steel desks, steel chairs, and steel tables from that period, and they're having a big revival. My friend, designer John Saladino, likes to use steel on the ceiling, too, to reflect the room and add sparkle in a low-key way.

Of course, the traditional place for steel is in the kitchen, in the form of marvelous stainless-steel counters and sinks—and lately much more.

If you think that stainless is cold and too contemporary for you, think again—and take a look at the pretty kitchen shown which combines the sleekness of steel with lots of warm, old-fashioned touches.

The sleekness of steel, acrylic, and slick black upholstery is handsomely paired with the old-fashioned charm of blue onion-patterned wallpaper in a convenience-oriented kitchen.

The steel is used for appliances and surfaces—including the top of a handy center island, which is partnered with a pair of acrylic-and-steel chairs. All the cabinetry is steel, too, lacquered black and trimmed with clear plastic handles. The old-fashioned charm is supplied in abundance by a traditional blue-onion-patterned wallpaper that sweeps across the walls and ceiling. It's the perfect foil for the kitchen's Old World white tilework.

MARBLE

When you think of marble, do you think of banks and office buildings? Why not think of your home, instead? Marble is a natural for home decorating in any room of the house. There's marble for flooring and marble for bathroom counters. There's marble for tabletops, and, for the adventurous, there's marble for walls.

I know a cook who swears by marble for rolling out her pastry. As you can imagine, all her kitchen countertops are sparkling white marble, and you should see how super that marble looks against the dark wood of her louvered-door kitchen cabinets! Wood and marble are also combined in her kitchen table, which has a white marble top and rich-looking wood pedestal base. The table is paired with four classic bentwood chairs with cane seats.

COLOR

Have you paid a visit to your local paint store lately? If you haven't, I suggest that you do so. Even when I'm not planning a paint job, I find the dazzling array of paint colors now on the market a terrific source of decorating inspiration.

But whenever I visit my neighborhood paint store, I'm always puzzled by one thing: With the bounty of colors on the market—not to mention the bounty of paint types and textures—why do so many people stick to the same old off-white, beige, and pale yellow tones? Granted, those bland shades have an important place in home decorating. But so do melon, terra-cotta, periwinkle blue, charcoal gray, tomato red, grass green, chocolate fudge . . . I could go on and on, but I'm sure you see my point.

For a color surprise in the kitchen, why not cut loose with shiny eggplant walls? I would play those gleaming dark walls against cabinets of light blond butcherblock laminate and cover the floor with pale straw-colored sisal matting. Appliances can be white. And for pure drama, how about a tomato-red sink? Accessories can be tomato red and apple green.

Please don't confuse eggplant with purple, however. Purple and its pastel relatives—lilac, orchid, lavender, violet—are colors to be used with care. I've seen many rooms spoiled by an overdose of heavy, heavy purple. Too bad!

If you want lots of purple, go the pastel way and mix in lots and lots of chalky white to keep things light and bright. The kitchen pictured features the look of wood teamed with orchid and lavender—and a handsome look it is! Upper cabinet doors are laminated in oak; lower doors are a pretty orchid hue. Wallpaper in the kitchen is an Art Deco design in the palest lavender, periwinkle blue, and white. And note that this pretty kitchen features lots of white—white molded plastic for breakfast table and chairs, plus white laminated countertops. Buttercup yellow is also used in the kitchen for accessories. Yellow plates, yellow cookware, and yellow accent pieces of crockery and molded plastic add a sunny note.

Plastic-laminate colors are also reaching over the rainbow, and I am certain we are about to see some exciting new looks in kitchens, using the new colors. A manufacturer of plastic laminates, which are used for countertops, walls, furniture, etc., recently sent me a sampling of the new color line. I was delighted to see tropic lime, brilliant green, hot pink, poppy, tiger lily, sky blue, pineapple, cyclamen, fuchsia, jasmine, and curry included in the color range.

It set me to thinking. What about a kitchen styled with alternating tropic-lime and bright white cabinets with a fuchsia countertop and splashback? Or a kitchen styled with alternating tiger-lily and hot-pink cabinets with pineapple counter top and splashback? It would be a real smasher with hanging kitchenware of lime green.

For those who want more color in their kitchens and more life in their colors, colored plastic laminate is available in widths of 2½, 3, 4, and 5 feet, and in lengths of 8, 10, and 12 feet. For the do-it-yourselfer, directions are simple.

A blend of orchid and oak, spiced with white and yellow, gives this pretty kitchen a different look.

The Kitchen Pep-Up

If you kitchen looks shabby, outdated or just blah, you can pep it up without breaking the bank on a complete remodeling job. Granted, new cabinets and countertops can give a kitchen new practicality and convenience, but the old ones might work just as well with just a face-lift.

My hat is off to the imaginative homemaker on a budget who knows how to use something old in a new way to refresh a tired-looking kitchen. A New England couple I know did this

—and turned a plain white kitchen into a distinctive food workshop to suit their life-style.

First, the white Beaverboard ceiling was stripped to expose the natural wood beams, which were then cleaned and covered with a clear sealer. Copper pots were hung from the newly exposed beams, and spotlights were installed for direct lighting on food-preparation surfaces.

Next, the plaster was removed from one wall to show off old birch, which was painted white.

Third, plain white metal cabinets and appliances were sparked with tomato-red plastic-laminate countertops and splashbacks, and above one chopping-board countertop an antique leaded-glass window was installed.

A unique feature of the kitchen was the use of colorful carpeting on the sides of the cooking counter dividing the room. The surfaces were covered with the same carpeting used on the floor—a rich royal blue, melon, green, and orange geometric pattern, treated to resist spills and stains.

Notice, too, that the island divider included shelves for cookbooks. A cookbook section is not only a useful addition to any remodeled kitchen, but to my mind it is a necessity. It can be an integral part of the dividing counter, as it is here; or it can be an old armoire outfitted with shelves; or it can be a wall of shelves supported on adjustable brackets, or a wall of stacked wooden cubes painted to enhance your kitchen decor and filled with cookbooks and other accessories.

The fact is, no kitchen ever seems to have enough space for all those accessories. In our country kitchen with blue-and-white gingham-checked vinyl walls and ceiling, my wife and I hung many baskets in light and dark colors on chains from the ceiling and filled them with various kitchen accessories.

MULTICOLORED WALLCOVERING

The multicolored wallcovering is not only a terrific kitchen pepper-upper, it's also a great problem solver that I use often in my decorating work. One of my clients, for instance, had this situation: Countertops in her old-fashioned kitchen were tomato red; floors were brick-red vinyl. The problem: how to bring together those clashing reds. The happy solution: a print wallcovering with both colors in it.

My choice was a giant-size strawberry pattern of brick red, tomato red, emerald green, and sunny yellow on a white background. To really tie things together, a matching fabric was used for tieback curtains at windows and for sash curtains behind glass cupboard doors. All wood trim was painted sparkling white.

A multicolored wallcovering can also be used to tie kitchen colors in with a different color scheme used in an adjoining dining room or living room.

PEGBOARD

Clearing away clutter is a remarkably effective way to make any kitchen look better almost instantly, and with storage space at a premium these days, many folks are hanging their storables on pegboards. Pegboard, which is actually perforated hardboard, comes in two thicknesses —¼ inch and ⅛ inch—and in several colors and finishes. If you can't find the color you want, however, unfinished brown pegboard can be painted any color of the rainbow to match your decor.

In the kitchen pictured, sparkling pegboard takes over all four walls to become the major decorative element in the room. The most attractive utensils—the shiny copper bowls and molds, the wooden boards, and the woven baskets—actually become part of the decor, while the unsightly items we all own, the dented pots and discolored pans, are hidden away in the cabinets below the sink.

Functional, yes. And this kitchen proves that functionalism can be a joy to look at. In addition to the pegboard display, there's the shiny brightness of parrot green and white for countertops and cabinet faces. And picking up the parrot green of the laminate is a ceiling papered in a wild geometric print of parrot green, ebony, and white. There's more fun at the window, where a shade, laminated to match the ceiling, brightens a grim view of a brick wall.

One of my friends even installed a pegboard

This "new" old kitchen features colorful patterned carpet on side surfaces of cooking counter as well as on the floor. No need to worry about spills and stains since nylon carpet was treated with carpet protector. Tomato-red plastic-laminate countertops and splashbacks add punch to white metal cabinets and appliances. From newly exposed old beam ceiling, copper pots were hung, and spotlights were installed for direct lighting on food-preparation surfaces.

ceiling in her kitchen and from it hangs strings of onions, cheeses, and salamis, as well as egg beaters and straw baskets filled with cookie cutters and small kitchen utensils. The pegboard was painted navy blue to visually lower a high ceiling, and it is most effective with the white patent-vinyl walls of the kitchen.

To give the pegboard in any room a finished look, by the way, make sure the edges are trimmed with stock molding from the lumberyard, painted to match or contrast with your wall color.

WALL GROUPINGS

To pep up a bare kitchen wall, scout around the kitchen—and the rest of the house—for things with which you can create an eye-catching wall grouping. Decorative groupings can be created from almost any collection of objects you can name—from priceless art objects and antiques to a gathering of $2 and $3 baskets purchased at flea markets and import shops.

One of the prettiest groupings I ever saw was nothing more than a clever kitchen-wall arrangement of wooden spoons of all shapes and sizes mounted on white-painted pegboard. Those spoons were not expensive, but they added a great deal of warmth and charm to an otherwise ordinary kitchen.

Many people collect china and pottery plates, and those plates—both patterned and plain—would make a super wall grouping. Such a grouping could even become the focal point of a country-style kitchen with rush-seated chairs pulled up to a pine trestle table. For color accents, pick a hue from one of the plates—Wedgwood blue, for example—and use that shade for draperies, chair pads, and place mats.

On the plain white walls of her kitchen, a designer friend of mine hangs an everchanging display of the fancy breads she makes as a hobby. On baking day, my friend makes an extra loaf or two for her walls. The loaves are sculptured into fanciful rounds, sunbursts, batons, and flower shapes. Thin, nearly invisible wire wrapped around the loaves provides a way of hanging them. The crusty brown loaves against white walls makes for a most unusual wall display—and a very personal one, too!

CEILINGS

Ceilings in older kitchens may be cracked or peeling, and are often too high for the size of the room. Such a ceiling will detract from the peppy new look you've chosen, no matter how well you've carried it out on floors, walls, and cabinets.

There are several ways to disguise a flawed ceiling. One is to cover it with vinyl wallcovering in a happy print. Another is to redo it with textured paint, applied with a brush, roller, or spatula for a stucco look that's particularly effective for "country" kitchens or the Mediterranean look. You might even add lightweight polyurethane-foam beams that you cut with a knife and apply with mastic; they look exactly like handhewn wood beams. A third way to hide an old ceiling, and lower it at the same time, is by creating an entirely new "dropped" ceiling with a do-it-yourself kit. The kit includes interlocking metal strips that form a large-square grid below the old ceiling, plus fiber-glass panels (individually removable for cleaning and access to fluorescent light fixtures) that rest on the grid and softly illuminate the entire kitchen.

But even if your ceiling is in perfect condition, why ignore the decorative potential of such a large area? I often advise clients, friends, and readers to paper or paint their ceilings with color. Whichever color you choose, remember that light colors will tend to make the ceiling look higher; dark tones—terra-cotta, navy, wine—will lower it.

A kitchen I saw recently was done with the coziness of wood and brick. Cabinetry was dark polished wood. Walls were brick. And for a touch of sunny brightness, the beamed ceiling was papered in a blockwork print of sunshine yellow, bronze, and lime green.

A kitchen that is functional as well as attractive features pegboard walls for storage and sparkling green-and-white laminate for countertops and cupboard fronts.

DON'T FORGET THE CORNERS

Who says the center of a room has to get all the attention? I believe that kitchen corners are just as important and have as much decorating potential.

Turn a dark, unused kitchen corner into a living garden by piling a stepladder with pretty green plants. Paint the stepladder a happy sunshine yellow, and light your garden with plant lights to keep it alive and well. Believe me, those green plants will turn a do-nothing, say-nothing kitchen corner into an exciting focal point.

Or turn an unused corner into a seating area. I am all for comfortable seating areas all over the house; I don't believe that a conversation grouping, a chaise longue, a sofa, or an easy chair must be reserved for the living room. I still recall a large kitchen where I spent many a pleasant afternoon. The kitchen, in an old city apartment, belonged to an artist friend of mine who loved to whip up fabulous gourmet meals when he wasn't painting. The kitchen conversation grouping—a chintz-covered sofa and club chair with a spacious end table in between— was his favorite entertaining spot. Here, friends could sit and watch the meal-in-the-making.

A corner too small for seating could be used to store a rolling cart—one of those handy little tables on wheels. With folks doing more and more informal entertaining in every room of the house, a rolling cart can be a great convenience.

In the kitchen, which is returning to favor as a popular eating and entertaining spot, a butcher-block rolling cart would be just the thing. When not in use as a serving piece, you can use the cart's top for preparing food. And, of course, you can move this handy work surface to wherever it's needed. Instead of a permanent bar in your family room or living room, for example, why not stock a rolling kitchen cart as a bar and wheel it where it's needed? Or if you, like many people these days, have taken to entertaining luncheon guests in your sitting room, set up a pretty skirted table—the skirt could match your spread or draperies—and roll in your luncheon for two on a rolling cart. You can also pile the cart with your barbecue supplies and roll it out to the patio or terrace.

You can make the butcherblock-and-chrome rolling cart a permanent kitchen accessory. Pair it with a matching table—and to pull up to that table, how about four swivel-base chairs upholstered in cheery orange vinyl? Pick up on the orange theme by painting cupboard doors orange too. For walls, how about a "with it" brown-and-white lattice-design wallcovering. Paint all trim chocolate brown and go brown for venetian blinds, too. That's a room you'll be proud to invite your guests into!

This "with it" kitchen is equipped for today's portable life-style with butcherblock-and-chrome rolling cart and matching table. Walls are covered in a brown-and-white lattice design, trim and venetian blinds are chocolate brown, and cabinet doors are painted orange.

7

The Bathroom

Many women dream of a bathroom reminiscent of early Hollywood, with a sunken tub of white marble, white marble floors and walls, and white chiffon curtains. I grant that a marble tub, marble floors, and marble walls can do a lot for a bathroom, but there are lots of other ways to make even a small bathroom beautiful today.

To me, the bathroom beautiful says color; it says flattering lighting; it says handsome accessories—faucets, towel racks, lemon soaps, shower curtains with a valance, apothecary jars on the vanity, hardware on vanity drawers, a vanity bench, plants hung in baskets from the ceiling or placed about the floor in attractive tubs.

Most of the things I just listed, you'll note, do not cost a great deal of money. Adding color to a small bathroom, for example, may require only a gallon of paint or a few rolls of vinyl wallcovering. You can make a shower curtain and valance yourself using either a patterned sheet or the fabric of your choice, teamed with a plastic liner from the dime store. Pick up some apothecary jars, too, while you're there, and some baskets for plants. With your savings, you may want to splurge on a really super lighting fixture to go over the vanity, or even a small crystal chandelier if it goes with your scheme. (A word about lighting: Never should the bath be lit with flourescent lights. This is the room where most of us get our first glimpse of our-selves in the morning—and a fluorescent light would send me right back to bed! If your bathroom comes equipped with a fluorescent fixture, replace it—and always buy flattering pink-toned bulbs for the bathroom, please.)

One imaginative and highly functional accessory you might try is a tall ladder used as a towel bar in the bathroom. I saw it done in a one-bathroom home recently and it was very effective. The ladder went from floor to ceiling and was painted fresh white to blend with the beige-and-white trellis wallcovering. Each member of the family had a towel of a different color —fire-engine red for dad, sunshine yellow for mom, apple green and deep blue for the children. The parents' towels hung high on the ladder and the children used the lower, easier-to-reach rungs. Another plus: The ladder, firmly secured to ceiling and floor, was placed so that when it came time for dad to change the light bulb in the ceiling, he could climb the ladder to reach the fixture.

Ladders can also be used for pretty storage racks. I like to see towels stacked on a Lucite stepladder in the bathroom. Or use a stepladder to hold green plants near a sunny bathroom window.

The point is, once again, that imagination is the key factor. No matter how small your budget and how bleak the bathroom you find your-

Decorate your breakfast room with the things you love; pretty tulip wallcovering was the choice here. White shell-back chairs with seats of green upholstery welted in white add lots of eye appeal.

Strawberry wallcovering is a kitchen favorite. The wallcovering and coordinating fabric here is my own design called Fraise Affaire.

This kitchen features cooking in the round; splash backs at counter surfaces are decorated with French flower, bird, and fruit tiles.

In this bathroom setting designed for Kohler, cabinetry is white and fixtures are rich chocolate. Wallcovering is my own Tau Yuan—a Chinese character design.

High Times by Carleton V is the wallcovering used in this old-fashioned bath. Heating pipes are painted black. Folding screen, with its painted trompe l'oeil ladder, conceals the bathtub.

This man's shower/bath is designed with beige marble walls; the cabinetry is painted hunter green and trimmed in beige. Ceiling is completely lighted.

The age of the big tub is here. And so is the age of the carpeted bath.

Get in the swing of things with hammocks, an inexpensive substitute for sofas. Floor pillows substitute for chairs.

A fur sofa throw, louvre-shuttered windows, supergraphic wall decor, and a Tiffany lamp over country table all say eclectic.

George and Martha Washington would have enjoyed this bedroom. Room is styled with chinoiserie wallcovering in yellows, greens, and browns. Love seat and bed-skirt are of a coordinating fabric.

A guest bedroom styled with a pretty flowered wallpaper is always a winner. Window valance is a great big bow.

self stuck with, there's plenty you can do to perk things up.

Decorating Around the Tilework You're Stuck With

There's no ignoring the tile that came with the place, because it represents a large expanse of color—usually institution green, washed-out pink, muddy peach, or watery blue. If you can't afford the major expense of retiling, you're going to have to work around the old tilework with a scheme that ties into it.

Let's begin by creating four exciting decorating schemes to go with those four most common tile colors. Then we'll move on to some others. If your bathroom tile is institution green and your fixtures are white, look for an awning-stripe wallcovering of rich emerald green and white. Choose a pattern that comes with a matching fabric, and use the fabric to make a shower curtain. Cover your floor tiles with an emerald-green carpet. Towels can be emerald green and rich chocolate brown. For accessories, go for brown wicker—and if there's a window, add a green plant or two.

If your bathroom tiles are washed-out pink and you want to minimize the prissy-pink look, choose a wallcovering of rich chocolate brown printed with small raspberry-pink flowers and grass-green leaves. Carpet can be chocolate, shower curtain a stripe of chocolate and raspberry. For towels, go toast beige and chocolate brown.

If, however, your bathroom is one of those with pink tiles and burgundy tile trim, here's a bold, beautiful look you can try. Paint walls a shiny burgundy red (or use patent vinyl if walls are pitted and cracked) and paint ceiling white. Carpet your wine-colored bath with thick, washable white fake fur! Shower curtain can be white, too, trimmed with burgundy ribbon. Accessorize with lots of shiny, shiny chrome, lacquer, and mirror baubles, and choose towels of fire-engine red, black, and snow white.

If your bathroom tiles are washed-out peach, try this simple Art Deco scheme: Paint walls high-gloss white (make sure you choose a pure white, not a washed-out off-white) and paint doors and trim glossy ebony. Choose a carpet in a black-and-white geometric and a shower curtain in silver and white. Decorate your white walls with colorful Art Deco posters. For towels, choose pure dove gray and black. Accessories can be mirror and chrome.

To lift the spirits of the watery blue-tiled bath, paper walls in a necktie print of sky blue and lipstick red on a shiny navy-blue ground. Carpet in rich navy-blue shag. Curtain your tub with shiny navy-blue vinyl trimmed with lipstick red and sky blue. For towels, lipstick red and navy blue would be super!

One time I saw an all blue bathroom with light blue tile on the walls and standard blue fixtures. The bathroom really came alive, thanks to a number of framed silk screens of different sizes that were hung on the walls. I must say that the yellow soaps in royal-blue soap dishes also helped, as did the royal-blue perfume bottles on the vanity. Brilliant canary-yellow towels, bath mat, and shower curtain were perfect in the room as the second color against the blue tile and fixtures.

So much for *those* four. Now on to some others you may find yourself stuck with. For example:

▶ *Blah beige.* This bathroom is a perfect candidate for the natural look of fern-patterned wall vinyl in shades of bright and dull green, yellow, and rich chocolate on pure white; beige shag carpeting; towels of forest green, canary yellow, and white; accessories of scorched bamboo and wicker. And if your bath is just a bit bigger than postage-stamp size, provide it with lounging luxuries—an acrylic bench, a dressing table, even a chaise longue.

Or try this scheme. Choose a beige moiré for walls and window shades. Edge shades in powder blue. Shower curtain can be pale blue; and for towels, a combination of beige, brown, and blue will do. I'd love to see rich chocolate brown hand towels embroidered with pale blue flowers to pick up the pale blue of a shag carpet. And if there's a corner that needs a special something, try a natural-straw basket filled with green plants.

▶ *Hospital white.* While a plain white bathroom with white tile, basic white fixtures, and an ordinary medicine-chest mirror may not thrill you, consider yourself lucky because there's no limit to the colors and prints it will go with. Or you could forgo color entirely and make that vision of the glamorous, all-white Hollywood bathroom come true!

If you opt for the glamour look, think of the details. Hang a crystal fixture from your white bathroom ceiling, and also find a crystal fixture to hang on the wall over your medicine chest. Use clear light bulbs only, not frosted, in these fixtures. Lay a white cotton shag rug wall-to-wall to cover the floor tile. For extra glamour, install a white Austrian-shade valance the entire length of your bathtub, and trim the valance with white ruching. For the shower curtain, white chiffon will be fine, provided you install a clear white plastic liner under it. Select white towels with a golden *fleur-de-lis* embroidered decoration and hang them on new brass towel racks and/or brass towel rings. Find a golden soap shell for the bathtub, and install new brass hardware on the drawers of a white vanity. If there is space for a small bench, select a brass piece upholstered in white vinyl moiré.

Here are a few schemes that are versatile enough to be used with more than one of the basic tile colors we've talked about.

Try pink-and-white candy-striped vinyl on walls above white, pink, or green tile. Shower and window curtains can be solid pink, hung on white rings. Choose mint-green cotton shag carpeting—make sure it's washable. Bathroom towels can be pink, white, and mint green, and, for the very flattering look, paint ceiling candy-cane pink. Save a bit of the candy-striped wall-covering to cover a wastebasket or tissue box. And in the candy-cane bathroom, place an apothecary jar with pink soap, along with perfume bottles and see-through jars for cotton, on a white wicker or Lucite wall-hung shelf.

Try a navy-blue bandanna look for a bathroom with light blue tile and white fixtures, with light blue tile and light blue fixtures, or with beige tile and white fixtures. Lay a rich navy-blue cotton-shag rug on bathroom floor. Shower and window curtains can be made of blue-and-white bandanna print, using a clear plastic liner

behind the shower curtain. Cover a bathroom wastebasket with the bandanna print too. And why not staple the blue-and-white bandanna print on bathroom walls? Paste white cord around the perimeter of the walls to cover the staples.

If none of these suggestions appeals and you really can't bear the color of your bathroom tiles, or if they're discolored or cracked, why not paint them with a ceramic epoxy? You can paint one row of tiles perhaps pale blue, and another row of tiles a sunny lemon yellow. This will create a carnival of colors on your tiled dado. Above the tile, I would suggest a vinyl wallcovering in a delicate flower pattern of daisy-yellow and green on a white background, and, if you like, you can paint your ceiling sky blue or sunny lemon yellow. The shower curtain can be bright white with borders of yellow, green, and blue, and shower-curtain rings can be brilliant green. (Again if you have a fabric shower curtain, be certain to use a plastic liner.) For windows, why not cover the shades with the same covering used on the walls?

A bright emerald-green washable shag carpet on the floor would be a wise choice, with bright orange, yellow, and green towels. Wicker accessories—such as a wastebasket, a hamper, and some hanging planters—would be pleasing eye-catchers. And for a light fixture, what about one of those inexpensive wicker pieces, painted bright green or sunshine yellow?

Three Great Looks for Bathroom Walls

SPANISH TILES

Real handpainted Spanish tile is a luxury few of us can indulge in. When I meet someone who loves the real thing but can't afford a whole room of tiles, I tell him or her to use handpainted tiles for accents. But if it's just the *look* you want —and lots of it—"Spanish tile" your bathroom walls with a self-adhesive vinyl in avocado green, royal blue, white, and lemon yellow. Car-

Bring sunny Spain to your bathroom with a Spanish-tile pattern in green, blue, yellow, and white in self-adhesive vinyl.

pet in rich royal blue, and carry out the Spanish mood with wicker accessories in avocado green. For towels, go avocado green and sunny yellow.

HERRINGBONE DESIGNS

I recently designed a bathroom using a beige-and-chocolate herringbone vinyl for walls and ceiling, and it looked terrific! Countertop was chocolate-brown laminate, outfitted with two bowls of lipstick red—I love a chocolate-beige-and-red scheme of things. Chocolate-brown ceramic tiles were used for floors and walls, with tub and toilet of fawn beige. Towels were lipstick red.

The manufacurers of vinyl floor tiles have shown us too that herringbone designs can be created on floors with their product. Can you visualize a bathroom with a herringbone pattern created of white and pearl-gray tiles? For towels and shower curtain, I'd suggest colors of mustard and white.

SHEET MIRROR

Sheet-mirrored walls add dimension to small bathrooms, creating the illusion that a room is wider or longer than it really is. But as the wall-covering, mirrors should always reflect something beautiful.

Singing star Dionne Warwick used sheet mirror on the doors of walk-in closets in her bathroom. The mirrors not only concealed the closet doors, they added lots of depth and glamour to the bath in the star's Hollywood home. Dionne's bathroom also has accessories worth reflecting: apothecary jars filled with soaps; perfume bottles; colorful towels and carpeting; plants; a sunken tub; and real amethyst and pewter fixtures.

Dionne is partial to a lavender-and-white scheme of things, with touches of green. Bathroom carpeting is an amethyst-and-white houndstooth design—the amethyst matching the handles on the bathtub fittings—and bath towels are printed with lavender and purple flowers on a white background.

The Victorian Look

A charming bathroom I once saw was done in an updated Victorian style. Walls and vanity were covered in a brocade-design vinyl wall-covering of Empire gold, celadon green, bronze, and white. Trim was colored a deep, gleaming chocolate brown to complement the burnished wood of an antique washstand and the frame of a Victorian mirror that hung over the sink. And flanking that mirror were two wrought-iron torchères with glass globes that would have looked right at home in a Victorian sitting room. Towels were Empire gold and chocolate brown, and bringing the whole look together was a plush carpet in lively spearmint green.

Mirrored closet doors in the bathroom of singing star Dionne Warwick reflect all her beautiful bathroom accessories—apothecary jars filled with soaps; perfume bottles; plants; colorful towels and carpeting; a sunken tub with real amethyst and pewter fixtures. Outside is a sauna with shower, both adjoining the garden.

(On following page)
The Victorian era lives again in a bathroom papered in updated version of Victorian brocade and carpeted in a lively spearmint-green plush.

8

The Family Room

The family room in many American homes is the heart of the house. It's where members of the family meet to relax, pursue individual interests together instead of alone in their rooms, and also where many American families—both parents and youngsters—do most of their casual entertaining. As such it's something of a decorating challenge: a multipurpose room designed to please the entire family, with space for each one's favorite indoor leisure activities, comfortable enough to feel completely relaxed in, attractive enough to invite guests into. It's a tall order, but one you can fill, and I'll help show you how.

Begin by deciding on a look that suits your family. It could be a contemporary or period look (or a mixture of both), an ethnic look, an outdoor look, a sporting look—whatever goes best with your life-style.

Plan the space you've allocated, however small, to include a special place—even if it's just a corner—for each member of the family.

Choose a color scheme that will please all of you (this may sound difficult, but with today's spectrum of colors and prints it's possible to work in a bit of everyone's favorite hue), and select practical materials for walls, floors, windows, and upholstery to suit the look and color scheme you've chosen.

Furnish with comfortable, attractive, functional pieces that coincide with the activities the room will be used for, and, lastly, accessorize with the family's favorite things.

Let's examine these steps in a bit more detail, starting with step one.

Choosing a "Look"

One of the things I, as a decorator, am thankful for is the range of inspiration that we have to work with in this country. Where else do you find ideas flowing from so many sources—French, English, Italian, African, tropical, plus our own Colonial American and American Indian–inspired designs? We can also turn for inspiration to our own favorite pastimes, building a look around sports or wildlife or seasonal pleasures. I'm thankful for this range of decorating inspiration because I can create rooms of beauty and originality without spending a fortune—and so can you.

THE FRENCH LOOK

If the look of French furniture is a look you like, adapt it to today's way of life and to the natural look of things that's taking the country by storm. A family room built around a French Provincial writing table and Louis XV chair would cer-

tainly be attractive, particularly if those wood pieces were stripped and bleached to a light, light shade. To complete the French flavor, house your family-room stereo, books, and bric-a-brac in a French Provincial armoire in the same bleached wood. (The armoire, you know, was a must in every French farmhouse back in Louis's day. In the American home of today, it would be an attractive change from book-shelves.) Paint the walls of your family room a warm melon with white trim. Upholster your desk chair in butterscotch leather, and, for extra seating bergère chairs in matching leather would be my choice. For carpeting, go rich grass green. Sofa can be a simple tuxedo style, covered in chocolate-brown corduroy and accented with toss cushions of scarlet, melon, and grass green. Or mix the look of France—bergère chairs—with African baskets and simple contemporary love seats. Upholster the love seats in brilliant scarlet wool and the bergères (with natural wood frames) in brown patent vinyl. Carpet in beige shag, and paint walls champagne beige with lipstick-red trim. Decorate walls with a colorful collection of African baskets.

THE TAILORED LOOK

I've just been shopping for a new wardrobe. Did you know that the stores are packed with the tailored look for both men and women? Shop windows are displaying glen plaids, houndstooth checks, pinstripes, and rich dark-colored woolens—all tailored into neat, fitted shapes.

What about giving your family room a touch of the same? I can think of so many tailored touches—tailored skirts for sofas and chairs; simple tailored draperies; upholstery of pinstripes or small plaids . . .

Let's try the tailored look in a family-room scheme of warm autumn tones. Walls are painted champagne beige; carpet is deep burgundy shag; sofa is upholstered in tailored beige-and-spice-brown houndstooth checks, accented with plump toss cushions of burgundy. For club-chair upholstery, my choice would be champagne-beige vinyl suede. Draperies are simply burgundy panels, hung from wooden poles.

THE NOSTALGIC LOOK

Nostalgia is the look of tomorrow. If that sounds like a contradiction, just go to your local furniture store and gaze at all the nostalgic looks on the market.

The biggest of these is golden oak furniture. Now that collectors of original golden oak have caused prices to skyrocket, manufacturers are turning out super reproductions of oak washstands, round dining tables, hat racks, bars—you name it.

To give your family room a nostalgic look, . how about a mix of old and new? Paint the sofa wall Gay Nineties red, and panel the other walls in oak. Furnish your family room with comfy seats, slipcovered in a zippy red-green-and-yellow plaid. Put in a golden oak bar and a pair of Gay Nineties slat-back chairs with seat pads of the plaid. Decorate walls with framed pages from old magazines or with framed turn-of-the-century postcards. Hang wooden venetian blinds at windows—and for fun, hang a wooden fan from the ceiling.

THE LOOK OF THE WILDS

Nature is the decorating news these days, and thus there are many wallcoverings and fabric designs on the market that represent natural elements—birds, animals, fish, trees, wildflowers. Fabrics that duplicate handsome animal hides are especially popular with decorators and conservationists. For example, there are ostrich and alligator Naugahydes used to cover Parsons-style tables, and I have seen chairs upholstered in vinyls that look like zebra skins. Fake furs that look like polar bear, tiger, zebra, or leopard skins are

Ancient inspiration from the American Indians of the Southwest is translated into a contemporary rug in colors of plum, scarlet, sunny gold, and cactus green. It's a perfect foil for plum-lacquered walls and a trio of trim sofas in leatherlike butterscotch vinyl, accented with brass and copper lamps and accessories.

popular for area rugs and accent pillows. I have even seen some white chinoiserie-style chandeliers that have woodcarved monkeys in the fixture design.

But you needn't have pelts and moose antlers for an effective wildlife theme. I liked a family room styled with a fabric design featuring polar bears, elephants, rhinoceroses, pandas, orangutans, spotted cats, and whales. The browns, yellows, reds, greens, and white in the pattern made it very versatile. In this comfortable family room with card table, cushy sofa, wing chair, and fireplace, the zoological print was used for sofa up-

holstery and for draperies. Walls were off-white, the carpet was caramel-colored, and accessories and occasional upholsteries were of bright red and russet.

Another attractive print features redwoods and Sequoias, the world's tallest trees, in a design of brown trunks and green bristlecone pine needles on a deep brown background that would be handsome and practical in a family room. With this fabric at the windows, I would like a tree-trunk-brown area rug, bordered in fern green, and green or brown grass cloth for walls. I would choose fern-green vinyl for club-chair upholstery,

Nature flourishes in this family room where a zoological-print fabric was used for sofa upholstery and draperies. Potted ferns and old brick complete a setting that says comfortable and homey charm.

Greeff Fabrics "Zoology" drapery and upholst

A dramatic red-and-black-striped graphic painted on white room-darkening shades and on white walls and ceiling is the focal point of this contemporary family room/den.

and I would cover the sofa in the tree pattern. A grouping of the new tree-stump tables now on the market would be perfect in front of that sofa.

THE CONTEMPORARY LOOK

Everyone knows the contemporary look—it's easy to recognize. But what is it exactly? In my opinion the contemporary look has certain basic elements: simple, clean lines for furniture; the uncluttered look of see-through furniture; bare floors accented with area rugs; pillows everywhere—on floors, sofas, chairs; bold geometric patterns; clear bright colors.

The family room is the perfect place for a contemporary scheme, I believe, because the contemporary style is easy to live with and, more important, easy to care for. In a room where the family snacks, children play, and feet, quite rightly, rest on the sofa, on tables—everywhere but on the floor—easy-care features are important.

A friend of mine planned her stunning red-black-and-white family room/den around a contemporary look that incorporates many of the easy-care features I've been talking about: a sofa with white vinyl upholstery that you can sponge off; bare wood floors, accented with a zebra-skin rug that needs only a once-over-lightly vacuuming; and laminated tables that wipe clean. Instead of draperies that need to be taken down and cleaned, there are supergraphics at the windows that climb the white room-darkening shades, go right up and over the ceiling, and down the white walls. The colors of the design—red, black, and white—pick up the room's clean, bright color scheme.

One word of caution in planning a contemporary scheme: The contemporary look can be cold and antiseptic unless you add some warm, happy touches—such as a bowl of flowers, a window box of plants, a collection of personal mementos or family photographs. Or how about a scattering of handmade needlepoint pillows, or a whimsical note like the bright red old-fashioned gumball machine on my friend's end table?

THE SPORTING LOOK

Hip hip hooray for the sporting life and the sporting look of tweed, plaid, corduroy, and the like! The fashion scene is bursting with the sporting look, and it's a look I like for decorating, too.

In a family room I like the sporting look of tawny fawn-beige vinyl suede for walls and sofa upholstery. And underfoot I picture a plaid carpet of beige, chocolate brown, and punchy tomato red.

Or how about the look of hunter-green corduroy upholstery teamed with light wood—paneled walls, hunter-green tartan draperies, and polished wood floors topped with furry rugs? On the green corduroy sofas I would like to see suede pillows of poppy red. And the sporting look should have sporting prints on the walls—prints of horses and hunting dogs in slim gold frames.

If you choose the sporting look, you might key it to your family's favorite sport. I myself have many happy associations with the rah-rah spirit of football games: the plaid lap robes; the camel's hair coats; the giant chrysanthemums; the bright red, green, and yellow football jerseys; the pennants waving against a clear blue autumn sky.

All those elements could be used in a room where the whole family gathers to watch its favorite teams.

I would start with walls covered in rich tobacco-colored vinyl pigskin suede. With those suede walls, I would like trim painted poppy red. Ceiling can be ivory.

I would cover a sofa and a deep club chair or two in a wool lap-robe plaid of zippy goldenrod yellow, maple-leaf red, and creamy ivory. For fun, you could use real blankets and use the fringe to skirt the chair and sofa! Add a luxuri-

ously comfortable recliner covered in pigskin—the real thing or look-alike vinyl—and make sure that the recliner, as well as the sofa and chairs, are arranged to give everyone an unobstructed view of the game.

Provide a large coffee table or a stack of trays for those Bowl-Game lunches and munches, and complete your football look with colorful pennants and a big brass bowl filled with giant yellow mums!

If baseball is your family's favorite sport, your scheme could start with a chocolate-and-cream wallcovering depicting the game, and draperies and slipcovers could be a snappy plaid of turf green, chocolate brown, and creamy white. Again, make sure the TV screen can be seen from any seat in the "house." You don't want anyone to miss those exciting plays!

A family room used for entertaining the after-tennis set could be designed for a lawn-party feeling. Use a green-and-white lattice-design wallcovering, and tent the ceiling in white cotton. Furnish with a mix of white laminated and lacquered pieces, clear acrylic lamps, and a pair of ruby-red lattice-design chairs. And underfoot, a new all-wool carpet with a tennis design in hunter green, pure white, ruby red, and chocolate brown would be very appropriate.

For all you sailors, there are scores of handsome print fabrics in a nautical mood on the market these days—prints of sailing ships, anchors, rope and chain. One of my favorites is a cotton print with vertical stripes of white rope on a royal-blue background.

I used this fabric in a den I designed for a seafaring client. We began by covering the walls with white sailcloth and painting the ceiling sky blue, then used rope to finish the wallcovering at baseboards and in place of crown molding. The blue-and-white rope print was used for draperies, hung from brass poles and rings, and also for seat pads on two captain's chairs that had been lacquered white.

Other furnishings included two comfortable love seats upholstered in white sailcloth with white rope welting; tall wooden bookcases to hold

"Tennis" design by Dick Ridge for Phoenix Carpet Co., Inc.

For entertaining the after-tennis set, the look is as breezy and fresh as a summer day with a new, all-wool carpet with a tennis design.

books, model ships, and a brass ship's clock; and cube end tables of brassbound teak. Lamps for those end tables were fashioned from a couple of old, squat ship's decanters, with shades of pierced brass.

The floor of the nautical den was bare polished wood planks that simulated a ship's scrubbed deck, and the white sailcloth walls were adorned with international code flags in snappy red, yellow, and blue.

Believe me, when you step into that room, you can almost feel the salt spray and smell the sea!

If your favorite outdoor sport is lounging in the sun with a beer in your hand and your hat over your eyes, there's a great family-room look for you, too!

Start by installing a hammock of white rope. (It's easy; just be sure your walls are strong enough to support the weight.) Furnish with easy-care vinyl seating in cheery sunshine yellow, teamed with tables and accessories of self-assemble tubular pieces in crisp black and white. To complete that fresh backyard decor, don't forget the greenery—and I mean lots of it—green growing plants hanging from the ceiling and sitting in pretty pots on the windowsill.

Lacy white wrought-iron garden furniture is another outdoor favorite of mine. Two of those

pretty garden chairs, with a small matching love seat, would be a pretty addition to a family room. Place them on a quarry-tile floor. Cover walls in a fresh green fern pattern on a chalk-white background. And for cushy pads on those wrought-iron chairs and love seat, how about covers of geranium pink? Your guests will think they're still in the great, green outdoors!

THE COUNTRY LOOK

The country look is everybody's favorite these days, and it's a natural for the family room because it goes so well with today's casual way of life.

The country look is barn siding for walls—whitewashed perhaps, Tom Sawyer–style. The country look is beams, brick, stone, stucco, patchwork, hooked rugs, calico. The country look definitely is *not* heavy draperies for windows, or —perish the thought—plastic covers for upholstered furniture, especially in a family room, where family members and guests should feel free to put their feet up and be comfortable.

Why not furnish the family room in sturdy butcherblock pieces? Butcherblock isn't just for tables these days; there are butcherblock storage units (I like the stackable style) and butcherblock upholstered pieces. In your family room, why not a butcherblock sofa covered in pumpkin cotton corduroy? Add a few antique pieces to round out your furnishings, and, just for fun, try a peppy patchwork carpet, patterned in gold, pumpkin, navy, nut brown, and white.

THE LOOK OF WOOD FLOORS

Oh, the beauty of wooden floors! For centuries wood has been the major material for covering floors, and it is still supreme. Granted, in medieval castles, you could be certain to see marble or stone floors in the entry halls, drawing rooms,

and baronial dining halls. But you can be certain you'd find wood flooring—most likely of oak planks or in a pattern of parquet—in the sleeping chambers.

There is nothing as lovely as a polished wood floor with beautiful graining. It can make a room's "look" all by itself. So if you have a beautiful floor, don't cover it up—let it be the focal point and set the tone for the entire room.

If you visit Early American homes, you will notice the sturdy wide planks of random widths on the floors. These boards came from the large trees of the early untouched forests, from the chestnut tree, the oak, maple, or birch, even the white pine. White-pine floors were generally painted or spatter-painted, and some were even stenciled with a pattern. The reason is that white pine is a soft wood. Oak or other hardwood floors were simply given a coat or two of protective wax.

When choosing wood flooring for a family room, you can pick exotic woods such as teak or mahogany from Africa, South America, Asia, if your budget is unlimited. If it's not, you will be selecting a hardwood (the harder woods are the most desirable). Hardwood floors can be laid in one or two different patterns or in a stripe. The parquet pattern, sometimes called the block or square pattern, is popular in apartments. You can create all different types of flooring designs with the blocks. I like them best when they are laid on the diagonal. As far as strip flooring is concerned, the wood lengths are best when laid in a way to give the room the longest look.

Consult your local lumber dealer about methods of installation of a new wood floor. One of the most important things to remember about wood floors is that they should always be installed on a wood subfloor. Today, plywood paneling serves as subflooring at very reasonable costs. And the costs to install plywood panels are less indeed than the costs to install separate wood underboards. If you plan a wide-plank floor in your family room, be certain the planks are thoroughly dry to prevent any possibility of expansion due to dampness.

Backyard living indoors? It's yours with a swinging rope hammock, a collection of green plants, and easy-care furniture.

A peppy patchwork carpet and natural butcherblock storage unit set the country mood in a family room designed for enjoyment and easy upkeep.

Creating Special Activity Areas

I believe that every member of the family should have a special place of his or her own, and, as I said before, it needn't be large. I know one dad whose special place is his leather reclining chair, and I know a mother whose special place is a sewing "room" made from a wide, shallow closet with folding doors. The sewing machine fits in neatly and is left open, ready for use; a series of small wood dowels holds threads and seambindings; and upper shelves store fabrics and patterns.

A workshop for dad could be made the same way. Remove the sliding doors from a closet and replace with space-saving foldaways or roll-up bamboo blinds. Cover the back and side walls of the closet with pegboard for hanging tools and other supplies, and put in a small workbench with storage space below. You can finish the floor of the closet and the adjacent area with washable self-stick vinyl tiles for easy cleanups.

If dad is an after-hours executive, his special place might be a corner of the family room, defined perhaps by a reproduction Oriental rug of rich royal blue, olive green, and gold. In the room pictured, a wallcovering of navy blue frosted with a leafy white bamboo-tree design further sets off the space. For work, there's a man-size antique pine desk, and for relaxation —or visitors—there's a deep button-tufted wing chair.

For a mother who needs space for work on household accounts or work brought home from the office, the same technique could be used with a different decor. The "office" might be a desk-and-bookshelf arrangement placed in a corner with a fresh scheme of green, yellow, and white. Paint walls sunny yellow with white trim, and for carpeting choose restful forest-green shag. Draperies and upholstery on a convertible sofa can be a small-scale plaid of emerald green, forest green, sunny yellow, tangerine, and white. Choose a desk of hardy white laminate, and flank your

convertible sofa with low, white file cabinets topped with bright yellow jar lamps.

A hobby center for parents and children can also be carved out of a family-room corner that isn't doing anything. Be creative and look for furnishings that serve dual functions. Friends of mine, who are part-time home craftsmen without an entire room to use as a home workshop, created a painting-and-needlework studio in a cozy corner of their family room—and everything connected with their arts and crafts can disappear when workshop time is over.

The family-room hobby center was styled with

A place of dad's own, in this case an office, can be carved out of a corner in a large family room. This study is defined by its area rug and wallcovering and it's decorated with man-size furniture—an antique kneehole desk and a generous wing chair.

"Ranchero" Naugahyde-covered wing chai

a vivid green-white-and-yellow color scheme. Yellow tile-patterned kitchen carpeting was laid wall-to-wall, and walls were covered with grooved random panels, placed at a 45-degree angle for a stunning chevron effect. Window trim, crown molding, baseboard, and decorative strips used to conceal the seams where the panels meet were painted off-white.

The chevron design was repeated in white-on-green window shades at three old-fashioned windows. One window was completely blocked out with shelving to store paints, brushes, and other art supplies, all cleverly concealed behind the window shade. Beneath the windowsills of the two other windows, white window shades decorated with green chevrons were installed to hide an air conditioner under one window and to cover a wall-hinged, drop-leaf worktable under another.

The entire hobby center fades into the walls of the family room when not in use: The white Lucite stool at the easel·is used at the family-room bar after workshop time; a wine-rack chest acts as a stash-away place for balls of yarn, half-finished appliqués and collages go into a flip-top sewing table, and wicker baskets hold rolled-up drawings.

Deciding on a Color Scheme

Many people today are in a color rut—usually avocado, gold, or, less often, red.

On the subject of color ruts, I received a letter saying, "After ten years of living with avocado green, I'm redecorating. I love the natural look and want to use beiges and browns in my family room, but I am afraid I'll be putting myself into another rut. What do you think?"

I think that decorating the "natural way" is not as likely to land you in a color rut, for the simple reason that naturals—particularly beige tones—are also neutrals, and that means they'll go with anything.

Many decorators have known this for years and have wisely decorated with neutral beige tones for major room areas—walls, upholstery, and floors. When a change is desired, all the decorator has to do is alter the accessory colors.

Visualize this family room: it is decorated in today's popular natural look, built around a sofa grouping upholstered in a geometric beige-tone fabric. The carpet is rich chocolate brown. The fabric is tough, and that means it will last for years, but its neutral coloration guarantees its versatility for a long time to come. Those beige tones can be accessorized with blues, reds, orange tones, with sharp greens, pinks, yellows.

In five years, I picture the same room this way: Colors then, if color forecasters are right, will be clearer and brighter—corals, blues, and mauves will be featured—so to the beige sofas, beige brick wall, and brown carpet, I would add those clear colors. In the center of the sofa grouping I might put down a thick plush area rug of clear sky blue, bordered in white. Instead of beige and off-white toss pillows, cushions of clear blue, coral, mauve, and lemon yellow would be my choice. The bamboo table might be painted white. The earth-toned print above the fireplace could be switched to a watery abstract of blues, corals, and mauves.

How's that for getting out of a rut? And that's only one way. I could have reaccessorized the room with yellows and sharp greens, reds and blues, purple and orange tones, too.

A DESERT COLOR SCHEME

If you think the desert is nothing but miles and miles of drab-looking sand, think again. I visited the Southwest recently, and take it from me, the desert is a colorful place and an inspiration to the decorator. Colors in the desert are muted, to be sure, but they are varied, too. I saw sand beige, of course, but I also saw rich rusts and browns, delicate salmon pink, and cactus greens. Topping many of those cacti were flowers in vibrant reds, yellows, and oranges. And what about brilliant blue sky? In my view it's certainly an important part of the desert color scheme.

A desert color scheme for the family room would be in step with today's popular natural look. Start with a neutral background of sand gray and beige for walls and carpet. Paint trim white. Continue your neutral theme by upholstering sofa and chairs with a rich twill in the same shades as the walls, and accent the sofa with toss cushions of soft, silvery sagebrush green and cactus-flower red. End tables and storage units can be pale bleached pine, oak, or ash. For draperies, my choice would be a nubby cotton in silvery green, hung from poles and rings of the

A versatile beige-tone scheme in a garden room is built around a sofa grouping upholstered in tough olefin. Chocolate-brown carpeting of hardy weave is suitable for indoor or outdoor use.

pale bleached wood. Lighting can be provided by chubby unglazed terra-cotta lamps shaded in off-white linen. And what desert room would be complete without a collection of hardy cacti in baskets and terra-cotta pots?

Chrysanthemum Colors

I love those subtle chrysanthemum colors— mauve, rust, sunny yellow, bronze, and frosty white. Look at a mixed bouquet of chrysanthe-

mums and you'll know why it's said that Nature is the best decorator!

I enjoy seeing those warm chrysanthemum colors in a family room. Try this scheme and see if you don't agree.

Paint walls chrysanthemum bronze. (Rich wall colors lend a cozy air to family rooms.) Paint ceiling and trim white. For carpeting, bronze shag would be my choice, and use that bronze tone for sofa upholstery, too—in velvet. Cover club chairs in mauve, and use mauve, yellow, frosty white, and leaf-green for toss pillows on your sofa. Some do-it-yourself needlepoint needlepoint cushions in chrysanthemum designs would be great, too!

Flank the sofa with polished brass trays for end tables. And for lamps, how about Chinese jars in frosty white with white shades. At windows, hang chintz draperies in a chrysanthemum print of burnished gold, oranges, blues, pinks, and mauves with green foliage on a creamy white ground. And don't forget to place some polished bronze planters, filled with live chrysanthemums, in front of those colorfully draped windows.

Potted chrysanthemums in all those pretty colors, are favorite decorative accessories of mine. I like them at windows; of course, and I also like them peeping from under an end table or peering down from the top of an armoire.

A "Brown Study"

A "brown study," according to Webster, is "a state of serious absorption or abstraction." I have a friend who took that expression literally. When she wants to think deep thoughts, she closets herself in a room she calls her "brown study." As the name implies, it is a room decorated in brown, and it certainly is a good place to get away from it all to think, read, or just be alone.

If you think an all-brown scheme sounds depressing, listen to my friend's scheme—it will change your mind.

Walls are painted chocolate brown with wide moldings and handsome old doors painted white. A tufted chesterfield sofa and a stately wing chair are upholstered in a lively floral of raspberry pink and white with spearmint-green foliage on a chocolate ground. Draperies are white, trimmed with chocolate tape. Carpet is chocolate. And those soothing brown walls are hung with softly lit oil paintings in carved, gilded frames.

That room convinced me that a brown study is a great idea.

A brown study/family room would be a great idea and a snug place to watch TV, entertain, or put up overnight guests.

Start with rich brown plywood-paneled walls, and line one wall with wood storage modules to hold television set, books, and hobby equipment. Furnish with two brown corduroy-covered love seats—make one of them a sleep sofa for guests—

and for contrast with all that warm brown, add two natural wicker chairs and a bleached-wood Parsons-style coffee table. Carpet in sand beige, and, for color, top that beige carpet with a lively geometric area rug of coin gold and brick red.

COLOR SCHEMES DESIGNED AROUND PLAIDS

In a family room, what could be cozier than plaid for those crisp autumn and winter days and nights? Plaid for walls; plaid for upholstery; plaid for draperies; plaid on the floor! I've said it before and I'll say it again: I love plaid. It's a perennial pattern that comes in endless color combinations and can have many different looks—from the Oriental look of Siam to the look of the Highlands to the rustic look of Americana.

If your family likes the natural look, as I do, why not use a plaid of natural beiges and browns for upholstery? On natural wood floors, a Navajo-inspired area rug in tans, grays, and browns that would team up beautifully with that plaid upholstery.

A plaid in warm tones of red is always a welcome sight—especially in a room with a colonial air. I saw one recently that had a glowing hearth as a focal point. Walls were whitewashed barn siding, and what a fresh, clean look they had! Love seats in that cozy country room were upholstered in a fall-tone plaid of reds and oranges with just a hint of Jack Frost white, and a chair was upholstered in cheery red tweed to match flame-colored wall-to-wall carpeting. Since no country room would be complete without lots and lots of gleaming rich wood, it was there on the sides of the love seats and armchair, and in the ample colonial-style coffee table as well.

If you choose that popular favorite, bright red-and-green to tan, team it with wood-paneled walls, stained wood shutters, and emerald-green carpets. Cover a sofa with the tartan, and use unfinished wood Parsons-style end tables, or, instead, a grouping of those new tree-stump tables I mentioned earlier. For lamps, why not two cubes covered in red suede with black shades?

Another scheme to try starts with a chocolate-and-black plaid used for walls, sofa, ottomans, and tieback draperies. Upholster a pair of fireside wing chairs in camel suede-look material; for

STRIPES

I have always believed the stripe was the decorating common denominator, because the stripe goes with almost everything.

Consider for a moment a family room decorated with a wallcovering of 3-inch-wide green and white stripes. The carpeting in the room is emerald green. Sofa and club chairs are covered in one of today's bright floral prints, perhaps wild emerald green and bright orange on a white background. The draperies are bright orange under a valance of the floral print. What a colorful scheme for the today look!

For the elegant, conservative look, visualize a family room with a dark-stained wood floor. The area rug under the mahogany game table is a ruby-red, blue, beige, and celadon-green Oriental. Walls are covered with a light-blue-on-white wallpaper. Draperies and valance are light blue, too, and wood trim and ceiling are white. But the sparkle of the room is the covering on the seats of the game chairs—a bright red, gold, and sky-blue stripe on a white background.

MIXING IT UP

If your family conference on a color scheme turns up the fact that you like a floral, the men in your family like plaid, and your daughter likes stripes, all is not lost. Flowers, stripes, and a plaid can be used in the same room—providing a color relationship exists among the designs. Indeed the use of the three designs in the same room is a growing look, especially popular with young homemakers.

I like the smart look of stripes, flowers, and plaids in a family room with a color scheme of chocolate brown, beiges, white, black, and parchment. Washable vinyl wallcovering for the window wall was a stripe of chocolate brown, white, and black. Other walls were covered in a washable vinyl floral design of large white flowers with black centers on a chocolate-brown background. A muted plaid of beiges and browns was introduced in sofa upholstery of a new soft, washable vinyl. Two deep, comfortable chairs were covered in parchment-colored vinyl, and carpeting was a lush parchment color. Table surfaces were of warm woods combined with steel and glass pieces. Instead of heavy drapery or curtains that require constant upkeep, very thin, silvery venetian blinds were used at the windows. Their horizontal lines always look well in rooms with vertical-stripe wallcoverings.

A COLOR SCHEME GOOD ENOUGH TO EAT

Here's a family-room decorating idea that's truly delicious. It starts off with a lush pineapple carpet, which will keep its bright look through years of youngsters' hustle and bustle. For wallcovering behind a love-seat-and-sofa grouping, use a washable vinyl of tangerine, coconut-white, and lime-sherbet waves. Curtains in the room can match the wallcovering. Love seat and sofa are covered in durable white vinyl that's soft and glovelike in texture, and for a coffee table, think wipeable white plastic.

Tangerine and lemon pillows would be appropriately luscious accents, and covers should be zippered for easy removal when soiled by sticky fingers.

New Products, New Ways

There are scores of new products on the market that can add architectural interest to bare square spaces and help you achieve the look you want with the added advantage of practicality. There are also lots of new ways to use things that were originally designed with only one function in mind. Here are some for you to consider in your family room.

SYNTHETIC BRICK

Many apartments and homes now lure occupants by offering the beauty of brick walls and fireplaces. But even if your home is not graced by natural brick, there are alternatives: vinyl brick for floors; brick-patterned wallpaper; and synthetic brick made of plastic or cement and gypsum for walls.

Synthetic bricks are the most effective because nowadays they look like the real thing and come in several styles—used brick, sparkling white, antique, and more. You can install the quarter-inch-thick bricks yourself, using a special mastic

World's "Luxera" carpet of Kodel III

Lush, lighthearted colors give this two-level family room a face-lift! Sturdy vinyl upholstery, white plastic furniture, vinyl wallcovering, and carpet of polyester are practical as well as bright.

Flowers, stripes, and a plaid are used successfully in this family room because there is a color relationship among the designs. Window wall is covered with vinyl wallcovering in a chocolate-brown, white, and black stripe. Other walls feature large white flowers with black centers on a chocolate-brown background. Sofa upholstery of new soft, washable vinyl is a muted plaid of beiges and browns.

that you apply to the wall and to the back of the bricks. As you press them in place, the mastic squeezes between the bricks to make genuine-looking mortar!

I would like to see "used brick" on one wall of a family room, with the other walls done in crunchy beige sand paint. For upholstery, I picture woolly flame stitch in beige and off-white; and for carpet, grass green.

Or how about a wall of "antique brick" facing a wall of white, with copper and patchwork accessories? White vinyl brick could be used on the floor, with furniture of rustic oak.

A cheery family room I once saw featured brick—real this time—for an entire fireplace wall. The room, in a northern climate, needed lots of warming up, so a color scheme of flame red and sunny yellow was the choice. A plush carpet of persimmon red not only looked warm, but actually helped insulate the room against wintry drafts.

If you like the more rugged look of stone, you'll also find synthetic fieldstone that duplicates the look perfectly.

Vinyl "Wood"

Rich wood for walls—you don't have to be a millionaire to afford it. There are many ways to achieve the wood-paneled look without much money—and without *any* wood! There are vinyl wallcoverings in wood grains and hardboard panels in wood tones.

Wood paneling, of course, is extremely popular for family rooms, and you'll find authentic-looking simulations on the market in all grains and shades. Team it with plaid or the "wildlife look" we talked about, or go for the elegant "English library" look.

Noiseproof Materials

If you crave peace and quiet, you should take that into consideration when decorating your family room, where children, music, television, and conversation can create a real din.

There are many attractive ways to noiseproof your room, the most obvious of which is acoustical tile, made to absorb sound. It's most often used on ceilings, and the newest types are easier than ever to install. But acoustical tile needn't be relegated to the ceiling; it's possible to use it on walls, too. Because it is a soft surface, however, experts recommend using the tiles above a dado—on the upper part of the wall only—where it won't be subject to nicks and marring.

Another great silencer is carpeting—for floors, of course, but today also for walls. Carpet on the walls works best with low-pile carpets backed in foam rubber (a good sound silencer on its own).

For that cozy family room try cork on the walls. You'll get peace and quiet as well as a wrap-around bulletin board for posting favorite family photographs, children's artwork, or whatever suits your fancy.

Friends of mine who wanted to ban the sound of noisy neighbors from their den took an unusual route: Walls were covered in dark brown quilting—the kind moving men use to wrap furniture. Carpeting was a thick, foam-backed shag in the same milk-chocolate color. The ceiling was white acoustical tile. A soft color scheme also contributed to the quiet mood of the room. Sofa and chairs were upholstered in an aquamarine-and-chocolate geometric. End tables were glass and chrome, topped with chrome-based lamps. And to complement those chrome tables, there were silvery, narrow-slat blinds at windows.

Prefinished Wood Tiles

If you love the look of wood floors as I do, you'll be happy to hear that it's now possible to lay a wood floor yourself using prefinished wood tiles. They come in a great variety of hardwoods, from exotic teak and karri wood to beloved oak, and the range of patterns is also large—everything from rustic random planks with pegs to diamond patterns inspired by French châteaus.

One of my favorites is a sporty herringbone effect in rich, red-toned karpa wood. (Karri, as you may know, is one of the world's hardest, most durable woods.) I picture that karri-wood floor in a family room with walls painted a soft ivory. For upholstery on sofa and club chairs, peppy emerald green would be my choice, and I would like to see colorful toss cushions of lipstick red, pumpkin orange, and sunny yellow on the sofa. Draperies can be ivory, hung over lipstick-red bamboo blinds. End tables can be plywood cubes covered in wood tiles to match the floor!

The cost of a wood floor is not as high as its lasting beauty would lead you to believe. According to New York City's Designed Wood Flooring Center, a floor of prefinished wood tile costs anywhere from $1 to $3.50 a square foot without installation, which you can do yourself. You can either use mastic (an adhesive you apply with a trowel) or use double-face tape. The tape—apartment dwellers, take note—allows you to remove the floor when you move.

Tiles should be laid on a dry, level surface such as concrete, vinyl-asbestos, or even wood. For those less fortunate folks whose floors buckle and bend, there are tiles available that actually flex to conform to your floor's ins and outs!

ORIENTAL RUGS

I never tire of writing about the beauty and versatility of Oriental rugs, both antique and modern. The antique rugs are considered by experts to be the more beautiful, but I personally favor a good-quality new Oriental for heavy traffic areas like the family room.

Antique orientals in poor condition should not be passed up, however. You can use damaged Orientals as pillow covers for the family-room sofa or floor. It's being done, you know. Particularly with kilims—Orientals woven flat, without pile. Look for ripped or badly worn rugs in antique shops. If you find a kilim, you can sew it at home, using the heaviest sewing-machine needle and heaviest thread you can find. The pile rugs are best done on a heavy-duty machine by your local tailor or dressmaker.

If you're a modernist, don't be afraid to use an Oriental rug with a contemporary scheme; the patterns are usually subtle enough to mix well with prints and patterned weaves for upholstery, draperies, and accessories. Try this family-room scheme and you'll see what I mean:

Paper walls in a plaid of chocolate brown and white. Lay an Oriental area rug of chocolate, sunny gold, and creamy white. Use a patchwork print of the same warm colors for Austrian shades at windows and for a table skirt. The sofa bed can be upholstered in rich chocolate-brown velvet.

Those patterns will work together, as long as they are the same scale and color.

QUILTS

Quilts are in the news these days as the popularity of patchwork quilts soars. But who says that quilts and the quilted look must be relegated to beds? I like the quilted look for upholstery, and I enjoy the quilted look on walls and ceilings, too. Not only does it absorb sound, it adds an extra dimension of luxury and eye appeal to any room in the house.

One family room I designed had the quilted look all the way. Walls were covered in chocolate-brown quilted suede cloth, trim was painted Chinese red, and the ceiling was sheet-mirrored for airiness. There were two buttery soft leather sofas in a warm tan. Club chairs were upholstered in a quilted cotton geometric print of sharp green, chocolate brown, royal purple, Siamese pink, and Chinese red on a black background. Draperies in the geometric print were hung under a quilted valance of the same fabric, and I chose a carpet of chocolate-brown shag.

For end tables in that family room, I selected contemporary brass and glass. End-table lamps were brass cubes with white shades—and the brass lamp bases were quilted. The look of quilted metal is often seen in stainless-steel kitchen fixtures for restaurants, but I like the look of quilted metal for the home, too.

WALLPAPERED FLOORS

Thanks to an exciting new product called polyurethane—a clear plastic coating you apply like paint—you can now wallpaper your floors and keep them looking beautiful for years!

To wallpaper the floor in a small area, first cut out a paper pattern of the area to be papered, lay it on a Masonite board, and cut the board to size. Nail or glue the board to your floor and then apply the paper as you would to a wall, using premixed vinyl paste. Let the paper dry for at least twelve hours before applying your first coat of polyurethane. A minimum of five coats of the plastic is recommended to keep your papered floor beautiful. Dry overnight between coats.

When I first heard of wallpapering floors from friends, visions of all the great possibilities flashed through my mind: stripes for hallway walls and floors, fields of colorful flowers for bathroom floors and walls, Portuguese tiles for the kitchen floor. . . .

For a small family room, why not paper walls in a ticking stripe of pale gray and white. Paper the floor in the stripe too, and then coat with polyurethane. For sofa upholstery, choose a plaid of gray, toast, black, and white. For chair upholstery, go pumpkin orange, and use the orange for sofa toss pillows, too. At your windows, hang woven roller-blinds of orange and toasty brown. And in that family room with its natty striped floor, how about using three or four large covered baskets for storage? Covered baskets in natural wicker make attractive catchalls for small toys, magazines, knitting yarns, and other family paraphernalia.

THE NEW VENETIAN BLINDS

I've had an on-again, off-again romance with venetian blinds for years—a real love-hate relationship. I loved the old wood-slat blinds (which today are collector's items), hated the bland, utilitarian aluminum blinds that replaced them, and love the new ones that have arrived to replace those!

Today you can purchase metal blinds in wood grains such as cedar, birch, and walnut, or in linen looks of beige, pale green, and gray-white. Also on the market are polished-aluminum blinds that reflect light—these mirrored, reflective blinds are exciting.

The newest look in venetian blinds is gingham —blue-and-white gingham, green-and-white gingham, yellow-and-white gingham, red-and-white gingham, or brown-and-white gingham. The new 1-inch-wide slats are threaded on cable tape of dacron polyester so thin that the tapes do not become a window feature. The gingham is printed on one side, and the shades are scrubbable.

When decorating a family room, why not try this scheme? Paint walls royal blue with white trim and use royal-blue-and-white gingham venetian blinds at windows. For flooring, go daffodil-yellow vinyl. And on the sofa, what about a sturdy royal-blue tweed, accented with gingham pillows in a variety of colors? A yellow-and-white gingham skirt for one end table could be topped with a royal-blue lamp with a white shade.

THE DRIP-DRY HOUSE

I was reminded recently of what a wonderful age we live in. My job was to decorate a house— top-to-bottom—for a family with four active young sons, and my client's major request was that I please, please, make everything washable!

Thirty years ago, that might have crippled a decorator. Today, nothing could be easier than achieving a beautiful, exciting, and completely washable room.

In the house I decorated, family-room walls were covered in poppy-red, leather-look vinyl. The wood floor was coated with polyurethane, which can be damp-mopped. Washable heavyweight cotton (preshrunk) was the choice for pole-hung draperies and slipcovers—a stripe of chocolate brown, poppy red, and grass green. Occasional tables and wall unit were also washable, thanks to glossy seal-brown laminate.

THE RECYCLED HOUSE

A young couple I know achieved the ultimate in finding new uses for old things. They furnished their entire country home with cast-offs.

In their family room, they paneled the bottom half of the walls with handsome old carved-wood interior shutters. First they removed the hardware and old finish from the shutters and bleached the oak to a pale blond shade. Then two strips of wood were attached to the walls— one at chair-rail height, the other near the floor—

An Oriental rug blends beautifully with two other patterns in shades of brown and gold in this family room with an up-to-date country look.

and the shutters were attached to the strips.

The walls above the paneled dado are painted white. Trim and floors are natural wood. The walls display more cast-offs: posters in cast-off frames, an old wood-framed mirror found at a local garage sale, and a collection of antique bottles dug up in a local dump.

At one end of the room, this clever couple installed a fireplace built of weathered brick salvaged from a demolition site. And they surrounded that old brick with a carved oak mantel discovered in an abandoned house.

The cozy cast-off family room looked anything but secondhand with its handsome country color scheme of black-and-white plaid linen upholstery, ruby-toned Oriental scatter rugs, and rich wine-red draperies, hung from cast-off wooden rods and rings.

Other rooms in the house held more innovations you could use in your family room: wooden porch columns, for example, cut down and refinished for use as plant stands; windows hung with handsome stained-glass panels instead of curtains; old clothes cut into strips and worked into colorful braided rugs.

Selecting Furniture

When you're ready to furnish your family room, you'll have decided on a look for the room, planned areas for special activities individual members of your family enjoy, and settled on a color scheme. All that's left is to select furnishings that suit your plan. You'll want easy-to-clean, practical pieces, but, beyond that, there are no hard-and-fast rules. If there is any such thing as a decorating Do or Don't, it's simply this: DO buy what you love and what's comfortable; DON'T listen to anyone who tells you not to.

Here are some family-room furnishings you may want to consider.

PLASTIC FURNITURE

Plastic is a dirty word to some people. And I will say that there are certain uses of plastic in decorating that are not my cup of tea—plastic slipcovers and lampshade covers, for instance.

But easy-care plastic furniture in cheery colors and gleaming finishes, handsome vinyl suedes and

leather, colorful laminates wipe clean—that's a whole different story, and it's a story I like. Try the plastic way of decorating in your family room. You'll never have to worry about scratched furniture, scuffing, or spills again.

Paper walls in tortoiseshell vinyl—tortoise is a rich, warm look for family room walls and there are many handsome tortoise vinyls on the market. Furnish your family room with a sofa and chairs upholstered in coin-gold vinyl suede, and go gold for wall-to-wall shag carpeting, too. Place a handsome molded-plastic game table and chairs in one corner. A rich chocolate brown for table and chairs would look super against those tortoise walls, and what a perfect place not only for games but for serving light suppers and snacks!

At windows, go plastic again, with vinyl window shades in handsome stripes of chocolate and wheat beige.

MIXING PLASTICS WITH WOODS

Many years ago a decorator might have told you never to use pink and orange in the same scheme. Today, pink and orange, as well as purple and orange, blue and green, and other "forbidden" combinations, are about as shocking as fog in London!

I recently visited a home where colorful periods were mixed, breaking all the old taboos. Abstract paintings, eighteenth-century French antiques, and very twentieth-century seating pieces, upholstered in nubby beige wool, all coexisted happily.

I asked the lady of the house how her unusual mix of furniture and paintings came about. She told me, "We inherited the antique furniture from our families, but the chairs and sofas were too fragile for everyday use, so we bought the modern sofas and chairs for comfort. And we purchased the paintings because we love them!"

Most people who love the look of wood paneling and wood floors, and also love the sleek look of contemporary molded plastic furniture, wouldn't dream of teaming the two. They think it's a decorating Don't. In fact, what could be more complementary than the cool looks of white or colorful molded plastic and the mellow warmth of wood?

Here's a family-room scheme that proves it: Floors and walls are random-width bleached oak.

Plastic is the name of the game in a family room that features a vinyl wall-covering and window shades and molded-plastic game table and chairs in rich chocolate brown.

Modular seating units with white plastic frames are upholstered in cool green-and-white plaid, brightened with flashes of shocking pink in accent pillows and paintings. A handsome molded-plastic bar on wheels makes a fine coffee table, and a white plastic desk makes this family room a home office, too.

"Feet-up" Furniture

Sitting ramrod tall in a straight-backed chair is not the way of today's moderns. And it's certainly not the way in today's family rooms. These days, everyone wants to be able to sit back and relax with their feet up.

I'm for that, with one reservation: I am opposed to feet on tables. Tables are meant to hold lamps, ashtrays, snacks, and drinks, not feet. Feet belong on ottomans, stools, recliners, and chaise longues.

One of my favorite ways of putting up my feet is on a softly upholstered ottoman that matches a deep, cushy club chair. The ottoman could also be part of one of today's snappy pit arrangements. Just make certain that the fabric on your

Chromecrafts modular seating ur

Mellow wood paneling is a warm backdrop for contemporary molded-plastic seating units, desk, and rolling cart. Seating units are upholstered in cool green-and-white plaid, brightened with shocking-pink pillows.

ottoman is one that can take the scuffing of feet: A removable, washable cotton slipcover, wipeable vinyl, or soil-hiding tweed would be my choice. Don't select delicate pastels or white covers or your "feet-up" furniture will go to waste. It has been my experience that no one but a lout will be tempted to put his feet up if he thinks a big, black, indelible mark will be the result!

Also part of the "feet-up" family is the longtime favorite chaise longue; I hope you're lucky enough to have room for a chaise in some part of your family room. Tuck a recliner in one corner and a softly cushioned chaise longue in another. Add a small love seat and a matching ottoman that can do double duty as a seat or footrest.

I would slipcover the love seat, chaise, and ottoman in washable chintz; a crisp geometric design of beige, dove gray, and white would be super. Choose a recliner covered in wipeable, leather-look vinyl of luggage tan. Paint walls luggage tan to match—or, better yet, use a matching vinyl on walls. Trim can be pale straw beige. At windows, hang draperies of the geometric chintz. And if there's room, why not build in foam-padded window seats? It's so cozy to sit with one's feet tucked up on a window seat. Cover window-seat pads with the printed chintz, too. For jaunty accents, choose emerald-green carpeting and a scattering of brass pots filled with green plants.

GAME TABLES

Tables for two may be romantic, but game tables for four are more practical in family rooms. The table for four can be the standard dining-table height of 29 or 30 inches, or the very popular 27-inch height. With the latter, however, remember that standard dining-room chairs will not work. There should be a 9- to 10-inch variance between the chair-seat height and the table, so seats of chairs used with the 27-inch table should, as a rule of thumb, be 17 inches high.

Some game tables have flip tops that open to seat six persons when the occasion arises. When selecting a game/snack table for the family room, think practicality. Easy-care plastic is always safe because it eliminates worry about stains, and the colors are great. Some plastic tables look like leather, others have a shiny patent finish, and lots have the look of real wood.

A stark white plastic party table for four with matching chairs had the look of now in a family room I visited. Everything was totally practical and easily maintained. The white sofa and grass-green Parsons tables were also plastic. The handsome black-and-white geometric-patterned carpet was durable and stain-resistant, backed with high-density latex foam rubber. It contrasted sharply with the cool green-white-and-pastel color scheme. Walls were grass green, with a white-painted serving buffet and storage cabinets recessed into the wall by the table for four. The window treatment added a garden look with white latticework panels and green-and-white-floral glazed-cotton curtains.

Game tables with checkerboard tops are also great for family rooms. There is hardly a day when I don't have a call from a friend or a client asking where to get a coffee table or a game table with a checkerboard set into the top. Fortunately there are some mighty attractive ones on the market.

The checkerboard and chessboard have the same number of squares, but while checker enthusiasts prefer a black-and-red board, I'm told that chess players would rather play on light-oak and dark-oak squares. I've seen glass-topped coffee tables, both squares and rounds, that have the checker-chess field screened directly onto the glass. One design I particularly liked was of gold and silver squares screened on the underside of the glass so the paint could not be scratched.

Parsons tables with a 14-inch-square playing surface are on the market also. If you already have a folding chessboard, why not place it on a 27″ x 30″ Parsons-style game table that's 29 or 30 inches high to accommodate normal-height side chairs. Your Parsons table can be any color that coordinates with your decor.

One chess player I know chose for his family room a Parsons-style table of white plastic laminate on which he placed a modern-style chess set. The room's decor went fun and games and squares all the way. Walls were covered with yellow-and-white checkerboard-patterned wallpaper. Draperies and sofa upholstery were a pattern featuring russet and cocoa-colored cats sitting on yellow and white squares, with a happy yellow canary perched on each cat's head. Carpeting was lemon yellow, and a white plastic coffee table was placed in front of the sofa. Lounge chairs of barrel-back design were natural rattan. The yellow-and-white checkerboard room was happy and gay.

Backgammon tables are popular, too, and many handy folks are creating their own special looks with handmade needlepoint covers for them.

But whichever style you choose, and whether you use it for games or for other purposes, game tables in my opinion add a certain note of elegance to the family room.

COFFEE TABLES

Because I'm so partial to planning groupings with the table-for-four arrangement, I've even used four lounge chairs on swivel bases around a large circular or square coffee table, in some family rooms I've decorated. The coffee-table-for-four arrangement is great for entertaining another couple.

For a country family room with terra-cotta-colored walls and sand-beige carpeting, choose

four club chairs upholstered in a tweed of pale blue, brown, and camel around a beigey-gray marble-topped coffee table.

PIANOS

Pianos play a happy decorating tune in any room, but they're special fun in family rooms.

A baby grand in walnut, mahogany, or shiny ebony black is perfect for a large family room if you can afford it. If space or budget won't allow it, there are many handsome small spinets on the market that will provide just as much enjoyment.

Spinet pianos can be specially ordered with decoratively finished backs if you'd like to place one perpendicular to the wall as a room divider in a small family room. Recently I saw a walnut spinet used this way—and to complete the division, louvered shutters, stained to match the piano finish, were installed from the top of the piano to the ceiling.

Pianos also provide additional surface area in a room. Have you ever seen a baby grand piano topped with a large shawl and lots of family pictures? I have. I am all for decorated piano tops but caution against overloading with too many accessories. Also, when placing a piano in a room, keep it away from hot radiators and cold exterior windows. Extreme heat and cold can harm a piano, so place your piano on an inside wall.

STORAGE PIECES

Storage space is a must for family rooms. Even those lucky folks with spacious attics and garages still want and need convenient space for items they use frequently. Hobbyists want hideaways for their knitting, sewing, tools, whatever. And mothers constantly try to make order out of the chaos of a family room strewn with children's toys!

The solution I favor for almost any family-room storage is the stackable or bunching storage unit. Stackables that snap together, bolt together, or simply—well, stack—require no installation and so can be moved from room to room or from home to home. There are plastic milk crate–type stackable cubes with handholds on the ends for transportability; there are solid cubes in wood or in attractive laminate finishes; there are skinny rectangular stackables for records and oversized books; stackable drawers; stackable wine racks; even stackable desk units. Just stack them up and you have instant—and good-looking—storage for books, records, games—you name it!

Stackables got their name from Monroe Rosenthal when he was a student at Columbia University and was studying almost daily in the university library stacks. He thought, Why not bring out bookcase units in standard sizes—24 inches, 36 inches, and 40 inches wide—that could be easily and securely stacked one on top of the other?

Monroe passed his idea on to his mother, owner of a furniture company in New York City, and in time they developed innumerable compositions of stackables. Some were 33 inches high, others were 82½ inches high. In fact, the Rosenthals even figured a way of creating a bookcase wall 12 feet long and 8½ feet high that turned a corner.

You could start with just such an L-shaped arrangement of white stackable bookshelves in any corner of your family room. Make sure there's enough shelf space for a television, a stereo, a bar, and your books and magazines. A natural wicker chaise will fit neatly into the angle of those shelves and you'll have every comfort near at hand—particularly if you place a wicker end table next to the chaise to hold a coffee cup, magazine, ashtray, or whatever.

Cover the chaise's upholstered pad in a rich flower-and-bird-design cotton of oranges, yellows, greens, sky-blue, and hot pink on a deep plum background. Paint walls that same rich plum, and all trim, ceiling, and doors white. Use the print

A table grouping for four in easy-care white plastic is an important element in this family room with a summer-garden look. Handsome black-and-white geometric-patterned carpet is stain-resistant and has high-density latex foam backing. Window treatment features white latticework panels and green-and-white floral glazed-cotton curtains.

Drexel-Heritage game table

This game room has all the necessary ingredients: a cozy color scheme of red and blue, plenty of seating for between-game conversation and for onlookers, and, of course, an elegant game table.

Checkerboards and chessboards play today's decorating game. In this family room with chess table setup, walls are covered with yellow-and-white checkerboard wallpaper. Drapery and upholstery feature a fanciful design of russet and cocoa-colored cats on yellow-and-white checkerboard squares.

for floor-length draperies, and hang those draperies from white poles and rings. Sofa and club-chair upholstery can be salmon, accented with cushions of the print. Carpet in the plum color of the walls, then sit back and enjoy.

To blend with a period family room, you might like one of the many attractive styles of bunching cabinets on the market. Put several cabinets together to form a wall unit to suit your particular needs.

In a traditional room with a bright airy look, why not a storage unit of shelves, drawers, and cupboards in a pale beige with bamboo trim? It makes a great focal point as well as a great storage solution. Paper walls in a summery apple-green-and-white floral, choose avocado green for sofa upholstery, and update a period chair with upholstery of sunny yellow vinyl. Tie the color scheme together with a rya-type rug in greens, blues, and white.

Another look I like is stackable bookcase units made of solid pine, cherry, walnut, or mahogany and filled solidly with books for an English-library scheme. In the library/den pictured, wall-to-wall stackables of amber mahogany are teamed with brick, rugged wood beams, and leather to particularly handsome effect.

Look for other furnishings with storage potential, too—end tables with shelves, drawers, or cupboards; coffee tables with storage features; hinged-top piano benches; even old office furniture. Paint is the secret behind turning blah office storage units into bright and useful accents for the family room. Old two-drawer filing cabinets can be prettied up with a coat of paint, and believe me, those deep drawers hold a lot. Bolt-together steel shelf units that look so grim in office gray come to sparkling life with a coat of yellow, red, green, or blue paint. Use one in your family room to hold books. Use another for the

television set and for your collection of *objets d'art.*

The family room pictured is an excellent example of how to choose furnishings with storage potential. The cocktail table provides handsome storage in two cupboard areas, and both the rectangular and round end tables also have plenty of drawer and cupboard space. A wall-size built-in bookcase is actually an example of storage within storage: Shelves not only hold books but also pretty baskets for attractive storage of small items. Those bookcases, in a rustic pickled-wood finish, provide a handsome backdrop for a pair of patchwork-covered love seats and a duo of paprika velvet-covered chairs.

THE ROUNDED LOOK

They're rounding out the cube these days—the square, hard edge of things is being softened. My prediction is that no longer will you be seeing so many room settings with squared-off sofas and squared-off lounge chairs grouped around a square coffee table. Rectangular and square end tables will be gone, too.

There are on today's market white modular wall units with the rounded look which can be assembled to make a family-room wall of bookcases or to form a desk unit. You can use rounded-off cubes as coffee tables or end tables, and you can even top those end tables with lamps advertised as "Rounded Cubes"—basic cube forms with rounded edges. The rounded-cube lamps come in many colors and would be a perfect choice in a chic family room.

If you'd like to try furnishings with the rounded look in your family room, you could start by painting walls a vivid marigold orange, using lacquer if walls are very smooth. Paint door trim and baseboard with white semigloss enamel. For carpeting, go soft and lush with luxurious spun nylon in contrasting tones of goldenrod yellow and nutmeg brown. (Shaded carpets in family

Storage woes in a multipurpose room are solved beautifully by a three-section bunching cabinet in a soft beige. A 100-percent-wool area rug provides bold contrast to the restrained traditional look of the room.

Heritage love seats

Style plus storage is provided in a family room with built-in bookshelves, baskets, and storage-minded occasional tables.

An easy-to-install wall of stackable bookcases, filled with treasured volumes, enhance this family room. The stackables are of amber mahogany. Carpeting is cherry red. Pagoda-shaped valances and draperies are a print of emerald green and forest green on a white linen background. Windows are treated with tortoise roller-blinds.

rooms are very practical.) Choose a rounded contour sofa in washable marigold-yellow nylon and a rounded glass coffee table surrounded by round hassocks in marigold yellow and nutmeg brown. They'll come in very handy for family snack gatherings. For storage, a white modular étagère-bookcase unit with the rounded-cube look would be my selection.

LEATHER

Leather is a great, versatile covering for family-room furnishings. And don't think that leather necessarily means the men's club decor—burgundy and dark green comfy pieces, generally overstuffed, sitting about on Oriental rugs. Today's leathers are light and bright—yellows, oranges, apple green, pinks—and they're used in lots of new ways.

Of course I'm not putting down the men's club look—there's nothing more pleasing to my eye than a warm, beautifully paneled library furnished with a deep green leather-covered sofa, a burgundy leather wing chair, and a club chair and ottoman upholstered perhaps in a plaid of rich red, forest green, and royal blue. Naturally, the plaid fabric would be used for draperies too, hung on brass poles with brass rings. And every library in the leather look that I like has a big fireplace with handsome brass andirons. I also like traditional desks with green, brown, or red leather tops, detailed with gold tooling.

But today's modern designers are covering the desk legs as well as the tops; and I've seen tables, end tables, and table desks completely covered in leather detailed with brass or steel nailheads. I know a great furniture designer and manufacturer who covers mirror frames in leather—some hexagonal, and others octagonal, rectangular, or square. I've also seen leather-covered folding screens—a great focal point in a family room; wastebaskets of leather; and benches completely covered in leather—tops as well as legs. There are rooms with leather-covered walls and window valances, and, of course, there are many upholstered furnishings available in leather.

DECOUPAGE FURNITURE

Get your scissors, your glue pot, and your creativity together and try decoupage, the cut-and-paste craft, to brighten your family room.

I was turned on to decoupage by my friend Barbara Barger of Boston, who began making decorative decoupage boxes as a hobby several years back. Today she's a real pro and her terrific decoupage boxes sell in some of New York's most exclusive boutiques. Barbara specializes in decoupage for boxes, but the technique needn't be limited to boxes; it can be used on tables, side chairs, old wooden trunks, desks—on any piece of wooden furniture that needs a lift.

Basically decoupage involves taking a picture —an old print, a map, a magazine or catalog illustration, for example—and gluing it to the object you're decorating, using white household glue. Finally, apply numerous coats of clear lacquer to seal and protect the design. Barbara uses seven to ten coats of lacquer, but she tells me that the new lacquers on the market need only an hour's drying time between coats.

Some of Barbara's designs use wine bottle labels, an idea you could use for the top of your family-room bar (or substitute beer bottle labels if you're fond of brew). Any of today's wide variety of unpainted furniture would take beautifully to decoupage. I'd like to see a family room enlivened with plywood-cube end tables decorated with decoupage. Or add a pretty touch to an Early American family room with decoupage on the backs of game chairs. Stain the wood a dark, dark color, then glue on your design—American eagles or wildflowers would be an authentic touch. Finally, lacquer the chair backs for shine and long wear.

The rounded look is all around the market. In this family room the stacked wall grouping has the rounded-cube look; round mushroom hassocks pull up to round glass-topped coffee table; and a rounded contour sofa invites recliners. Carpeting of luxurious spun nylon completes the soft look.

Accessories

Table topics—what's on tabletops and what is not on tabletops—are the subject. When you and your friends sit down in your family room, your eyes are naturally drawn to what is at eye level—the tabletops. Too often what we see are piles of magazines, books, and old newspapers; overflowing ashtrays; assorted knickknacks plopped down at random.

Don't get me wrong, I'm not one for surgically perfect tabletops with little china figurines marching in neat formation; I'm all for magazines and books on family-room tabletops. But keep magazines neat and don't leave the dog-eared retreads out. Keep books stacked and use markers to keep your place. Books laid facedown not only look messy, the books themselves suffer and eventually will break.

Accessories on tabletops should relate to each other and the rest of the room. If you have a big fat lamp on an end table, don't park your favorite collection of miniatures at its base. The miniatures will be dwarfed by the lamp. If you want those miniatures on display, put them in an attractive glass or acrylic case on the table. The case will bring your collection and the lamp into harmony.

I love plants on tables, but I don't love seeing moldy clay pots or plastic pots. If you're a plant person, by all means display your greenery, but conceal an ugly pot in an attractive container. A basket, china cachepot, or gleaming copper pot will do.

I also like fresh flowers on tabletops, but if that's impractical, a bowl of fruit will do. I like a white porcelain bowl filled with lemons and oranges; they not only look beautiful but lend a pleasing scent to the air.

Ashtrays are probably the most common tabletop accessory, but they needn't be common in appearance. Choose your ashtray as carefully as you choose a sofa or chair. I like to use antique plates as ashtrays, and I love giant crystal ashtrays that sparkle under an end-table lamp. In fact, I believe that all ashtrays should be of generous size—but not because they'll hold hundreds of butts! Overflowing ashtrays are not only unsightly, they give an unpleasant odor to a room.

I like showing off prized collections in a family room—paintings, sea shells, stamps, coins, butterflies, pressed flowers, statues, firearms, or whatever. For maximum effect, group your collection in one place; don't scatter it hither and yon all over the room. A couple of things here and there without what in French is termed *raison d'être* rarely if ever add up to much decorative appeal.

A client of mine had collected antique firearms for many years. He kept them in drawers, in back hallways, in trunks, in the attic, and in the basement. When planning a modern family room for his new home, I suggested that the firearms be the focal point. So the firearms were hung on bleached wood walls, and everything else in the room was left very simple. Floors were dark-stained polished wood; windows were covered with natural beige linen roll-up shades; and upholsteries were flaxen and tweedy. The room was most handsome, if I do say so myself.

Group your favorite collections on a wall, in a curio cabinet, on shelves, or on a tabletop. And if your room is French-styled, don't think that your collection has to be French; it might very well be modern in feeling, such as glass-cube paperweights.

I happen to love duck decoys, although I'm not a duck hunter myself, and I have many friends and acquaintances who collect duck decoys of natural and painted wood. One friend displays his collection on shelves in a wood-paneled den. All the deep armchairs and the sofa are upholstered in the red-and-black plaid of a hunter's jacket, and even the lamps carry out the theme—the bases are duck decoys and the parchment shades are painted with duck-hunting scenes. With its plaid upholstery, wooden shutters, and vases of dried cattails, that den is as cozy as can be.

For those who prefer one or two decoys to an entire collection, there are many ways to effectively display a single "feathered friend." There are duck-decoy lamps like the ones my friend has, which are handsome in a family room or library. And duck decoys look smart as bookends, too. I also like the look of a duck decoy or two peering from among a grouping of plants, or a duck-decoy centerpiece for the coffee table.

If you want even more of the duck theme in

your family room, look for a duck-print wall-covering in earthy brown and beige tones on a creamy ground. Hang heavy off-white cotton draperies from heavy wooden poles and rings. And fill a pine corner cupboard with duck decoys!

Maximizing the Minimum

We have all heard of the Stone Age, the Bronze Age, the Iron Age, and the Space Age. But have you heard of the Spaceless Age? Probably not, because I just invented it. That's my term for the decorating era in which we live—the era of small apartments, dining areas instead of dining rooms, postage-stamp bathrooms. If you're lucky enough to have any space at all that can be designed as the "family room," it's apt to be minimal, and it will require special treatment to make the most of it. Here are some of my thoughts:

Color in the small family room needn't be white or washed out, as many people think. Intense color adds personality to small rooms, whereas whites and pastels do nothing but enlarge them.

Color schemes built around one color are super for small rooms. For instance, a floor color can be picked up for walls, wrapping the whole room with the color.

Furniture in a small room should, of course, be small in scale; otherwise it won't fit. But small

Small rooms have maximum effect—both decoratively and functionally—when the right colors and furniture are chosen.

Syroco's love seat, chair, and tables

does not mean stingy. Look for upholstered furniture that takes up little floor space but is plumply pillowed. A love seat and chair of molded plastic would be a good choice, upholstered in a color that contrasts with the walls.

Tables and case goods (the industry term for storage units) should be portable and multipurpose. Molded-plastic tables, for instance, can be removed when a large party is in the offing, or moved in front of the sofa for TV snacking anytime. And a rolling bar cart con be pushed anywhere—even into a closet when it's not needed.

Window treatments in small rooms should be simple, please. No great swathes of fabric or eye-popping patterns.

The small family room pictured is a good example of what I'm talking about. The terra-cotta of a natural tile floor is picked up for walls, wrapping the whole tiny space in a wash of warm russet. A molded-plastic love seat and chair are upholstered in a contrasting patterned tweed in oatmeal tones, teamed with portable plastic end tables and rolling bar. And the off-center window is flanked by a pair of do-it-yourself raw wood screens, giving it the illusion of greater width, while the window itself is covered with understated beige narrow-slat blinds.

BASEMENTS AND ATTICS

If you've been searching for unused space to convert to a family room or den, you may think you've looked high and low—but have you really?

For a family of avid gamesters, why not take unused basement or attic space and turn it into a game room, with a handsome game table as a focal point? A cozy color scheme in that leisure room could be rich blue and warm red with just a touch or two of wheat gold.

Start by painting walls a rich blue. Carpet in red shag. Comfy club chairs for between-game conversations can be upholstered in blue and gold velvet. Onlookers might enjoy a love seat upholstered in a subdued diamond print of soft red and off-white.

Or take your cue from this room in an attic that began as a drab storage space. It was transformed into a spacious family room after insulation, wallboard, and a trio of washable wallcoverings put it on the road to its new life. To make it extra inviting, a carpet of warm rusty orange was added—and extended up and over a sleeping platform built under the eaves. A large supporting beame, running up the wall and across the ceiling, acted as a divider to set the sleeping platform off from the rest of the room, creating a snug alcove effect. To further define the area, a geometric wallcovering of lemon yellow, white, and chocolate was used inside the alcove, while a coordinating stripe was used outside. Note also the inviting look of those soft, rounded furnishings we talked about earlier.

If you like the wood look, why not create a wood-paneled hideaway in that unused attic space? Those sloping ceilings are especially cozy when complemented by dark wood and wood-grained mullion windows. For coziness underfoot, choose rich shag carpet in tones of brown, gold, and beige. And furnish your attic nook with a love seat or sofa bed covered in plushy beige corduroy and a comfy chair upholstered in butterscotch leather. Set off the wood-paneled walls with accessories of gleaming pewter, copper, and brass.

An attic family room (and instant guest room) becomes something special with the addition of a cozy sleeping nook. A trio of washable wallcoverings and a sculptured carpet make the room easy to care for.

Magee's "Viva" carpet of Enkaloft nylo

*Den under the eaves gets the cozy treatment with wood-paneled walls in a dark,
rich hue and with rich shag carpet of nylon in tones of brown, gold, and beige.*

9

The Guest Room

The guest room is a room that is visited often around our house come summer. And our guest room certainly proves that guest rooms needn't be large to be comfortable.

Ours is in the attic of our old country farmhouse. The floor is covered in practical straw-colored sisal matting and the walls and sloping ceiling are painted our favorite sky blue. For privacy and light control, there are white louvered shutters at the window.

To pick up the blue of the walls, we've covered the daybed with a blue-and-white antique quilt. My wife, Suzanne, likes to sleep guests on soft old linen sheets and pillowcases she buys at auctions.

For reading and relaxing, guests have a choice of an old "twig" rocker or a cushy chaise longue covered with another old blue-and-white quilt.

And our guest room emphatically says, "Welcome to the Varney family," thanks to a collection of family pictures we've hung on the walls.

Be a guest in your own spare room and see if you're happy. Spend an evening there; sleep there; and when you wake up, ask yourself these questions: Did I enjoy myself? Were all my needs for comfort fulfilled? If your answers are yes, then your guest-room decorating is on keel. If your answers are no, you have some work to do.

Some people I know think in terms of using their shabbiest old furniture in the spare room. I don't mind old furnishings freshly painted and reupholstered for a guest room, but I strongly object to guest rooms full of furniture that looks like attic junk.

At the other extreme are those people, who concentrate all their energy, time, and money on selecting color, furniture, fabrics, then wonder when they're done why the room still looks dead. The reason is simple—they've forgotten that a room is more than a collection of fabrics and furniture; a room is a place for reading, for relaxing. Instead of designing guest rooms for comfort, many people design rooms that are pretty to look at—period.

These same people are often guilty of thinking that a beautiful room is a room that's always neat as a pin, with a place for everything, and everything in its place. I was once a weekend guest in such a home: There were no books, no magazines, no radio or television visible; not a scrap of paper marred the perfection of the decor. In short, there were no signs of life. Believe me, I was mighty happy to get back home where I could lay down the newspaper without feeling like a litterbug!

So if you want your guest room to come alive, by all means think color, think furniture, think room arrangement, but think about all these things in terms of what will make a guest feel welcome in your home.

Refurbishing the Spare Room

A fresh coat of paint or new wallcovering in happy colors works magic in cheering up the spare room. And a guest room that says a warm welcome should also, of course, have a comfortable bed, not one that has seen its day. Some other important items on the guest-room checklist: pretty spreads and sheets; soft carpeting; a good reading lamp (or lamps), plus reading material; a chest of drawers; a comfortable chair; pictures on the wall; fresh curtains, and—one last tip—shutters or opaque window shades so those who like to sleep late on holiday can do so.

A brass headboard would be a nice decorative touch for the guest bedroom, or why not consider a wrought-iron headboard? Wrought-iron furnishings, once relegated to the terrace or sun porch, have made their way inside the home. In a guest room I decorated with pale, pale apple-green walls and white trim, a wrought-iron headboard painted antique forest green was most effective. So was the bedspread of emerald-green and apple-green leaves with big purple flowers on a white background. Two antique-green wrought-iron-based chairs, one with an ottoman, said a happy hello with their brilliant purple-and-white-striped cushions. Walnut-stained wood furnishings—a long dresser and two night tables—were refinished with antique-green paint, and the trim on the chest was white. A deep purple shag rug covered the floor, and white crisscross curtains were hung at the windows. End-table lamps were brass with white pleated shades.

Since a guest room has to please many tastes, avoid frills and overly feminine prints. And if your guest room also doubles as a workroom, decorate with soil-hiding easy-to-clean materials. Today's patterned, drip-dry sheets are a good way to begin.

Everyone likes the clean look of a geometric print, so for bed linens you might choose a windowpane check in fresh grass green and white. Top the bed with a matching comforter. Paint walls soft lemon yellow and all trim white. A jumble of mismatched furniture can be unified

and rejuvenated by spraying all pieces sparkling white, using washable enamel. Replace all hardware with round wooden knobs spray-painted lemon yellow. At windows, hang draperies of the sheet fabric over matchstick blinds sprayed white. Underfoot, a rug or carpet of grass green would be my choice.

If today's natural look is your thing, try a beach-inspired guest-room scheme built around a sky-blue carpet and beige-and-white bed linens. Walls can be painted sand beige with white trim and ceiling. Make draperies and chair-pad covers from the sheet fabric, and for more of that fresh seaside feeling, look for furniture of natural wicker or bamboo.

"Good Looks" for the Guest Room

Here are some other schemes you might try for a guest room that's sure to please visitors.

The tropical look. To me, the tropics are palettes of fresh, natural color—sea and sky blue, palm green, sunshine yellow, sparkling sand, bougainvillea scarlet, and, of course, splashes of white everywhere. The tropics also mean louvers for windows and door—a convenient and pretty way to keep out sun and let in soft tropical breezes. And the tropics wouldn't be the tropics without airy wicker furniture. I would certainly never think of doing a tropical room without it.

Start with a coat of palm-green paint for walls. Furniture can be white wicker—old porch furniture refurbished with a coat or two of paint is just the thing. For more tropical flair, choose a trellis-floral print in hibiscus pink and palm green on white for bedcover and curtains, and go hibiscus pink for seat pads on those wicker chairs. Underfoot, my choice would be a mossy green easy-care nylon carpet. And be sure to add some live green plants in wicker, raffia, or terra-cotta pots. Don't make it a jungle, however, in a room where people will be sleeping.

Light against dark. One of my favorite and most dramatic decorating looks uses dark walls as a backdrop for light furniture.

Visualize light against dark in a guest room. Walls are painted a rich avocado green, and the

Bigelow Trevira Star carpet

Fieldcrest's "Mixed Emotions" bed linens

The freshness of the seaside is captured in a beige-and-sky-blue guest room decorated around a fresh blue carpet and beige-and-white patterned sheets. Furnishings of wicker and bamboo enhance the natural theme.

floor is covered with a dark, dark avocado-green shag carpet. Sounds dark and dreary so far, doesn't it? But now, paint trim and woodwork white and fill the room with natural wood furniture. (You can pickle or bleach it for the lightest look possible.) And with your natural wood, use wicker—in a headboard, perhaps, or for night tables. At windows, hang a geometric print of melon, yellow, and hot pink on a white background. Use the same print for a bedspread, and for the bedskirt choose hot pink. To make things even livelier, add a pink ginger-jar lamp with a white accordion-pleated shade; a mirror framed in a melon-yellow-and-white crisscross-patterned cotton above the chest of drawers; a straw basket planter or two; and some colorful modern paintings over the headboard.

In a modern guest room/sitting room, why not

Shaheen carpet of Enkalure II nylon

A guest room with a touch of the tropics has palm-green walls, airy white wicker furniture, and mossy-green nylon carpet.

set contemporary furniture against dramatic dark chocolate walls and carpeting? Furniture in the room pictured is edged with polished aluminum to heighten the light-dark effect. A Thai-look, multicolored quilted bedspread and bright chaise cushions add a splash of contrast color, and, for added sparkle, sheer draw curtains are accented by a silvery bamboo design.

Blue and white. There is hardly a person I know who dislikes a blue-and-white color scheme. It's an in-between scheme that is always effective.

There are many blue-and-white fabrics on the market, in stripes, floral prints, geometrics. And when shopping blue and white, think about blue-and-white wallpaper. White lattice on a blue background would be a good choice for your guest room—especially if it's a small room, since the openwork pattern will visually enlarge it.

In the room shown, walls, drapes, and sofa bed were done in a classical blue-and-white print of blue flowers and leaves on a white background. As an end table by the sofa, a 30-inch round table was skirted in royal blue moiré and accessorized with a handsome white porcelain lamp and

Dark chocolate-brown walls and carpeting provide a dramatic backdrop for white-lacquered furniture. And for added gleam, each Orient-inspired piece is banded in silvery polished aluminum that's picked up in the silver bamboo print on curtains.

shade. White openwork chairs with seats covered in rich royal blue give a light and airy look, and are easy to move. Coffee tables are actually white-painted luggage racks with glass panes placed on top. They were planned to be easily moved when the sofa is opened.

Matched prints. I like the matching-fabric-and-wall-covering look in a small guest room where a variety of patterns would be overwhelming. It's also a good way to unify rooms that are broken up by doors, windows, and cabinetry.

In a pretty guest room I designed, a white Oriental floral on a peony-pink ground was used for walls, bedspread, upholstery, and draperies. All furniture was white, and on the floor there was an Oriental carpet of soft blue and rose pink.

Companion prints. For those who want some contrast to the one-pattern look, there are companion patterns—prints in the same colors but with slightly different designs. The companion to a floral stripe, for instance, might be the stripe alone. If no companion print is available, choose

This traditional room sparkles in blue-and-white polished cotton, used for walls, draperies, and for upholstery on a sofa bed.

a stripe or check in the colors of your main print.

Let's try it in an Early American guest room, using a floral and a check.

For walls, we'll use a print of delicate white miniflowers on a brick-red background. Use matching floral fabric for laminated window shades and for a fitted daybed cover. For contrast, choose a small check of brick red, lemon yellow, and white for bolster covers, bedskirt, and seat pads on occasional chairs. Storage space for guests can be provided by a George Washington–style chest. A matching desk, with white china knobs, can double as a dressing table.

The nook look. What could be cozier for a guest room than a sleeping nook fitted right into the wall? The sleeping nook started way back when, in northern Europe, where cupboard beds were built right into the wall to keep out the icy north wind. Today we have central heating, but I still enjoy creating the look of the sleeping nook. And a charming look it is.

The alcove bed works best with a single bed, which makes it ideal for the guest room. You can create a nook between built-in closets, built-in bookshelves, or, more simply, with draperies. Still another way is to set your nook bed into a bay-window recess and hang draperies in front of the bed to enclose window, bed, and all.

Why not build deep floor-to-ceiling bookcases on either end of your guest-room wall, leaving room in between for a twin bed. Paper the wall behind the bed in a colorful Indian-inspired block print of brown, beige, pumpkin, wine, and emerald green. Use a matching fabric for a fitted bedcover and for tieback draperies to hang in front of that "built-in" bed. Make toss cushions of the print and also in solid colors of pumpkin, emerald, and wine.

If your guest room has a short wall, just the length of a bed or a trifle longer, you can create a welcoming nook without expensive built-ins. All you need is draperies! Hang the drapery panels in front of the bed, so that they partially conceal the head and foot. Tie back the draperies with matching or contrasting fabric and add a shaped valance, hung from the ceiling, to conceal the drapery hardware. Finish the look by draping the bed and the wall behind the bed in the same fabric.

And here's another idea for a tiny guest room.

A bouncy check and floral combination for walls, upholstery, and window shades is accented by mellow pine furniture in an Early American guest room.

Plymwood's Sugar Hill pine furniture

If there's a little-used closet in that room, take off the doors and turn the closet into an alcove for the bed! You could paper the alcove with one print and the other walls with another that co-ordinates. Try a plaid for the alcove, and cover the other walls with a floral companion. I believe in soft, restful colors for the guest room, like our own sky blue, or the soft dawn pink, robin's egg blue, lavender, and beige of many floral prints.

Even in a small room, guests need a place to sit, so with this soft-colored scheme I'd choose a mint-green lacquered chair. Add a pink-skirted table and, for storing belongings, a graceful lowboy.

The beamed scheme. Wood beams immediately say country to me, and that can be a rural region anyplace—France, England, Spain, New England, the West, etc. Today, as you know, there are imitation beams that look like real wood and can be very easily installed on walls, ceiling, or both to give any room in your home the popular country look.

Recently I saw a colorful guest room/sitting room with an Indian theme that was enhanced with imitation wood beams. The rich wood-stained beams were applied to stucco walls and ceiling to form panels, and were also used free-standing to visually divide the space. The beams were even applied to the headboard wall to accent a tepee-shaped recess and form the basis of the popular Indian look. The quilted cotton bedspread was made by the Wahpeton Sioux Indians in South Dakota and featured tepee-shaped tribal motifs in feather red, corn yellow, and white appliquéd on forest green. Carpeting was warm russet polyester shag.

Old-fashioned chenille. If you're thinking of throwing out your old chenille spreads, why not think again? The spreads could be used as bed-skirts—how pretty a white chenille bedskirt would be with a navy-and-white gingham bed-spread; or as curtains—dotted chenille curtains with ball-fringe trim would be effective. And can you picture a round table skirted in white chenille? The table should have a clear glass top to protect the fabric and to provide a flat surface on which to place lamps, picture frames, and other accessories.

I once saw a guest bedroom with walls cov-ered in dotted white chenille. Chenille-covered walls may sound a bit strange at first, but, let me tell you, it was a mighty handsome look. The chenille fabric was also used for drapery hung on pale blue curtain rods with matching rings. Carpeting was pale blue. For bedskirt and chaise-longue upholstery, pale yellow was used. Natur-ally the bedspread was white chenille with ball fringe.

Try chenille with painted furniture, or team it with maple or pine furnishings for the look of a New England farmhouse. I once used chenille bedspreads, ecru with white dots, at the guest-room windows of a wood-ceiling-beamed country house. The spreads-turned-curtains, complete with ball-fringe edges, were perfect at windows. Walls were painted ecru, trim was white, carpet-ing was sage green, and the bed was covered in a leaf print of sage green, champagne, and white. The country look was completed with a pine end table, white porcelain lamps, and lots of live greenery in straw baskets.

Tissue paper for furniture finish. My wife and I once visited friends whose country weekend

Imitation wood beams, so easy to install, enhance the ceiling and walls of this guest room/sitting room with an Indian theme. Beams also accent a tepee-shaped recess on headboard wall. Bedspread is forest green with tribal motif appliquéd in feather red, corn yellow, and white. Carpeting is warm russet-orange polyester shag.

house had been furnished with wood chests, chairs, and tables purchased in the raw-wood state and then finished with tissue paper. It was a great look. In the guest bedroom, the chest and night tables were first coated with a yellow-gold water-mixed paint base, which dried effectively to a texture. After the paint had dried, squares and rectangles of ordinary tissue paper in gold, yellow, and white were applied overlapping to the painted wood surfaces with lac-quer, then finished with several coats of the lacquer.

The golden yellow tissue-paper finish was most effective against walls lacquered brilliant red. Windows were treated with goldenrod-yellow louvered shutters, and carpeting was chocolate brown. Bedspreads and the upholstery on club chairs were of the same print—chocolate-brown, goldenrod-yellow, wheat, and red flowers on a white background.

A Final Word

I hope by now you've realized the decorative and functional potential of even the smallest spaces in your home, and I hope you've been helped to maximize this potential through the many looks, color schemes, furnishing styles, new materials, and imaginative uses of old materials we've discussed throughout the book. Adapt them as you wish, using your own imagination and creativity to bring personal warmth to your home, and remembering always that pretty alone isn't what you're striving for—it's a look that says welcome, a happy, comfortable atmosphere that makes friends and family glad they're there.

DATE DUE

25-370

CONTRA COSTA COUNTY LIBRARY